Oh Say Can You See

Unexpected Anecdotes About American History

JOHN WHITCOMB

AND

CLAIRE WHITCOMB

WILLIAM MORROW

AND COMPANY, INC.

NEW YORK

Library of Congress Cataloging-in-Publication Data

Whitcomb, John.
    Oh say can you see.
    Includes index.
    1. United States—History—Anecdotes, facetiae, satire, etc. 2. United States—History—Quotations, maxims, etc. 3. Quotations, American. I. Whitcomb, Claire.
E178.4.W44   1987   973   87-10964
ISBN 0-688-06547-3

Printed in the United States of America

First Edition

1 2 3 4 5 6 7 8 9 10

BOOK DESIGN BY BARBARA BACHMAN

Co-Author's Note

A badly lit airport restaurant is an odd place for inspiration to strike, but some ideas will not be deterred. We were meeting my brother at Kennedy Airport and paused for a family dinner. My father explained that he was retiring from teaching. In that case, I said, he should put down his stories and write a book with me. The result is *Oh Say Can You See*.

Though this book has been a father-daughter effort, it is a natural outgrowth of the Whitcomb family's pursuit of history. When my brother Jonathan and I were young, we'd be packed into the blue Plymouth station wagon and taken to see all the log cabins Lincoln ever slept in. We'd follow the Oregon Trail, keep our eyes peeled for gold at Sutter's Mill, and relive the shoot-out at the OK Corral. Family dinners were often spent listening to my father's tales long after our plates had been emptied, for we were unwilling to clear the table and break the spell.

Oh Say Can You See has been a pleasure to work on, since it has made history a family presence once again. My mother, Helen, a writer, has helped shape it with her fine editorial skills. Jonathan, with his keen memory, has made sure we didn't miss his favorite stories. Naturally, many more anecdotes could have been included in this book, but containing America's history within two covers is no easy task. *Oh Say Can You See* reflects what intrigued us—and, we hope, you.

—*Claire Whitcomb*
New York, February 1987

CONTENTS

PART VIII: *Words and Wisdom*

PART IX: *The Political Process*

PART X: *Joys and Sorrows, Love and Death*

CONTENTS

PART I

All in the First Family

Presidents on the Presidency

1. GEORGE WASHINGTON "My movements to the chair of Government will be accompanied by feelings not unlike those of a culprit who is going to his place of execution."

2. THOMAS JEFFERSON "Never did a prisoner released from his chains feel such relief as I shall on shaking off the shackles of power."

3. JAMES K. POLK "The Presidency is not a bed of roses."

4. JAMES BUCHANAN, TO INCOMING PRESIDENT ABRAHAM LINCOLN "If you are as happy, my dear sir, on entering this house as I am in leaving it and returning home, you are the happiest man in this country."

5. ABRAHAM LINCOLN Being president is like "the man who was tarred and feathered and ridden out of town on a rail. . . . A man in the crowd asked how he liked it, and his reply was that if it wasn't for the honor of the thing, he would much rather walk."

6. ULYSSES S. GRANT "Being President would be highly unfortunate for myself, if not for the country" (a sentiment voiced before he seriously considered accepting the nomination).

7. RUTHERFORD B. HAYES "I am heartily tired of this life of bondage, responsibility, and toil" (spoken when refusing a second term).

8. JAMES A. GARFIELD "My God! What is there in this place that a man should ever want to get in to it?"

9. GROVER CLEVELAND "My little man, I am making a strange wish for you. It is that you may never be president of the United States." His advice was offered to a youthful Franklin D. Roosevelt.

10. THEODORE ROOSEVELT "No President has ever enjoyed himself as much as I have enjoyed myself."

11. WILLIAM HOWARD TAFT "I'm glad to be going—this is the loneliest place in the world."

12. WOODROW WILSON "The office of President requires the constitution of an athlete, the patience of a mother, the endurance of an early Christian."

13. CALVIN COOLIDGE "I thought I could swing it."

14.   HARRY S TRUMAN "Being a President is like riding a tiger. A man has to keep on riding or be swallowed."

15.   JOHN F. KENNEDY "The pay is good and I can walk to work."

Presidential Imbibers and Abstainers

1.   FINICKY IN THEIR OWN FASHION Bess and Harry Truman enjoyed their old-fashioneds before dinner—until they moved into the White House. There they found the drinks were simply not up to snuff. Bess asked for them a little drier, but the result still didn't satisfy her. "They make the worst old-fashioneds here I've ever tasted!" she complained. Finally the butler dumped two big splashes of bourbon and some ice in a glass. Bess and the president were pleased. "Now that's the way we like our old-fashioneds," said Mrs. Truman.

2.   A LARGE LIQUOR CLOSET James Buchanan, a wealthy bachelor, was a serious but controlled drinker. When he was living in Lancaster, Pennsylvania, just prior to his presidency, he liked to use his Sunday drive to church as an excuse for a trip to Jacob Baer's distillery to pick up a ten-gallon cask of "Old J.B. Whiskey," a brand he thought to be the finest. "The Madeira and sherry that he has consumed would fill more than one old cellar" wrote John Forney, editor of the *Lancaster Intelligencer*. At the White House, Buchanan once asked a supplier not to deliver champagne in small bottles "as the article is not used in such small quantities."

3.   NO INHIBITIONS ON PROHIBITION When the Eighteenth Amendment to the Constitution became effective during Warren G. Harding's administration, the president banned liquor at all official White House dinners. But whiskey flowed two evenings a week when Harding held his private "poker cabinet." Tobacco smoke hung in the air, feet were on the desk, and the spittoons rang. "Trays with bottles containing every imaginable brand of whiskey stood about," wrote a disgusted Alice Roosevelt. "The Duchess," as Harding called his wife, went about mixing drinks for the "boys."

4.   A TEMPERAMENT FOR TEMPERANCE Rutherford B. Hayes's wife, "Lemonade Lucy," set the moral tone of the White House—

morning prayers, no smoking, dancing, or card games, and no alcoholic drinks at dinners or receptions. At night there were hymn sings. After one official dinner, Secretary of State William Evarts remarked: "It was a brilliant affair; the water flowed like champagne."

5. LIBEL TO DRINK When a small Michigan newspaper said Theodore Roosevelt "lies and curses in a most disgusting way; he gets drunk, too," the Bull Moose candidate sued. The trial, which took place after his defeat for a third term, was a media event. His own star witness, Roosevelt admitted to maybe a glass of champagne a month, but never whiskey or brandy unless ordered by a doctor. The jury found the publisher guilty of libel, and Roosevelt was awarded damages of six cents.

6. BEER AND BRATWURST As a young lawyer and politician in Buffalo, New York, bachelor Grover Cleveland loved to spend his evenings in the beer gardens, singing songs, drinking stein after stein of beer, and eating hearty amounts of German fare. He did not appear visibly drunk even after several steins of Bavarian beer, but the beer and food did have a visible aftereffect—he gained one hundred pounds during his first fifteen years in Buffalo. Cleveland's nieces called him "Uncle Jumbo." By the time he reached the White House he had given up his beer-garden life-style, but the weight stayed with him.

7. NO DRUNKARD Abraham Lincoln said of his vice-president, "Andy ain't a drunkard." But when Andrew Johnson was being sworn in as vice-president, he "evidently did not shun Bourbon county, Kentucky, on his way here" a reporter for the *Herald* wrote. According to one eyewitness, Johnson had to be assisted to the chair by the sergeant at arms and two doorkeepers. His problem was probably weakness from a fever and some medicinal whiskey, but his detractors made the most of it.

8. LOG CABINS AND HARD CIDER In the election of 1840, the *Baltimore Republican* ridiculed the Whig candidate William Henry Harrison: "Give him a barrel of hard cider and a pension of two thousand a year and our word for it, he will sit the remainder of his days in a log cabin by the side of a 'sea coal' fire and study moral philosophy." Actually, Harrison was the son of a wealthy Virginia planter who lived on a beautiful estate in North Bend, Ohio, but his supporters latched on to the "log cabin and hard cider" phrase and ran a campaign that portrayed war hero "Old Tippe-

canoe" as a man of the people. Incumbent Martin Van Buren was overwhelmed and Harrison went to the White House.

9.   TOO DRUNK TO COUNT After duty in the Mexican War, Captain Ulysses S. Grant was stationed at an isolated post 240 miles north of San Francisco. He was lonely away from his wife, Julia, who had given birth to a son he had never seen. With his captain's pay too meager to bring his family west, Grant became an alcoholic. He was warned about his drinking by Colonel Robert Buchanan, who had Grant write out his resignation with the understanding that it would be dated and sent in if there was another problem. There was. One day Captain Grant, acting as paymaster, was too drunk to count out the money. Colonel Buchanan ordered him put under arrest. He was given the choice of either resigning or facing trial. Grant, the man who was to achieve the highest army rank since George Washington, resigned in disgrace.

10.   GOING TOO FAR Woodrow Wilson's Secretary of the Navy Josephus Daniels was an ardent prohibitionist. He issued an order forbidding liquor on all U.S. Navy ships—an order that got him in trouble with his boss. The president participated in Washington's Birthday ceremonies at Mount Vernon on a cold, rainy February day. Returning to the navy yacht *Sylph* wet and thoroughly chilled, he ordered a Scotch and soda.

"I'm sorry, Mr. President," an apologetic steward said, "This is a Navy ship and no alcoholic beverages are allowed." Wilson turned on his secretary of the navy: "Confound it, Daniels, this is going too far."

Trying Out for Commander in Chief

1.   WINNING THE SILVER STAR When the U.S. entered World War II, Congressman Lyndon Johnson wanted to get into uniform. He traded an influential congressional post for the rank of lieutenant commander in the navy but complained that he "looked like any other junior officer."

Initially stationed in San Francisco, he appealed to President Franklin D. Roosevelt for a more active job. FDR sent him on a special presidential mission to assess American morale and military strength in the South Pacific. LBJ insisted his duties required him to go on a combat bombing raid. "I think you're stupid," the tail gunner on the mission told him, but Johnson wanted to get involved in something dangerous. He certainly did.

As LBJ's B-26 bomber neared its target, an engine failed and the plane had to break formation. It was jumped by Japanese fighters and hit several times. The pilot managed to escape by heading into a weaving, skidding dive.

Commander Johnson then returned to Congress, his seven months of war service ended. For his "marked coolness in spite of the hazard involved," he was awarded the Silver Star medal. The pilot and the crew, who continued fighting in the war, went unrewarded.

2. SOLVING A MILITARY DILEMMA In 1832 Abraham Lincoln borrowed a horse and went to fight in the Black Hawk War—a frontier clash with Indians led by Chief Black Hawk. Lincoln, who had volunteered to serve for thirty days, was elected captain, an honor that he said gave him more satisfaction than any later success.

Leading his unruly company was no easy feat. Lincoln's first order was met with "Go to hell." He quickly learned to ad lib. When a dispute arose over which company should have a certain campground, Lincoln wrestled another commander to settle it. When his company was marching twenty abreast across a field, he realized that they were coming to a fence with a narrow gate and he couldn't think of a command to "turn the company endwise." Lincoln improvised, announcing, "this company is dismissed for two minutes when it will fall in again on the other side of the gate."

When his thirty days were up, Lincoln reenlisted for another twenty and then an additional thirty days until the Indian problems were over. On the night he was discharged, his horse was stolen and he had to navigate the two hundred miles home largely on foot and on the backs of friends' horses.

He earned ninety-five dollars for his eighty days in the war.

3. HOW TO BECOME A HERO On August 2, 1943, Commander John F. Kennedy was at the helm of the PT-109, on night patrol in the South Pacific. At 2:30 A.M. the Japanese destroyer *Amagari* roared out of the darkness and, before Kennedy had a chance to react, sliced through the PT-109. The survivors spent the night on the damaged hulk, hoping to be rescued. Discouraged and thirsty, the next day they began a four-hour swim to the nearest island. Kennedy swam the breaststroke, pulling a wounded crewman by holding the cords of the man's life jacket in his teeth.

The next night Kennedy braved the channel currents and tried unsuccessfully to intercept PT boats. He returned exhausted, his feet badly cut by the coral. The beleaguered crew spent the next four days trying other rescue plans, but their saving grace came when two natives paddled up in canoes. Kennedy quartered a co-conut with a sheath knife, and on the smooth inner side of the shell inscribed an SOS message and sent the natives off for help.

Since JFK was Ambassador Joe Kennedy's son, his rescue was page-one material for the August 20 edition of *The New York Times*, which proclaimed him a hero. After he became president, Kennedy was asked by a small boy just how he had become a war hero and JFK replied, "It was absolutely involuntary. They sank my boat."

4. SWEPT AWAY In December 1948, Navy Lieutenant Jimmy Carter was on night duty on the bridge on his submarine, the U.S.S. *Pom-fret*, which was riding on the surface recharging its batteries. Suddenly an enormous wave crashed over Carter's head and across the sub. Unable to keep his hold on the railing, Carter found himself swimming inside the wave with no sense of what was up or down. Had the current been broadside, he would have been lost. By pure chance, the wave set Carter down on the submarine's gun turret thirty feet from the bridge. He felt he was watched over by Providence and said, "I don't have any fear at all of death."

5. LEARNING ABOUT WAR EARLY Andrew Jackson was just thirteen when he went off to fight in the Revolution. An expert horseman, he enlisted in a cavalry unit and served as a mounted messenger. He knew the South Carolina roads and proved so valuable that he was rewarded with a pistol.

The following April, in 1781, young Andy and his older brother Robert were captured by British raiders. A dragoon officer "in a very imperious tone" ordered Jackson to clean his boots. When he refused, the officer swung at him with his saber, slashing his head and arm severely. At the disease-ridden prison camp his wounds were neglected. He and his brother were fed bread and water.

Eventually the boys' mother was able to obtain their release in a prisoner exchange. Jackson retained the scars and hatred of the British for the rest of his life.

6. TALL IN THE SADDLE Young George Washington was an aide to British General Edward Braddock during the French and Indian War when his outfit was ambushed on the way to attack Fort Du-quesne, a French outpost at the forks of the Ohio River. Washington was suffering from chills and a fever, which he called the "bloody

flux." The previous day, he had been so weak he'd had to stretch out in a wagon. Nevertheless, when the battle came, he fought bravely. Two horses were shot out from under him. A bullet tore through his hat and three others burned tracks through his uniform.

General Braddock, fatally wounded, gave what was to be his final order. He sent Washington for reinforcements nine miles away. Washington had to use all his remaining strength just to hold the saddle and stay on his horse. When he returned he found that he had been reported dead. In all, he had spent twenty-four hours either fighting or in the saddle.

Presidents on the Right and Wrong Sides of the Law

1. FIGHTING CRIME WHILE READING TOLSTOY Theodore Roosevelt was deputy sheriff of Billings County, Dakota Territory, when "three hard characters" stole his boat, worth at the most thirty dollars. Incensed and convinced it was his duty to capture lawbreakers, TR and two ranch hands built a makeshift craft and floated downriver in pursuit. A blizzard had just subsided. Temperatures reached zero. Floating ice made the river hazardous, but a hundred miles downstream they surprised, captured, and disarmed the incredulous thieves.

No cameras were on hand when deputy sheriff Roosevelt arrested the three thieves who stole his boat in the Dakotas. However, after two were released from jail, he reenacted his capture with an unidentified ranch hand filling in for the third thief.
THEODORE ROOSEVELT COLLECTION, HARVARD COLLEGE LIBRARY

Roosevelt's ethics ruled out the usual western solution—hanging. They had to be turned over to the nearest law, which involved poling downstream amid the ice jams for eight days. Food ran out except for soggy unleavened cakes. The prisoners could not be tied up or their hands and feet would freeze.

TR read Tolstoy and Matthew Arnold between turns at guarding them. For the last forty-five miles he herded them into a borrowed wagon and walked behind them carrying his Winchester. He arrived in Mandan after thirty-six sleepless hours, turned over his prisoners to the local authorities, and received his fees as deputy sheriff and mileage for three hundred miles, a total of fifty dollars.

2. TWINKLE, TWINKLE LITTLE STAR Growing up in Dixon, Illinois, Ronald "Dutch" Reagan didn't need to be convinced of the problems of drinking—he had a firsthand example with his father, who was an alcoholic. But once he and a friend did finish off a bottle of homemade wine—a gift to Dutch from a neighborhood couple for teaching their kids to swim. The two took a walk through the town and Dutch climbed on top of a stoplight, a short cement post in the middle of an intersection.

He was happily sitting there when the police chief came by in his Model T Ford and asked Dutch what he was doing up there. "Twinkle, twinkle little star. Who do you think you are?" was Reagan's reply. The chief took him in and he was fined one dollar.

3. "OFFICER, DO YOUR DUTY." President Ulysses S. Grant was racing along in his horse and carriage heading toward the White House when a police officer ran out from the sidewalk and grabbed the horse's bridle. He was dragged half a block before he could stop the carriage to dole out a speeding ticket. When the officer found out whom he was ticketing, he hesitated.

"Officer, do your duty," Grant said. The presidential rig was taken to the police station while the president returned to the White House on foot. Later Grant wrote the officer's superior commending him for what he had done.

4. "BIG STEVE" THE HANGMAN Stephen Grover Cleveland began his political career as an assistant district attorney of Erie County, New York. In 1871 he became the county sheriff. Even then Cleveland was developing his reputation for being hard-working and conscientious. He said he would not ask someone else to do something he wouldn't do himself. Twice when criminals needed to be hanged, he placed the noose around the condemned murderer's

neck and sprang the trap door. Cleveland, whose weight veered toward 250 pounds, was sometimes called "Big Steve" in his early years, even though he preferred his middle name. His enemies called him "the Hangman of Buffalo."

5. TAKING NO CHANCES When Senator Lyndon Johnson accepted the vice-presidential spot on John F. Kennedy's ticket in 1960, he wanted to be sure to return to Washington no matter what. So he convinced the Texas legislature to pass a special law permitting him to run for the vice-presidency and the U.S. Senate at the same time.

6. ACCIDENTAL ARREST In 1853 Franklin Pierce ran down an aged woman while driving his carriage back to the White House. The president was arrested by a Washington constable, but when the police found out who he was, the charges were dropped.

7. PLAYING HOOKY On December 12, 1778, the journal of the Virginia State Assembly noted: "Ordered the Sergeant of Arms to take into custody the following members of the House, to wit: Thomas Jefferson . . ." Even though it was against the House rules, Jefferson and many of his fellows liked to seek fresh air and amusements during the tedious periods of the Assembly proceedings. In the course of the term he was taken into custody several times, but discharged after paying a fine.

8. THE PRESIDENT AS COP Woodrow Wilson loved to go motoring but always insisted that his chauffeur keep within the speed limit. When his car was passed by a speeder, Wilson fumed that the offender should be arrested. He even wrote the attorney general to find out if he had the power to make the arrest himself. He thought that as president he had the "powers of a magistrate" and wanted to "hold up some scoffing automobilist and fine him about a thousand dollars." Wilson was talked out of it.

Life in the White House

1. STALKING GAME ON PENNSYLVANIA AVENUE In 1801, the first year of Thomas Jefferson's administration, carpenters framed off part of the unfinished East Room to create a makeshift bedchamber and office for the president's private secretary, Captain Meriwether Lewis, who arrived overland from Detroit with a string of

mud-spattered pack horses. Lewis was less a secretary than a protégé whom Jefferson, an old friend of the family's, was preparing to head a great western expedition.

Left to his own devices, twenty-seven-year-old Lewis would go out to hunt along Pennsylvania and other of Washington's untamed avenues. The squirrel and game he caught would be turned over to the White House cook.

2.   OPEN-DOOR POLICY Until well into the nineteenth century, the White House was never locked. In Martin Van Buren's term a drunk wandered in and spent the night on a sofa.

3.   SLIPPING INTO SOMETHING COMFORTABLE In Dolley Madison's era, Washington's streets were still notoriously muddy. When guests came for her drawing-room receptions, which lasted from dusk till about nine P.M., they exchanged their boots and heavy shoes for slippers, which did less damage to the carpeting.

4.   A VIRTUAL STATE OF SIEGE Throughout the 1800s, the president faced a consistent and unwelcome string of guests in his house—the office-seekers who lined the corridors outside his office and even positioned themselves on the stairs leading to the family quarters on the second floor. William Henry Harrison complained that he was so besieged by office-seekers that he could not properly attend to "the natural functions of nature."

5.   "WHAT A LIFE!" President Harry Truman described his solitary meal in the White House: "I have to eat alone and in silence in a candlelit room. I ring. Barnett takes the plate and the butter plates. John comes in with a napkin and a silver crumb tray—there are no crumbs, but John has to brush them off the table anyway. Barnett brings me a plate with a finger bowl and doily on it and John puts a glass saucer and a little bowl on the plate. Barnett brings me some chocolate custard. John brings me a demi-tasse—about two good gulps of coffee.

"My dinner is over. I take a hand bath in the finger bowl and go back to work. What a life!"

6.   SHE SLEPT WITH A SABER When the War of 1812 heated up, friends tried to convince Dolley Madison to leave Washington, which the British seemed certain to attack. "I am determined to stay with my husband," Mrs. Madison replied. Militia were stationed on the White House lawn. For peace of mind, Dolley began sleeping with

a Tunisian saber beside her bed, a souvenir of the war with the Barbary pirates.

7.   A DEMOCRATIC WAY TO DINE Thomas Jefferson, with his firm belief in egalitarianism, always seated his guests at a circular table, a principle borrowed from King Arthur.

8.   A DECORATING DISASTER Jackie Kennedy broke down and cried when she saw the White House in 1960. Outgoing First Lady Mamie Eisenhower had given her a one-hour tour, during which Jackie made use of a wheelchair as she hadn't fully recovered from the Thanksgiving Day birth of her son, John junior. Jackie thought the White House looked like a hotel furnished during a January clearance sale.

9.   ISN'T ANYBODY HOME? President Franklin Pierce was inaugurated at noon on March 4, 1853, but because of a severe snowstorm the parade back to the White House was canceled. Pierce dropped off outgoing President Millard Fillmore at his hotel and went on alone to the White House where a big crowd was waiting to shake his hand. It was getting dark when the last guest departed and Pierce was exhausted. He had been kept awake the night before by drunken revelers and a band called the New York Continentals who serenaded him outside his hotel window.

   Pierce and Sidney Webster, his secretary, decided to retire early. They lit candles and went upstairs to the living quarters where they found the servants had left everything a mess: Pierce's possessions were strewn about in boxes and so were Fillmore's. The furniture was pushed against the walls, the beds were stripped and dismantled, and no fresh linen could be found. There were no servants anywhere. The president and his secretary slept on mattresses on the floor that night.

10.   TURNING BOTH CHEEKS Huge animal heads from Theodore Roosevelt's administration were still mounted in the State Dining Room when the next president, Woodrow Wilson, took office. Wilson shuddered and had the table moved to another end of the room so that his back would be to the mounted heads and he and his family could look out at the White House lawns and gardens.

11.   NOSES PRESSED TO THE WINDOW The Hardings came into the White House like a fresh breeze and opened the gates that had been shut tight during World War I and throughout Woodrow Wil-

son's long illness. Warren Harding and his wife, "the Duchess," were small-town Ohio and liked it that way. They didn't mind when tourists walked right up and snapped pictures of each other up against the white porch pillars. When they pressed their faces against the windows, Florence Harding pulled up the window shades and smiled. "It's their White House," she said. "Let them look in if they want to."

12.   A SPITTING IMAGE During John Tyler's administration, Congress was tight-fisted about funds to fix up the White House. Tyler had to use his own money to pay the light and fuel bills. No doubt cleaning was also a problem as it was an era of constant spitting. Charles Dickens, waiting to see Tyler, noted how those waiting in the same room "bestowed their favors so abundantly upon the carpet."

13.   TO MARKET, TO MARKET Indian fighter William Henry Harrison, Old Tippecanoe, lived up to his image as a man of the people. When he first moved into the White House, he liked to walk to the city market, a basket under his arm, to do the daily shopping. However, he curtailed his marketing when he found out that hundreds got up early to watch him or, worse, pester him with petitions.

Home Improvement at the White House

1.   PRIVY TO PRIVACY When the White House was first built, it had a wooden outdoor privy. Thomas Jefferson, the second president to live there, thought it beneath the dignity of the office and ordered it demolished. Two indoor water closets were built instead. When the city commissioners ordered them, they specified, at Jefferson's instruction, that they be ones "of superior construction, which are prepared so as to be cleansed constantly by a Pipe throwing Water through them at command from a reservoir above."

2.   A KITCHEN CRISIS Until Millard Fillmore became president in 1850, the White House kitchen had no stove. Meals were cooked just as in colonial times, in a big open fireplace with kettles and pots on a maze of hooks and cranes. When Fillmore purchased the first stove, which was described as "small hotel size," the black

cook was so bewildered by all the pulleys and drafts that she became infuriated. To appease her, the president had to go over to the Patent Office and find out how to operate the new contraption.

3. FEW MODERN CONVENIENCES President Benjamin Harrison's family included his wife, two married children, three grandchildren, Mrs. Harrison's father, and her widowed niece—a total of eleven. In 1889 they moved into the White House, which had only two water closets, but each bedroom was equipped with a chamber pot. Mrs. Harrison commented on the "straits the president's family have been put at for lack of accommodation."

4. THE POLKS WERE IN THE DARK When James K. Polk was president, the Capitol and some Washington streetlights were being illuminated the modern way—with gas—so Congress thought it was a good idea to extend the new technology to the White House.

Sarah Polk, however, didn't like giving up candlelight. She refused to have workmen touch her favorite chandelier in the Blue Room. Society thought her old-fashioned, until the night of the first gaslighted White House reception. At 9:00 P.M. the gas company turned off its plant and darkness reigned everywhere at the White House—except in the Blue Room.

5. ALL WIRED UP AND NO ONE TO TALK TO The first White House telephone arrived on May 10, 1879, and was hung on the wall of the telegraph room. Its wires went out the window to the Treasury Department where there was another phone. President Rutherford Hayes used his phone rarely because there were hardly any phones in Washington. What he did find useful, however, were the surface-mounted speaking tubes that let him talk to other offices or the doormen in the entrance hall.

6. THE UNSHOCKABLE HARRISONS When the White House was wired for electricity in 1891, President Benjamin Harrison and his wife, Caroline, were afraid of getting electrical shocks when they touched the switches. Lights in the downstairs parlors and halls were turned on at dusk by a servant who found them still burning when he returned the next morning.

7. NO MORE WASHTUBS The first bathtub with hot and cold running water was installed in Franklin Pierce's administration. Before 1853, most presidents had bathed in painted tin tubs. Water was heated in a kettle. Since the tubs became hot, they were lined with linen towels to protect the skin. Pierce's bathroom was deco-

rated with wallpaper to simulate oak paneling and a floorcloth with a tilelike pattern.

8. TRUMAN AND THE BULLDOZERS At a 1947 Truman reception in the East Ballroom, one of the massive crystal chandeliers suddenly began to sway and make a tinkling noise, a result of someone walking on the floor above. Talking died out and guests moved to the room's perimeters. Truman had already noticed that his bathtub was sinking into the floor and the leg of his daughter Margaret's piano had come through the dining-room ceiling. The president had had enough and called for a thorough investigation.

The analysis was unanimous—the White House was about to cave in. The aging framework had been weakened over the years by holes drilled for gas pipes and electrical wires. Two of the three experts suggested demolition, but Truman opted for a total renovation. He and his family moved out to Blair House while the interior of the White House was stripped to a shell. Bulldozers sat on the ground floor. Beams were carefully taken down and numbered. A new foundation and steel framework was built and the house totally reassembled.

9. AIR CONDITIONING COMES TO THE WHITE HOUSE From July to September 1881, President James A. Garfield lingered on the edge of death. He'd been shot in the back and the hot Washington summer made his condition even more unbearable. One Baltimore engineer came up with a way to cool the president's bedroom. Chilled air was piped from an adjoining cast-iron chamber that was filled with hanging strips of terry cloth. These were constantly sprayed with ice water from a pipe and served as a primitive refrigerator for the air that was drawn into Garfield's room.

During the Taft administration, the presidential bulk necessitated the installation of a specially made tub.
CULVER PICTURES

10.   RUB-A-DUB-DUB President William Howard Taft was six feet two inches tall and well over three hundred pounds. The White House tub was literally too small for him. When he took a bath, he often got stuck and had to be pulled out. Taft wisely ordered a new tub which was so large that four workmen could sit in it to pose for a picture.

11.   PRESIDENT ARTHUR CLEANS HOUSE After James Garfield was assassinated, the new president, Chester A. Arthur, came to look over the White House and pronounced it "a badly kept barracks." The widowed Arthur was urbane and luxury-loving and refused to move in until it was fixed up.

If Congress would not vote the money, he said, "I will go ahead and have it done and pay for it out of my own pocket. I will not live in a house like this." He had twenty-four wagonloads of furnishings removed, including mattresses, old stoves, lace curtains, and spittoons. They were sold at auction and netted six thousand dollars, largely because people were willing to pay for White House souvenirs.

During the refurbishment Arthur ran the government from a friend's mansion. Finally, in December 1881, he moved into the White House, four months after taking office. Still dissatisfied with the taste level of the house, he called upon the decorator of the hour, Louis Comfort Tiffany, to recolor rooms and even design one of his famous stained-glass screens for an entry hall. It was dismantled by a later administration.

First Children

1.   BABYING RUTH President Grover Cleveland created a sensation when he married pretty young Frances Folsom in the White House. So naturally their little baby, Ruth, was the center of attention. Her name was even borrowed for the candy bar.

In those days crowds swarmed unchecked on the White House grounds. Once, when baby Ruth was being taken out on the South Lawn, admirers insisted on picking her up and patting her, much to the distress of the nurse. Protective of their privacy, the Clevelands rented a suburban Washington house where they spent much of their time, and they summered in Maine. The president treated the White House primarily as an office.

2.   THE PRESIDENT IN WONDERLAND "I can do one of two things. I can be President of the United States or I can control Alice. I cannot possibly do both," said Theodore Roosevelt of his free-spirited eldest daughter.

3.   UNTAMABLE TAD The president's favorite, young Thomas Lincoln, was nicknamed "Tad" because as a baby he had a large head and squirmed like a tadpole. Tad had a cleft palate and couldn't read at age twelve. He adored his father, who would carry him piggyback through the White House while Tad let out war whoops. Lincoln's policy toward his undisciplined son was "Let him run." Tad whittled the rosewood furniture and even drove a team of goats through the ballroom while riding a kitchen chair behind them.

4.   THE HIT OF THE PRESS CONFERENCE When Caroline Kennedy was three, she romped in a play yard her mother had designed. Built under the trees by the West Wing, it had a rabbit hutch, barrel tunnel, leather swing, and slide. As her menagerie of pets grew, lamb pens were added plus a stable for her pony Macaroni, which she loved to ride around the grounds.

Three-year-old Caroline Kennedy upstaged her father when she wandered into a 1960 press conference in Jackie's high heels.
UPI/BETTMANN NEWSPHOTOS

Upstairs at the White House, Caroline had a playroom that included a sandbox filled with sand ordered from the national parks. Low bookcases were added and it became a nursery school for ten pupils whose parents shared the expense of the teacher's salary with the Kennedys.

Once Caroline stole the show at her father's press conference when she wandered in among the wires and lights wearing her pajamas and a robe and flopping about in her mother's shoes. Her younger brother, John, discovered a trap door on the front of his father's desk in the Oval Office and would hide in there, peeking out occasionally to surprise visitors.

5.   OFF TO PUBLIC SCHOOL Amy Carter liked to roller-skate around the big white pillars at the White House entrance and play in the tree house that her father had built for her. When it came to school, Amy looked like the other kids, walking to the public school with a book bag on her back. However, a Secret Service agent followed her everywhere. Since the time of Theodore Roosevelt, no presidential children had attended public school, but Jimmy Carter, conscious of his democratic image, wanted his daughter to attend a Washington elementary school. On her first day Amy entered through a mass of TV cameras, news reporters, and onlookers.

When Jimmy Carter was running for reelection and about to debate Ronald Reagan on TV, he talked with Amy beforehand and she said "the atomic bomb is the most important issue." When President Carter quoted his twelve-year-old daughter's opinion in the debate, his opponents and the news media ridiculed it and Carter admitted that quoting Amy was a mistake.

6.   A FATHER'S PRIDE AND JOY Margaret Truman, like her father, enjoyed playing the White House piano. She was in her middle twenties and had aspirations of becoming a professional pianist. When *Washington Post* music critic Paul Hume gave one of Margaret's performances a devastating review, the irate president wrote him, "I never met you, but if I do you'll need a new nose and plenty of beefsteak and perhaps a supporter below."

7.   THE PRESIDENT POPS AN ENGAGING QUESTION "Heck, I dated Luci when her father was only a Vice-President," one of teenaged Luci Johnson's boyfriends told a reporter. Luci, who liked to do the frug and the monkey at White House parties, usually kept the press hopping with her romances.

She gave reporters the slip, however, when she had a blind date at Marquette University in Milwaukee. Luci wore a blond wig and used a false name. Her date was Patrick J. Nugent, her future husband. Later, when he proposed, President Johnson found out about it on the news ticker and was furious about being scooped. Luci and Patrick had flown home to tell LBJ but decided not to say anything because Johnson was recovering from a gallbladder operation.

Finally, three weeks later, the president came to Luci and said, "What's all this I read in the papers?" As she tells it, "That was when we sat down and reasoned together." Whenever Luci "reasoned" with her father, she was almost sure to get what she wanted.

PART II

Fortunes and Fates

Runaways

1.   NOT VERY BROTHERLY LOVE When seventeen-year-old Benjamin Franklin boarded a boat for New York, he told the ship's captain he'd gotten a girl pregnant and was escaping marriage. Actually, he was escaping apprenticeship to his brother James, a Boston newspaper publisher. James had been sent to prison for criticizing the British authorities. To prevent the paper from being seized, he had put it in Ben's name, which meant that he had to cancel his younger brother's indentures. Secretly, however, he had made Ben sign new indenture papers that required him to remain an apprentice until he was twenty-one. When James got out of jail, Ben decided to run away, gambling that his brother would not prosecute because it would mean revealing the ruse of the secret indentures.

Young Franklin sailed for New York but couldn't find work, so he walked across New Jersey and got a ride down the Delaware River by helping with the rowing. Broke and munching on a penny loaf of bread, he arrived in Philadelphia, the city where he would make his fortune.

At the age of forty-two, Franklin, the fifteenth son of a candlemaker, was so successful that he retired and devoted the rest of his long life to his country and his many interests.

2.   A $10 REWARD FOR A FUTURE PRESIDENT Andrew Johnson was born in a log cabin on the North Carolina frontier and never went to school a day in his life. His father, a handyman, died when Andrew was three. His mother supported the family by sewing and washing.

When her son was barely thirteen, she apprenticed him to a tailor in Raleigh, Virginia, signing the papers with an X and giving his age as fourteen. One night, Andrew threw a stone and accidentally broke the bedroom window of a widow who had two "right smart" daughters. The widow threatened to "persecute," a serious concern to an apprentice, so on the night of June 15, 1824, Andy slipped away.

An ad in the *Raleigh Star* offered a ten-dollar reward for his return. Johnson ended up in Tennessee, where at eighteen he married a sixteen-year-old schoolteacher who taught him to write. He trained himself in public speaking by entering debates. In 1828 he ran for alderman, then became representative, senator, and governor of Tennessee. He was picked to be Lincoln's vice-president during the Civil War because he was a loyal Democrat from a border state. When Lincoln was assassinated, the runaway apprentice became president.

3. A PENNY REWARD Legendary frontiersman Christopher "Kit" Carson made his first move west at the age of two when, in 1811, his family left Kentucky for the Boone Lick district of Missouri. There his father was killed by a tree limb that fell while he was burning a clearing in the forest.

Kit grew up on a farm and at fifteen was apprenticed to a saddler in Franklin, Missouri. He had no schooling and was reared on tales of Indian fights and adventures. Within a year he decided to run away and join one of the wagon trains headed west to Santa Fe.

A local newspaper ad offered a one-cent reward to anyone "who will bring back said boy." No one claimed it. Kit Carson went on to become a hunter, Indian fighter, and soldier whose adventures became part of the folklore of the West. In 1841 he guided military explorer John C. Frémont on his landmark expedition. "With me Carson and truth are one," said Frémont, whose writings about his expedition first gave Carson his national reputation.

4. BETTER THAN SMITHING In February 1822, Jim Bridger, the man who would discover the Great Salt Lake and Yellowstone's geysers, was apprenticed to a St. Louis blacksmith when he heard about an ad calling for "enterprising young men." Bridger, who was illiterate, had to have the ad read to him. It announced a beaver-hunting expedition, which sounded better than smithing, so eighteen-year-old Bridger ran away and didn't see a town again for the next seventeen years.

5. $700 FOR LIBERTY Frederick Bailey, a slave, hopped a train out of Baltimore in 1838 hoping not to be recognized. Dressed as a sailor, he carried borrowed papers and money given to him by a free black woman, Anna Murray, his future wife. Once north, he took the last name of Douglass as a disguise.

The safe route would have been to live quietly, but Frederick Douglass proceeded to speak up against slavery. His protests, based on the beatings and humiliations of his own experience, made him a national figure. Since skeptics doubted a slave could be so eloquent, Douglass published his autobiography *and* the name of his master. Friends feared for his safety, so he went to England. There, about seven hundred dollars was raised to buy his freedom—a liberty that came eight years after his escape.

6.   HOMER UNDER A TREE In the spring of 1809, Sam Houston, the future president of the Republic of Texas, was sixteen years old and in a state of rebellion. He had helped his mother and his brothers clear their four hundred acres of Tennessee wilderness, but settling in to farm work was not for him. The family tried to interest him in tending their store, but young Sam was only motivated by reading. Alexander Pope's translation of the *Iliad* had him hooked. He had memorized more than one thousand lines and in time was able to recite almost the entire five hundred pages.

When he was upbraided by his two older brothers, James and John, for reading instead of working, Sam Houston decided to run away the next day. It wasn't until several weeks later that the family heard that Sam had crossed the Tennessee River and was living with the Cherokees. His mother sent her two sons to plead with him to come home. The boys found Sam stretched out under a tree reading Homer. He told them he "preferred measuring deer tracks in the forest to tape and calico in a country store." Then Sam politely asked to be excused because he desired to "read in peace."

It was nearly three years before Houston returned to the white settlements.

7.   THE MAN WHOM POCAHONTAS SAVED John Smith, the son of a tenant farmer, had himself apprenticed to a merchant in hopes of going to sea. When the merchant tried to keep Smith at a desk, he ran away to fight the Turks. His adventures included substituting for a prince in a fight with a royal Turk who had issued a challenge for single combat. Smith ran his opponent through with a quick thrust of his lance; his trophy was the severed head. Smith accepted and won two other such challenges and received a coat of arms showing "three Turkes heads." Later he was taken prisoner, manacled, and sold as a slave. He managed to kill his master and escape back to England after a long wander through the Ukraine.

In 1607 he headed to sea again with the expedition that settled Jamestown. Initially, Captain Smith played a minor role among the "gentlemen" settlers. But when hard times hit, it was Smith's leadership that forced the men to work and saved the settlement from starvation. At Jamestown, he was captured by the Indians and was about to be executed when Chief Powhatan's thirteen-year-old daughter, Pocahontas, rescued him in what is now a famous schoolbook episode. In 1609 Smith left Jamestown and later explored other areas of the New World.

They Died Broke

1.   A PENNILESS FOUNDING FATHER In 1824 an ad in the *Richmond Enquirer* offered "the Estate of Thomas Jefferson, deceased" for the "payment of the testator's debts." Jefferson owned thousands of acres and many slaves, but, like many planters, he tended to outspend his income and died bankrupt. In his last days he had the additional burden of providing hospitality for the many distinguished guests who came to honor him. Aware of his situation, a sympathetic Congress started its famous library by paying Jefferson twenty-five thousand dollars for his books. Friends tried to organize a lottery to sell off some of his land, but it didn't raise nearly enough money. In 1831 Monticello was sold by Jefferson's heirs to James Barclay, a druggist, who tried to establish silkworm production on the land. When it proved unsuccessful, Monticello went into a century of neglect and decay.

2.   HE WAS NO MIDAS In 1848 John Sutter was living quietly on his forty-nine-thousand-acre California ranch when gold was discovered at his mill on the American River. As the news spread, Sutter's help left in pursuit of riches. Gold seekers streamed in, destroying his fields and squatting on his land. There was no law to protect him. Bankrupted, Sutter finally came to Washington, D.C., in 1866 to try to get reimbursement for his losses.

For the next fourteen years Congress considered various bills to compensate him. Sutter grew old and discouraged. Finally, on June 11, 1880, Senator Daniel W. Voorhees introduced a joint resolution to pay Sutter fifty thousand dollars. But it was an election year and Congress adjourned on June 16 without taking any action. Sutter gave up hope and went into a deep depression. His condition was so alarming that Senator Voorhees was urged to come to Sutter's hotel room to assure him that the bill would pass first thing in the next session.

Senator Voorhees agreed but he was delayed a day, and it was just one day too many for John Sutter. When the senator arrived he found that the seventy-seven-year-old pioneer had died earlier that afternoon.

3.   UNABLE TO COPE James Marshall found the tiny specks of gold in the tailrace of Sutter's mill that started the great gold rush

Jes. W. Marshall

THE DISCOVERER OF GOLD IN CALIFORNIA

In his impoverished old age, James Marshall sold his autograph for cash.
THE BANCROFT LIBRARY

of 1849. But Marshall, a loner, was decidedly strange, or "notional" as they said. He was unable to cope with what he called the grabbers and prospected only haphazardly, surviving by doing odd jobs such as gardening. As a sympathetic tribute to his discovery, California awarded him a pension of two hundred dollars a month in 1872 but after a few years let it lapse. Marshall fell into straits so dire he even sold his autograph for money. Just before he died in 1885, California rejected a new request for help. After his death, a nine-thousand-dollar monument was erected in his honor at Coloma.

4.   HONORED IN JAIL In low temperatures India rubber was hard as a rock, but in heat it became soft and gummy. Its useful possibilities absorbed inventor Charles Goodyear to the point of monomania. He tried curing rubber with everything he could think of— salt, soup, ink, cream cheese. When he thought he had the problem solved, he made hundreds of pairs of rubber shoes and sold them only to have them melt into a stinking mass on the first hot day.

In pursuing his experiments, he put himself and his family through the tortures of extreme poverty. Several times he was thrown in debtor's prison. He had to sell his child's schoolbooks to get food. His family lived on potatoes and wild roots. Then one day he was cooking a batch of rubber when some accidentally spilled on the stove and "charred like leather" instead of melting. Using sulfur and heat he perfected the process that he called vulcanization, producing the rubber we know today in so many products.

Financial success continued to elude Goodyear even though honors came his way. His display of rubber products was the hit of the Great Exposition in Paris in 1855. Napoleon III was so impressed by it that he awarded him the Cross of the Legion of Honor. But it was delivered to Goodyear at a French debtor's prison. Business failures in the United States had ruined him. He could not meet the notes he had signed and was jailed at Clichy. Finally, money received from a license procured his freedom in time to accept a ride through the Bois de Boulogne with Napoleon III. He fascinated the emperor by demonstrating rubber pontoons for bridges. His last years were spent in Washington, D.C. Just before his death in 1860 he was denied an extension on his rubber patent. He left his heirs two hundred thousand dollars in debts.

5.   DUPED BY THE "YOUNG NAPOLEON OF WALL STREET" In 1884, Ulysses S. Grant's assets amounted to the $81 in his wallet. His wife, Julia, had $130 in her cookie jar. Everything else was lost in the collapse of Grant and Ward, a firm founded by the ex-president's son, Ulysses S. Grant, Jr., and Ferdinand Ward, dubbed the "young Napoleon of Wall Street." Young Grant had offered his father a chance to invest in the firm when, on paper, his investments had quadrupled and becoming a millionaire seemed certain. Ulysses S. Grant, Sr., put his life savings of $100,000 into the firm and even induced Mrs. Grant to part with her savings. No one realized profits were accruing because of Ward's manipulations, which included pledging the same security for more than one loan.

On Sunday, May 4, 1884, Ward came to Grant with the news that the firm would go under Monday morning unless he received a $150,000 one-day loan. The embarrassed ex-president went to call on William Henry Vanderbilt, hat in hand. Vanderbilt gave him $150,000 but specified, "To you—to General Grant—I'm making this loan, and not to the firm." Like many others on Wall Street, Vanderbilt knew more about the "young Napoleon" than the naïve Grant did. Ward put the $150,000 in his own pocket and the firm failed. He was sent to jail and Grant was broke. Had it not been for admirers who sent him money, sometimes anonymously, Grant could not even have paid the grocer and would have been forced into bankruptcy.

To make a living, Grant began writing about his Civil War experiences, encouraged by Mark Twain, who became his publisher. He knew he was dying of cancer. Days before his death he completed his memoirs, which later brought financial security to his family.

6.   THE GREAT DREAMER Pierre Charles L'Enfant was a French volunteer who came to America at twenty-three at his own expense to fight for freedom. He designed Federal Hall in New York City, originally the U.S. Capitol. George Washington, who was sworn in as the first president on its balcony, liked L'Enfant's work so much, he asked the Frenchman to plan the new capital city. L'Enfant rejected the usual rectangular layout as lacking "a sense of the real

grand and truly beautiful." He envisioned a city of wide radiating streets, circles, malls, and parks.

L'Enfant's vision was not matched by practicality or discretion. He overspent prodigiously, antagonized the city commissioners and Congress, and, finally, irritated Washington, who fired him. His fee had not been agreed to in advance, but Washington thought $2,500 to $3,000 would be liberal. L'Enfant's bill was a fantastic $95,500. He disdained compromise offers. In 1810, Congress voted him $1,394.20, which his creditors seized before he could turn it down. Gradually poverty engulfed him, and when he died on June, 14, 1825, his estate was a few maps, books, and surveying instruments valued at $45.

The first modern city planner was buried in an unmarked grave and forgotten. His plan for the capital was often ignored until 1901, when its importance was belatedly recognized. Since then L'Enfant's spirit has governed the design of the city. In 1909 his remains were disinterred, carried to the Capitol to lie in state, then reburied in Arlington National Cemetery on a hill overlooking the great city he had designed.

Wills

1. WHAT DID THE WIDOW WANT? In 1876 gossip flew when a wealthy widow, Sarah Dorsey, invited Jefferson Davis to live in a cottage on her six-hundred-acre Mississippi estate, Beauvoir. Davis was financially troubled and in need of a quiet place to write his account of the Southern struggle. The newly widowed Mrs. Dorsey was passionate about the Confederate cause and in need of a way to fill her days with meaning. Helping Davis looked like the perfect project. He loved her oaks and magnolias, so decided to settle in, insisting on paying fifty dollars a month to cover expenses, including his servant's board.

The arrangement suited everyone except Davis's wife, Varina, who had been in Europe at the time. She was furious that Mrs. Dorsey, her girlhood friend, was taking Davis's dictation. For a while she refused to visit Beauvoir, but finally her jealousy abated and she came and helped him on his book.

In November, Sarah Dorsey died of cancer with Jefferson Davis at her side. When her will was read, he was surprised to learn she had bequeathed everything to him, including Beauvoir and three other plantations. Her will referred to him as "my most honored and esteemed friend" and said, "I do not intend to share in the ingratitude of my country towards the man who is in my eyes the highest and noblest in existence."

2.   FRANKLIN'S PENNY SAVED "My fine crab-tree walking stick, with a gold head curiously wrought in the form of a cap of liberty, I give to my friend, and the friend of mankind, General Washington." That was among the items Benjamin Franklin included in his will. He also included a unique bequest—£1,000 each to Boston and Philadelphia to be used for loans to young mechanics who had, like Franklin, been apprentices.

The loans, which were intended to help the "young married artificers" set up their businesses, had to be repaid with interest set at rates that were low but not too low. Franklin didn't want to make it too easy for the young men. In both cities the funds have grown. After one hundred years Boston had $391,000 and withdrew some for a technical school. It still expects to have $4 million by 1991. The Philadelphia endowment helped fund the Franklin Institute.

3.   A PRECAUTIONARY MOVE Before British General Sir Henry Clinton sailed to aid Lord Cornwallis at the battle of Yorktown in 1781, he sent a copy of his will home to England and left another with his mistress, Mrs. Braddeley, in New York.

4.   FDR'S DEAL "If it embarrasses mother," Franklin Roosevelt told his son James, "I'm sorry. It shouldn't but it may." He had just left half the interest income on his estate to his faithful private secretary, Missy LeHand. Despite rumors about an affair, it appears likely that FDR maintained only a platonic intimacy with his secretary. However, Missy LeHand never married and devoted much of her life to Roosevelt.

5.   A FEMINIST IS NEARLY CUT OFF "Your first lecture will be a very expensive one," wealthy Judge Daniel Cady told his daughter Elizabeth Cady Stanton. He was opposed to her feminist lectures and threatened to disinherit her. "I intend that it shall be very profitable," she shot back. Her father claimed to have disinherited her a number of times, but when he finally died in 1859 he left her a handsome sum of fifty thousand dollars.

6.   FREE AT LAST George Washington's will provided immediate freedom for his "mullato man," William Lee, "as a testimony of my

sense of his attachment to me, and for his faithful services during the Revolutionary War." In addition, Washington provided him with "an annuity of thirty dollars during his natural life." His will also freed the rest of his slaves, but only on Martha's death, because the slaves that he had owned prior to the marriage were mixed together with hers as families. In Martha's will, she did not free her slaves.

7. FOUNDING THE SMITHSONIAN James Smithson's will began: "I bequeath the whole of my property . . . to the United States of America." Smithson was an Englishman who had never even set foot in the United States when he died in 1820. His purpose was to found "an Establishment for the increase and diffusion of knowledge among men." The value of the estate was over five hundred thousand dollars and came to the U.S. in 105 bags, each filled with one thousand sovereigns. The U.S. used it to found Washington's Smithsonian Institution in 1846, now known as "the nation's attic."

Unrewarded Heroes

1. FIRED FOR GAINING AN EMPIRE President Polk was irritated at the slow pace of the treaty negotiations at the end of the Mexican War and recalled his envoy, Nicholas Trist. However, the message took three weeks to reach Trist. At that point the Mexicans suddenly seemed on the verge of agreeing to the American terms. Trist disobeyed his orders and stayed to negotiate a treaty that gave the United States California, Nevada, New Mexico, Utah, Arizona, and parts of Wyoming and Colorado, all for about fifteen million dollars, just the arrangement Polk had wanted. Polk sent the treaty to the Senate but failed to change his mind about Trist.

Trist returned to Washington to find out he had been fired in disgrace. He was so destitute he took a clerk's job for a railroad. Twenty-three years later Congress voted him the back salary he was owed for negotiating the treaty with Mexico.

2. THEY GAVE HIM A SECONDHAND SWORD Wresting the Ohio Valley from the British during the Revolutionary War hadn't been easy for George Rogers Clark. At the battle of Vincennes, for example, he set out in mid-February 1778, crossed two hundred miles of frozen swampland, and didn't eat for the last two days of the march. But his suffering paid off. It was his brilliant victories

that forced England to surrender this vast territory at the end of the Revolution.

Clark had paid for part of the expedition's expenses out of his own pocket, as was the practice at the time. He even put up his own land for security. He expected to be reimbursed by Virginia, the state that had sent him on the expedition, but payments became bogged down in the bureaucratic shuffle. Clerks had trouble understanding the hardship prices he'd paid in the wilderness when supplies were scarce. His problems were further complicated when Virginia ceded the Ohio territories to the federal government. The U.S. agreed to pay Clark's bills but the papers were somehow lost. In 1913 they reappeared in a Virginia attic.

What the Virginia legislature did do was offer Clark congratulations and send him a secondhand sword, which, they assured him, the previous owner "had used but little." Clark was so disgusted he broke the sword in two and kicked the hilt into the Ohio River. He had lost his lands and was penniless.

The rest of his life was spent fighting financial ruin, ill health, and depression. In his old age, paralyzed and helpless, he was voted a new sword by Virginia and a pension of four hundred dollars a year. In 1928 the United States spent one million dollars for a memorial to Clark at Vincennes.

3. THE HISTORY BOOKS OMIT A HERO Except for George Washington, there was no greater figure at the end of the Revolution than Tom Paine. His writings, such as *Common Sense*, had been crucial in promoting the cause of independence. Washington counted on him, not only for his keen prose but because Paine could rally the soldiers when they were tempted to quit in the darkest days of the war. When the men would not listen to the pleadings of officers, who did not share their hardships, they could be swayed by Private Paine, an enlisted man who had callouses on his hands.

After the Revolution, Paine fell from grace. His first sin in the eyes of the public was his book *The Age of Reason*, thought to be an atheistic treatise. His second sin was criticizing President Washington. When "the father of our country" didn't help Paine get out of a Parisian jail during the French Revolution, he called Washington "an imposter" and wondered whether he had "abandoned good principles" or whether he had "ever had any."

Paine returned to the United States destitute. His old revolutionary friends had advanced to positions of power, but they were unable to help Paine because he was so publicly despised. A Boston newspaper, for example, referred to him as "a lying, drunken, brutal infidel, who rejoices in the opportunity of basking and wallowing in the confusion, devastation, bloodshed, rapine and murder, in which his soul delights."

Paine spent his last years on a farm in New Rochelle, a Tory holding that had been given to him after the Revolution. He died in poverty and his grave was defaced. It was not until the latter part of the 1800s that his name made its way into the history books.

4. HE READ THE ENEMY'S MIND After Pearl Harbor, the U.S. Navy received intelligence reports of a huge Japanese invasion fleet heading across the Pacific, its destination unknown. Commander Joseph Rochefort, head of the navy's code unit at Pearl Harbor, believed that the target was Midway, a key base in the mid-Pacific. Others, especially those at headquarters in Washington, disagreed. Intercepted messages from the Japanese only identified the target as "AF."

Rochefort decided to test his Midway theory. He asked the island to broadcast a false message saying that the evaporators used to produce fresh water from sea water had broken down. Sure enough, intelligence intercepted from the Japanese said "AF" had a water problem. This convinced Rochefort that Midway was indeed the Japanese target. The navy used Rochefort's unit's information, which has been called the most important intelligence in the history of naval warfare, to concentrate forces at Midway and defeat the Japanese in what proved to be the turning point in the Pacific war.

Admiral Nimitz recommended Rochefort for the navy's highest noncombat award—the Distinguished Service Medal. Then bureaucratic infighting began. A group of code-breakers in Washington was bitterly opposed to recognizing Rochefort. He was denied the medal. Hurt and disgusted, he asked for sea duty. He was assigned to a floating drydock. In 1985, nine years after his death, he was awarded the Distinguished Service Medal.

5. HE PAINTED THE CEILING Sixty-year-old Constantino Brumidi, lying on a scaffold on his back 180 feet up in the air, painted the great scenes on the Capitol dome. Like Michelangelo's Sistine ceiling, the paint was applied to wet plaster, which meant that if the plaster dried before it was colored properly, it had to be ripped out and the process started anew. Particles, paint, and dust fell on Brumidi and got in his eyes. Some of the figures he painted were fifteen feet high so as to appear life-size from the rotunda floor far below. He was paid about ten dollars a day and worked at the Cap-

itol for twenty-five years, decorating friezes and corridor ceilings, until in 1880 a scaffolding accident forced him to give up his labor of love.

A few months later, Brumidi died at the age of seventy-two, his great paintings incomplete. A pauper, he was buried in an unmarked grave with no recognition for his artistic accomplishments. Seventy years later his grave was rediscovered and given a proper tombstone. In 1949 Congress voted to erect a monument to him.

Pride Before a Fall

1. UNFORTUNATELY, HE GOT WHAT HE ASKED FOR Captain William Fetterman had said, "Give me 80 men and I'll ride through the whole Sioux nation." That was the number of men he led out of Fort Phil Kearney on December 21, 1866.

The fort was in dangerous Indian country and an armed guard was needed whenever the men left for such chores as cutting wood. On December 21, a group of Indians led by Crazy Horse attacked a wood-cutting detail and Captain Fetterman, at his own request, was assigned to lead the relief force. They had strict orders not to pursue the Indians beyond Lodge Trail Ridge, but Crazy Horse lured the cavalrymen over the ridge and into a narrow valley where they were ambused by Cheyennes, Arapahos, and Sioux.

The entire force was killed and horribly mutilated. Fetterman and Captain Brown had bullet holes through the left temples from weapons held so close as to leave powder burns, indicating that they had saved a last shot for themselves rather than fall into the hands of the Indians.

2. UNDERESTIMATING "THESE SAVAGES" At the time of the French and Indian War, British General William Braddock told Benjamin Franklin: "These savages may, indeed, be a formidable enemy to your raw American militia, but upon the King's regular and disciplined troops, sir, it is impossible they should make any impression."

Braddock organized two thousand men to attack the French Fort Duquesne, in present-day Pittsburgh, rejecting all advice of George Washington and other "colonials" on his staff. Before they reached the fort, the British were ambushed by the French and Indians. Braddock refused to let his men take cover behind trees, sometimes beating them with his sword if they attempted to do so.

*British General Brad-
dock, who refused to lis-
ten to "colonials" such
as George Washington,
was ambushed and mor-
tally wounded in the
French and Indian War.
His men buried him in a
roadbed and ran wagons
over the grave so that
the Indians would not
find and mutilate
his body.*
COURTESY OF THE NEW-YORK HIS-
TORICAL SOCIETY, NEW YORK CITY

More than half his force died in the battle. Braddock fought bravely.
Four horses were shot out from under him. He was fatally hit while
mounting the fifth. "Who would have thought it," he kept mut-
tering.

3. "MY PLANS ARE PERFECT." The newspapers called him
"Fighting Joe." When President Lincoln made him commander of
the Army of the Potomac, Union General Joseph Hooker announced, "My plans are perfect . . . may God have mercy on General Lee, for I will have none." Soon thereafter, on May 2, 1863, a
Confederate force half the size of his army defeated him at Chancellorsville. Robert E. Lee attacked him from the front while Stonewall Jackson surprised Hooker from behind, nearly cutting Hooker's
army in two. It was one of the worst Union defeats of the war.
Hooker asked to be relieved of his command and was transferred
to fight in the West.

4. HOPEFULLY IT WASN'T HELL In the War of 1812, British
General Robert Ross invaded and burned Washington and then
headed to Baltimore. On his way he stopped for a leisurely country
breakfast at the farm of Mr. Gorsuch. When the general left, Mr.
Gorsuch asked if he would be returning for supper. General Ross
replied, "No, I'll eat in Baltimore tonight—or in hell."
A few minutes later he moved out with an advance guard to re-
connoiter and was shot by a Baltimore militiaman. Ross fell from
his horse, mortally wounded. The discouraged British called off the
attack on Baltimore. Ross's remains were returned to England in a
barrel along with 129 gallons of Jamaican rum as a preservative.

5. A "RIDICULOUS" IDEA Before America's entry into World War I, the British luxury liner *Lusitania* was scheduled to sail from New York to England through the German submarine blockade.

Although it was a passenger ship, the *Lusitania* was rumored to be carrying ammunition. The Germans put announcements in American newspapers warning passengers not to travel on the ship. Among those who boarded anyway was millionaire Alfred Gwynne Vanderbilt. Reporters cornered him on the promenade deck and asked about the German warning. Vanderbilt's answer: "Ridiculous! The Germans would not dare make an attempt to sink the *Lusitania*."

On May 7, 1915, the *Lusitania* was sunk by a German submarine off Ireland. Of the 1,924 passengers on board, 1,198 were lost, including Alfred Gwynne Vanderbilt, his valet, and 126 other Americans.

6. SEWARD'S TRUE FOLLY Senator William H. Seward was the leading Republican in the nation. He was so confident his party would nominate him for president in 1860 that when he went home to Auburn, New York, to await the news, he rented a cannon and had it set up in his front yard. He wanted to announce his nomination with a bang. Invitations were extended for a giant celebration. Then the word arrived that the Republicans had picked an Illinois lawyer, Abraham Lincoln, as their candidate. The party was canceled. Seward worked for Lincoln's election and served as his secretary of state.

Visions, Dreams, and Omens

1. AN ANGEL COMES TO NEW YORK STATE On the night of September 21, 1823, Joseph Smith was kneeling by his farmhouse bed. A light filled his room and the angel Moroni appeared, standing in air wearing a loose robe of exquisite whiteness.

The angel told the eighteen-year-old Smith that a record engraved on golden plates was buried on a hill near his home in Palmyra, New York. No one else has ever seen them, but Smith translated the tablets, published the material as the *Book of Mormon*, and founded the Mormon Church.

2. THE LORD DICTATES A BEST SELLER Harriet Beecher Stowe was sitting in church during a communion service when she had a

vivid vision that became the heart of her novel—the loving slave Uncle Tom being beaten to death by the cruel slave driver Simon Legree. It moved her to tears. She went home and began to write what was to become America's most controversial best seller, *Uncle Tom's Cabin*.

3.   JESUS INSPIRES A DANCE In 1890, after the Indians had been subdued and confined to reservations, Kicking Bear and other Indians saw a vision of Christ returned as an Indian who told them that the earth would be covered with new soil which would bury all white men. The new land would have sweet grass, running water, and great herds of buffalo. Those Indians who danced the Ghost Dance would be suspended in air as this wave of new earth came and then would be set down on this new land where only Indians would live.

Kicking Bear brought his message to the Sioux reservation and the resulting frenzied Ghost Dances panicked the whites. The army attempted to halt the spread of the dancing, a move that led to the shooting of Sitting Bull during an attempted arrest and the slaughter at Wounded Knee.

4.   A MOTHER RECALLS HER SON After her son Willie died at the White House, Mary Lincoln was so bereft that she sought out a spiritualist who called himself Lord Colchester. In a darkened room he convinced Mary that various rappings were loving messages from Willie. At the White House, Mary often had visions in which her dead sons visited her. Once she saw Willie standing at the foot of her bed. Other times she saw little Eddie, who had died long before when the Lincolns lived in Springfield.

5.   CUSTER WAS DOOMED Shortly before the Battle of Little Big Horn, Sitting Bull submitted to ritual torture, which included cutting out fifty pieces of flesh from his chest and arms. He then had a vision in which pony soldiers were upside down.

This was interpreted to mean that the Indians would be victorious in an encounter with the U.S. cavalry. When General George Armstrong Custer attacked the Indian encampment at Little Big Horn, the Sioux decided to stand and fight, something they would not have done had the omens been bad. The result was Custer's last stand and the army's worst defeat in the Indian wars.

6.   WHAT LINCOLN FORESAW Just after his 1860 election to the presidency, an exhausted Abraham Lincoln came home and threw himself on a lounge. In a bureau mirror he saw a double reflection

of himself. When he got up it vanished, when he lay down it re-curred, though, as he wrote, "I noticed one of the faces was a little paler, say five shades, than the other." A few days later the ghost "came back again."

Mary Lincoln told him she "thought it was a 'sign' that I was to be elected to a second term of office, and that the paleness of one of the faces was an omen that I should not see life through the last term."

Several weeks before his assassination, Lincoln dreamed that he was hearing distant sobs in the White House and was wandering from room to room trying to find the people who were making them. In the East Room he was startled to find a funeral bier on which a corpse lay draped in vestments. Soldiers stood guard; mourners passed by. When Lincoln asked who had died, he was told it was the president.

7. ROOSEVELT GETS OUT THE CRYSTAL BALL Mr. and Mrs. William Howard Taft visited President Theodore Roosevelt at the White House in 1906. TR got them alone in the library, and sat down in a chair as if in a trance. Closing his eyes, he intoned in a deep voice, "I am the seventh son of a seventh daughter, and I have clairvoyant powers. I see a man weighing three hundred and fifty pounds. There is something hanging over his head. . . . At one time it looks like the presidency. Then again it looks like the chief justiceship."

"Make it the chief justiceship," Taft urged.

"Make it the presidency," said Mrs. Taft. Her influence prevailed and Taft declined the Supreme Court nomination. Two years later he became TR's handpicked presidential successor. He served one unhappy term and then Woodrow Wilson appointed him Chief Justice of the Supreme Court, which he enjoyed immensely.

8. INSTRUCTED TO KILL "In a dream I saw President McKinley sit up in his coffin, pointing to a man in a monk's attire in whom I recognized as Theo. Roosevelt. The dead President said, 'This is my murderer, avenge my death.' " So wrote John Schrank on September 15, 1901, the day after McKinley was shot.

Schrank ignored this otherworldly calling for exactly eleven years. Then on September 14, 1912, at one-thirty A.M., he had another vision. "While writing a poem," he said, "someone tapped me on the shoulder and said, 'Let not a murderer take the presidential chair. Avenge my death.' I could see Mr. McKinley's features." Roosevelt had already sat in the presidential chair for seven years and after four years of retirement was running for a third term.

This time Schrank responded to his vision. He bought a fourteen-dollar Colt and set out after TR, who was campaigning. In Milwaukee he got within six feet of Roosevelt, who was entering a car, and shot him in the chest but didn't wound him seriously.

Schrank denied insanity, comparing his visions to those of Moses and Joan of Arc. He requested that the bullet and pistol be given to the New-York Historical Society.

Lincoln's Son: Invited to Three Assassinations

1. 1865, FORD'S THEATRE Abraham Lincoln's oldest son, Robert Todd Lincoln, was invited to join his mother and father at Ford's Theatre the night John Wilkes Booth fired his fatal shot. But that morning Robert had returned from a wearying trip to General Grant's headquarters. He asked to be excused.

President Harding (left) was fated to die in office, but it wasn't because of the Robert Lincoln jinx. When the aging Lincoln attended the 1922 dedication of his father's memorial in Washington, D.C., no assassins' guns were fired.
ROBERT TODD LINCOLN'S HILDENE

News of the assassination reached him at the White House. Immediately he hurried to the boardinghouse across the street from Ford's Theatre where his father was lying unconscious. As he approached the tiny room he could hear his father's labored breathing and his mother's pitiful cries. He stayed until death came in the morning, when he took his sobbing mother to the White House.

Later he made an excursion to Ford's Theatre and saw the vacant chair he was to have occupied. It was situated between the door where Booth entered and his father's seat. Robert felt he could have thwarted the assassination and blamed himself for not attending the play that night.

2.   1881, THE WASHINGTON, D.C., TRAIN STATION President James A. Garfield invited his secretary of war, Robert Todd Lincoln, to join him on a trip to Williams College, from which the president had graduated twenty-five years earlier. Lincoln went to the railroad station to explain that he couldn't attend and arrived just in time to see Garfield shot down in the waiting room.

3.   1901, THE TEMPLE OF MUSIC President William McKinley invited Robert Todd Lincoln to meet him at the Pan American Exposition in Buffalo, New York. Hundreds had gathered at the Temple of Music to shake McKinley's hand. As Lincoln approached, he saw a group gathered around the president, who had just been fatally shot.

Sometime afterward a reporter asked Lincoln if he was planning to attend a particular presidential reception, and he replied, "No, I'm not going and they'd better not invite me, because there is a certain fatality about presidential functions when I am present."

Illegitimacy in America's Past

1.   A TURNCOAT SON It was Benjamin Franklin's illegitimate son, twenty-one-year-old William, who had helped with the famous kite experiment. The two were close and the elder Franklin used his influence to have William appointed governor of New Jersey. But when the Revolution came, William split with his father and sided with the British. He was declared a traitor by New Jersey patriots and forced to flee. He returned to England and his father disowned him. "Indeed nothing has ever hurt me so much . . . as to find myself deserted in my old age by my only son," said Franklin, who died a wealthy man but only left William a barren tract of land in Nova Scotia.

2.   THE BOY COULD BE MINE Bachelor Grover Cleveland was campaigning for president when it was discovered that he was supporting an illegitimate child. Actually, Cleveland wasn't sure the child was his, as other men had also been regular visitors to the mother, Maria Halprin. She had named the child Oscar Folsom Cleveland Halprin just in case. But Cleveland was the only bachelor, so he had shouldered the responsibility. "The boy could be mine. I don't know," he admitted. The Republicans were delighted and subsidized a popular song that went:

Ma! Ma!
Where's my pa?
Gone to the White House
Ha. Ha. Ha.

When Cleveland supporters heard of the scandal, they rushed to the candidate and asked what they should do. "Tell the truth," Cleveland said. His forthrightness and honesty helped him win the election.

3.   HIS MOTHER JAILED As John Adams put it, Alexander Hamilton was "the bastard brat of a Scottish pedlar." He was born on the island of Nevis in the West Indies to a woman whose husband divorced her, charging that she "has given herself to whoring with everyone." He had her thrown in jail for it.

After serving her term she lived with Alexander's father, James Hamilton. Their illegitimate son began to work in a large shipping office, and by the time he was fourteen he was in full charge. Hamilton was so talented that the local merchants took up a collection to send him to college in America. He soon joined the Revolutionary cause, became a trusted aide to Washington, and at thirty-two became the first secretary of the treasury of the United States.

4.   SHE FELL IN LOVE WITH A FRENCH REFUGEE John Charles Frémont, the famous explorer and "Pathfinder of the West," was first candidate for president from the new Republican party in 1856. He was also an illegitimate child. His mother, a high-born Virginian, was only seventeen when she was married off to sixty-year-old John Pryor. At twenty-nine she fell in love with a young French refugee. Pryor learned of the relationship and threatened to kill his wife, but the young couple fled to Savannah, where John Charles Frémont was born in 1813.

5.   THE PRESIDENT'S DAUGHTER In February 1919, Senator Warren G. Harding was shocked to find out that his mistress, Nan Britton, was pregnant. Harding was deathly afraid that his wife would find out and he wanted Nan to have an abortion, but Nan was filled with romantic excitement.

They continued to meet in run-down hotels, and at the end of her fifth month he gave her a sapphire ring surrounded by diamonds, declaring she could "not belong to him more utterly" even if they had been "joined together by fifty ministers." He sent her to Asbury Park, New Jersey, to have their baby and the affair continued as Harding moved up to the presidency.

After Harding's death, Nan, not getting what she thought she deserved from the Harding estate, wrote a book called *The President's Daughter*. New York publishers wouldn't touch it but it was printed privately. Nobody reviewed it, but word-of-mouth sales increased until it became a phenomenal best seller. The daughter in question graduated from high school in 1938 using the name Elizabeth Ann Harding and listed her father as Warren G. Harding on her college application.

Thanks, but—

1. A LAXATIVE FOR MISS LIBERTY The Statue of Liberty, paid for with the centimes and francs of the French people, was formally given to the United States in 1884, but it couldn't be installed because the American people had been slow in raising money for the pedestal.

To the rescue came the makers of Castoria laxative with an offer of twenty-five thousand dollars, "provided that for the period of one year you permit us to place across the top of the pedestal the word 'Castoria.' Thus art and science, the symbol of liberty to man, and of health to his children, would be more closely enshrined in the hearts of our people." The money was declined.

2. THE OFFER TO END ALL OFFERS Charles A. Lindbergh's spectacular solo flight from New York to Paris made him an instant hero. He had very little money but the chance to make millions by accepting one of the countless offers to exploit his name. The strangest proposal came from an unknown admirer who didn't want to see a hero cheapened by having to advertise products. He offered Lindbergh one million dollars to make no endorsements. When asked what he expected in return, he replied, "Not a damn thing." Lindbergh said no thanks.

3. A BONANZA REFUSED When South Carolina seceded from the Union in 1861, Federal Fort Sumter in the Charleston harbor was a thorn in her side. Initially, both the North and South refrained from armed conflict over the issue, but South Carolina farmers took action by refusing to sell fresh meat and vegetables to "foreigners."

The troops in Fort Sumter were beginning to face starvation when suddenly a boat sent by a humanitarian South Carolina army quartermaster arrived with two hundred pounds of beef and bags of vegetables. The soldiers joyfully began unloading this bonanza and were carrying it into the kitchen when Major Robert Anderson, Fort Sumter's commander, found out about it. He had them send it right back. Anderson said thanks but he could not accept charity from the Confederacy. Provisions must be obtained "in the manner prescribed by law."

4.   IF ELECTED I WILL NOT SERVE Buffalo Bill Cody was a famous army scout and a dashing figure in 1872, when his friends decided to elect him to the Nebraska legislature without telling him. Cody came back from a scouting mission and became aware of his victory at the polls when a lot of men in front of the general store greeted him with "How do you do, Honorable." Cody felt that his election was "highly complimentary, and I appreciate it, but I am no politician and I shall have to tender my resignation." He did hang on to the salutation "Honorable," which he felt was rightly his.

5.   WASHINGTON ABDICATES THE THRONE Colonel Lewis Nicola, an officer on Washington's staff, wrote his Commander in Chief proposing that the new nation be a monarchy with George Washington as king. Washington replied that he read the suggestion "with abhorence." He added emphatically: "If I am not deceived in the knowledge of myself, you could not have found a person to whom your schemes are more disagreeable."

6.   ROOSEVELT RIDES NO MORE War was a "bully" thing as far as Theodore Roosevelt was concerned. In the 1898 Spanish-American War he organized a headline-stealing regiment that included cowboys and polo players. When World War I came along, Roosevelt was ready for an encore. The former president went hat in hand to see Woodrow Wilson, a man he had accused of weakness for delaying U.S. entry into the war. TR offered to organize a division. Applications to serve under Roosevelt came in at a rate of one thousand a day. A special office on Fifth Avenue was set up to handle the requests to volunteer. Wilson turned him down flatly. Georges Clemenceau, who was soon to be France's prime minister, published an open letter to Wilson saying the French soldiers needed "something approaching a miracle . . . send Roosevelt." Wilson's position was unaltered. Less than two months later, on July 4, 1917, when the first American troops paraded through Paris, the French cheered, *"Vive les Teddies!"*

Bets

1. THE PRESIDENT WHO LOVED POKER Mrs. Louise Cromwell Brooks was an attractive and wealthy widow who met Senator Warren G. Harding when the two were trapped in a Senate elevator together. When Harding became president, he and his friends liked to go to her town house for a night of poker. He once challenged her to a game, "just the two of us—winner names the stakes." She won and named a set of White House dishes as her prize. The next day she received a barrel of china stamped with the mark of the Benjamin Harrison administration.

2. THE MISFORTUNES OF WAR British General Burgoyne, called "Gentleman Johnny," went home to England in the winter of 1776 to promote the idea of his leading an invasion army south from Canada to divide the colonies in two. At the fashionable Brooks's Club in London he wrote in the betting book: John Burgoyne wages Charles Fox one pony (fifty guineas) "that he will be home victorious from America by Christmas Day, 1777."

On October 16, 1777, he surrendered his whole army and was taken prisoner at Saratoga. It was a stunning victory for the Americans, led by General Horatio Gates. Burgoyne wrote his conquerer: "The fortune of war, General Gates, has made me your prisoner." Burgoyne was allowed to return home to England, where Charles Fox was paid off by the club manager. Burgoyne's soldiers remained prisoners in America for the rest of the war.

3. A SOCIAL GAFFE Gouverneur Morris told James Madison that he didn't believe George Washington was as austere and formidable as he was made out to be. Madison said he would buy him a handsome dinner, if, on the next social occasion, Morris would go up to Washington, clap him on the back, and give him a friendly greeting. Morris did it and Madison bought the dinner, but Morris was so shaken and abashed by Washington's chilling reaction that he admitted he would never do anything like that again.

4. A RAILROAD WAGER Union Pacific crews building the first transcontinental railroad from east to west set a one-day record of eight and a half miles. Charles Crocker, in charge of construction for the Central Pacific, boasted that his crews, working from west to east, could lay ten miles in a day. Thomas Durant of the Union

By the time the champagne was uncorked at the completion of the first transcontinental railroad, Charles Crocker, head of the Union Pacific, was ten thousand dollars richer because of a savvy bet on the speed of his track-laying crews.
UNION PACIFIC RAILROAD MUSEUM COLLECTION

Pacific bet ten thousand dollars against it. On April 29, 1869, Crocker took a select crew and worked them from sunup to sundown with only a short break for lunch. They laid ten miles plus two hundred feet, or 3,520 rails and 55,000 spikes.

5.   INSPIRATION BY THE BARREL Thomas Edison's friend Batchelor was convinced the inventor couldn't make a talking machine, even after witnessing a makeshift experiment that produced a faint "hello." He wagered a barrel of apples that the idea wouldn't work. When Edison did get his machine to talk, his assistant "nearly fell down in his fright. I was a little scared, myself," Edison wrote. "I won that barrel of apples from Batchelor, though, and was mighty glad of it."

6.   SHE SHOULD HAVE TALKED IT OVER A woman sat down next to Calvin "Silent Cal" Coolidge at a dinner party and said, "You must talk to me, Mr. Coolidge. I made a bet today that I could get more than two words out of you." "You lose," said Coolidge.

Fired

1.   TRUMAN TELLS IT LIKE IT IS Commander in Chief Harry Truman explained why he dismissed five-star general of the army Douglas MacArthur: "I fired him because he wouldn't respect the authority of the President. That's the answer to that. I didn't fire him because he was a dumb son-of-a-bitch, although he was, but that's not against the law for generals. If it was, half to three-quarters of them would be in jail."

2.   AN ENFANT TERRIBLE Major Pierre L'Enfant, a French engineer and architect who had served in the Revolution, impressed President George Washington with his plan for the new Federal City, a visionary scheme with radiating streets and parks. Washington decided to hire him to design the president's house and the Capitol.

L'Enfant was brilliant but uncooperative. The only authority he recognized was the president's, an attitude that quickly provoked a fierce feud with the commissioners in charge of the new city. They complained quietly to Washington, but when L'Enfant imperiously tore down a house that was in the way of one of his new streets, they were furious. The situation became so messy that once when L'Enfant left town, his assistant was arrested for carrying out his orders. Reluctantly, Washington decided to fire him. On February 27, 1792, he had Thomas Jefferson write a letter saying "your services must be at an end." A competition was launched to find a suitable design for the first federal buildings. L'Enfant's designs for the White House and the Capitol have since been lost.

3.   NOT BEFORE BREAKFAST When Secretary of War Edwin Stanton was fired in 1867, he barricaded himself in his office and had the War Department surrounded by soldiers. He refused to leave because the man who had fired him, President Andrew Johnson, was defying a new, though constitutionally questionable, law. Passed over Johnson's veto, the law forbade the president to fire a member of his own cabinet.

Johnson designated a new secretary of war, Adjutant General Lorenzo Thomas, but Stanton refused to be ousted. When Thomas tried to take up his new job, Stanton issued an order for his arrest. A marshal served the warrant in the morning before breakfast. Thomas appeared before the judge, was released, and went to Stanton's office where the two got into a shouting match as to who was secretary of war. Each ordered the other out.

Finally, they calmed down. Stanton offered Thomas a drink. On leaving, Thomas said, "The next time you have me arrested please do not do it before I get something to eat."

Stanton hung on to his job until Johnson's impeachment trial. When the Senate failed to convict the president in May 1868, Stanton resigned.

4.   ONE DRINK TOO MANY When FDR's son John returned to the White House late one night, he found his father, who liked to retire early, still up in his chair. The crippled president had been

ringing for his valet to help him get from the chair to the bed; but his servant, Irvin McDuffie, after one drink too many, had fallen asleep himself. Roosevelt decided McDuffie had to be fired but couldn't bring himself to do it. While the president was out of town, the First Lady handed out the pink slip.

5. GROSS NEGLECT OF DUTY Presidential guard John F. Parker was "detailed to attend and protect the President Mr. Lincoln" on the night of April 14, 1865, the night when the president went to Ford's Theatre. Parker was a former policeman with a spotty departmental record. When John Wilkes Booth fired his fatal shot, Parker, who was not at his post, may even have been off having an ale with the coachman.

On May 3, 1865, a departmental trial investigated the charge that Parker had allowed "a man to enter the President's private Box and shoot the President." On June 2 the charge against him was dismissed even though others only remotely connected with the assassination received harsh treatment. Parker was permitted to go back to his old job of guarding the president, now Andrew Johnson. Somehow the records of his trial were lost.

Three years later he was found asleep on his beat and fired for "gross neglect of duty."

PART III

War Games

The Army-Navy Game Is Played at Santiago de Cuba

It was fortunate that the 1898 Spanish-American War, fought over Cuban independence, was a romp for the U.S. because at times the army and the navy seemed to be more concerned with fighting each other.

1. TOO TIRED TO HELP The land war was the army's job, but getting troops to the island of Cuba necessitated getting involved with boats—the navy's specialty. The army hired transports and brought its men from Tampa, Florida, to Santiago de Cuba, but then could not find enough small boats to get them ashore. The secretary of the navy begged "leave to inquire" how the army intended to get the troops onto the beaches, for the navy crews "ought not to be fatigued" by such work. The problem was complicated by the captains of the commercial transports that the army had hired. They refused to risk their ships anywhere near the invasion beach. Since the army obviously could not get its troops ashore without help, the navy was forced to exert itself.

2. THE NAVY LOSES THE GLORY Though the army had captured Santiago and forced Spain to surrender, Admiral William Sampson felt that the navy, which had contributed to the victory by destroying the Spanish fleet, should get equal credit. He expressed his views to the army commander, General William Shafter, and Shafter agreed, but somehow the army was late getting the news about the arrangements for the grand surrender ceremony to the navy. By the time the navy representative arrived, it was all over. The navy representative then asked if he could add his signature to the surrender document, but the army denied the request. The army was not about to share the glory with the navy.

3. THE STRUGGLE FOR PRIZES At the beginning of hostilities, the War Department had offered prize money for the capture of Spanish commercial ships. After the surrender, the navy became aware that the army was claiming the ships remaining in the harbor as prizes. The navy was understandably upset because ships were a navy matter. It sent crews racing into the harbor to board the ships but found the army was already there confronting navy men with fixed bayonets. Navy Lieutenant Frank Marble then conned the army officer in command into believing that it had all been ar-

ranged for the navy to take over. When General Shafter discovered the navy steaming away with his prizes, he was "exceedingly wroth."

In the end, control of the ships in the harbor really didn't matter because the attorney general ruled that they were not subject to prize money.

How They Fought in the Days of Sail

1.   SPLINTER TACTICS Sailors traditionally fought barefoot, a fact enemies used to their advantage. Cannons were loaded with glass splinters and rusty nails and fired at close range. The U.S.S. *Constitution*, "Old Ironsides," used such a splinter tactic in its famous battle with the British ship *Guerrière* in the War of 1812. The *Guerrière*'s deck was strewn with bodies, pieces of bodies, blood, and sharp fragments that had to be swept away before firing could continue.

2.   ALL FIRED UP One good way to rout an enemy sailing ship was to set him on fire. Tarred ropes, canvas sails, and wooden decks and masts were all highly inflammable, so cannonballs would be heated in a furnace on the deck. When they were white hot, they were loaded and fired into an enemy ship where they would start burning timber.

3.   A LABORIOUS WAY TO ESCAPE A hazard of all sailing ships was becoming becalmed. This happened to the *Constitution* off the New Jersey coast during the War of 1812. It managed to escape seven British ships by kedging, a tedious tactic possible in coastal waters.

To kedge, all the rope on board was tied together into two ropes, each one half a mile long. Then an anchor was tied to one rope and it was rowed out as far as possible and dropped. The crew literally pulled the ship forward by the men seizing the rope and walking from the bow to the stern. While this was being repeated, the other rope with a second anchor was rowed ahead.

When the British discovered the *Constitution*'s tactic, they began to do the same. Just then a fortunate breeze came up. American Captain Isaac Hull demonstrated his expert seamanship by letting out his sails immediately. Without stopping, he swooped by, hauled up his rowboats, and made his getaway.

4. STINKPOT TOSSING A weaker ship could sometimes overpower one with superior firepower if it could get in close enough to lash the two ships together. Then sailors and marines could board the enemy ship and the battle would become a hand-to-hand fight and often a matter of sheer guts. Stinkpots—earthen jugs filled with rotted fish, saltpeter, and brimstone—would be tossed from the rigging down the enemy's hatches, forcing the enemy crew to the deck gasping for air where they would be shot down by marines.

5. BAILING OUT Sailing ships were often at sea for six months at a time. As much as 48,500 gallons of water and 8,000 gallons of rum were stored in the hull. One way to assure a speedy getaway was to lighten the ship. In escaping from the superior British ship *Guerrière*, Captain Hull of the U.S.S. *Constitution* ordered 2,335 gallons of the precious water thrown overboard but kept all his rum.

6. A SLOW MATCH IN HIS TEETH Another weapon for closeup fighting was an iron grenade with a fuse that had to be lighted before it was tossed.

In the famous sea battle between John Paul Jones's ship, the *Bonhomme Richard*, and the British ship *Serapis*, Jones managed to lash the two ships together. Then William Hamilton, an enterprising Scot, climbed the American ship's rigging with a heavy bucket of grenades in one hand and a smoldering slow match between his teeth. He inched his way along the yardarm on his stomach high above the deck of the *Serapis* until he saw a hatch about fifteen feet to the left of his perch with its cover partly off. He lit the grenade fuse, swung his arm to gauge the distance, and lobbed it onto the enemy deck. There it exploded. Hamilton made a devasting hit with a second grenade. It bounced off part of the hatch and fell through the opening, exploding among piles of ammunition. First came a searing flash, then a series of explosions. At least twenty British sailors were killed, and others, their clothing on fire, jumped into the sea.

7. NAME THAT FLAG Running up a false flag was a standard *ruse de guerre*. Most vessels carried a trunk full of flags to use as the occasion demanded. Fighting was a guessing game and sometimes captains guessed wrong. Before any firing began a ship was supposed to show its true colors, but often it was too late and the potentially weaker ship had already opted to run from the more

powerful one. On one such occasion, the mighty *Constitution* chased an "enemy" privateer, which threw twelve of its fourteen new cannons overboard attempting to lighten its load and escape. Then each side recognized the other as American.

8. LICENSE TO RAID Privateers were vital to weaker naval powers. With a letter of marque, a commercial captain, whose ship was usually armed already, became a privateer with a license to raid. He could attack any enemy ship and keep half of all he captured. Naturally many privateers became rich. During the Revolutionary War more than six hundred British ships were taken. After the Civil War, privateering ceased, but Congress still has power under the Constitution to "grant letters of marque."

When Wars Were More Gentlemanly

1. A CIVILIZED PLEA Dr. William Thornton was the head of the U.S. Patent Office during the War of 1812. When the British invaded Washington, D.C., and began to set fire to the Capitol, the White House, and other public buildings, Thornton rushed outside. With histrionic flair he warned the British that "to burn what would be useful to all mankind would be as barbarous as to burn the Alexandria Library, for which the Turks have been condemned by all enlightened nations." The British agreed and spared the Patent Office.

2. GIVING THE ENEMY A FIGHTING CHANCE In the Civil War, land mines were a new technology viewed with horror. Confederate Secretary of War Randolph ruled that hidden land mines could be used "to repel an assault," but not "merely to destroy life and without other design than that of depriving the enemy of a few men." He also ruled against shooting enemy soldiers who were bathing.

3. WASHINGTON'S PROMISE In the French and Indian War, George Washington found himself trapped in a valley and surrounded by enemy forces. Hastily he built Fort Necessity, but his chances of fending off an attack were slim. The French offered him unusual surrender terms. If he promised to march out and not re-

turn, his men could escape with their guns and their honor. Washington agreed and the French gained a victory without bloodshed.

4. RESPECT FOR THE PATRIARCHS Mount Vernon, George Washington's historic Virginia home, was neutral ground to both sides in the Civil War. So was the late President James K. Polk's house in Nashville, Tennessee, where his widow still lived.

5. PRISONERS AT MONTICELLO In 1779, while the Revolutionary War was still being fought, it was not unusual for German and British officers to dine at Monticello. They were prisoners of war, part of the four thousand captured at the Battle of Saratoga and sent to Virginia. Thomas Jefferson loved their spirited conversation and especially their music. His humanitarian instincts also compelled him to help make their imprisonment more endurable, but indeed their confinement was of the most casual nature. The officers lived in rented houses and the privates all farmed. The German General Baron Riedesel even lived with his wife at Colle, a small estate near Monticello. The baroness, who wrote home that she had raised "turkeys weighing fifty pounds," delighted Jefferson with her risqué stories and Italian songs.

6. THE RED CARPET FOR A PRISONER When the British marched on Washington, D.C., in the War of 1812, American Commodore Joshua Barney knew he would soon be their prisoner. He was gravely wounded and had ordered his men to leave him behind as they retreated.

A British corporal found the injured American commodore, but Barney refused to surrender to an enlisted man, so Admiral Cockburn was summoned. Barney told him, "Well, Admiral, you have got hold of me at last." Cockburn was gracious: "Do not let us speak of that subject, Commodore. I regret to see you in this state." The wounded American was immediately given medical help and set free. A party of stretcher-bearers was ordered to take him to his comrades at nearby Bladensberg. He was escorted by a captain who was assigned to see that he was well attended to.

7. HE ESCAPED IN HIS NIGHTCLOTHES Confederate General Nathan Bedford Forrest, a brilliant cavalry leader, led a predawn raid on Union-occupied Memphis, a town he and his men knew well. Sentries alerted Northern General Washburn of the attack and he managed to escape in his nightclothes. In his haste he left behind his general's uniform, which the Southern troops seized as a consolation prize.

When Forrest discovered this, he returned Washburn's uniform under a flag of truce. The grateful Washburn had Forrest's Memphis tailor make a fine Confederate general's uniform and sent it to him under a flag of truce.

8.   MISS LIVINGSTON APPEALS TO A GENTLEMAN In 1780 the British launched a surprise raid on New Jersey Governor William Livingston, hoping to take him prisoner. Disappointed by his absence, they decided to snare his confidential papers. Brigadier Stirling led the search. When he approached a locked secretary, the governor's quick-thinking daughter Susan begged him not to open it. "In here are letters that I have exchanged with a certain gentleman," she told him, her voice trembling. "If *you* are a gentleman, sir, you will not disturb them." Stirling heeded her call to honor, but made her promise to lead him to her father's papers. She then climbed the library ladder and handed him down papers from the top shelves. They were her father's old law briefs, but the British officer rushed away without reading them.

9.   VICTORY DINNERS The night after the British surrendered at Yorktown, ending the Revolutionary War fighting, the victorious Americans and their French allies invited defeated British officers to a banquet. A round of dinners followed with both sides entering into the jovial camaraderie.

10.   STARTING THE WAR ON A POLITE NOTE Major Robert Anderson, Union commander of Fort Sumter in Charleston harbor, was surrounded by South Carolina forces and running out of food. When he gallantly refused to surrender, he received a note stating, "By authority of Brigadier-General Beauregard, commanding the Provisional Forces of the Confederate States, we have the honor to notify you that he will open the fire of his batteries on Fort Sumter in one hour from this time." The time was 3:20 A.M., April 12, 1861. Anderson shook hands with the Southern emissaries and one hour later the great American Civil War began.

Ruses That Worked

1.   DOUBLE-DECEPTION D-DAY To throw the Germans off the track of the June 6, 1944, invasion at Normandy, the Allies used a double fake. They planned a false invasion of Norway, dubbed For-

titude North, as well as a false one at Calais, given the code name Fortitude South. The idea was that the Germans would realize that Fortitude North was a fake and then believe that the real invasion would be at Calais.

To make the deception credible, a huge invasion base was built on the English shore opposite Calais. Rubber tanks and wooden guns were stored in fields. Tank tracks crisscrossed the countryside. Dummy runways were lit so they would be picked up by German night reconnaisance. Along the shore, obsolete boats and inflated landing craft were positioned. Radio traffic from a fake headquarters poured out twenty-four hours a day and loudspeakers played recordings of airplanes warming up.

The double fake confused the Germans sufficiently that the Allies suffered relatively light casualties when they landed on the beaches of Normandy.

2. WASHINGTON LEAVES THE CAMPFIRES BURNING After surprising the Hessians at Trenton, Washington was entrenched behind Assunpink Creek. Lord Cornwallis, with a superior force of eight thousand men, hurried to Trenton seeking revenge. He arrived in the late afternoon and decided not to attack until the next morning.

It was a mistake. During the night Washington slipped away. He ordered the wheels of the cannon and the hooves of the horses wrapped in rags to deaden their sound on the frozen ground. He left the campfires burning and assigned a work party to noisily build fortifications where the British would need to cross the creek. Cornwallis awoke to find Washington gone and, as an aide said, he was "in a most infernal sweat . . . at being so outwitted." By marching all night, Washington was able to capture Cornwallis's supply base at Princeton.

3. THE SMALL BOYS FOIL THE JAPANESE In October 1944, General Douglas MacArthur was ready to make good on his promise to return and liberate the Philippines. The Japanese, who controlled the islands, planned to put up an all-out fight when MacArthur's troops landed, the moment when they were most vulnerable. But they could only risk what was left of their battered navy if the main American carrier force was lured away. The unenviable job of decoy fell to Admiral Ozawa, who led a force south from Japan. He sailed with aircraft carriers but only a few aircraft. He fully expected his fleet to be destroyed.

As the American invasion began at Leyte, the main Japanese battle squadrons approached quietly from the opposite direction, winding through the islands. Meanwhile, Admiral Ozawa tried desperately to attract American attention—he sent out radio messages and brought his force within range of American search planes.

Finally he was sighted and Admiral William F. "Bull" Halsey took the bait. He raced off with more than sixty ships and hundreds of planes to chase Ozawa's seventeen ships and two dozen aircraft. The Americans were left to defend the beaches with the "small boys"—destroyers, unarmored merchant ships with converted flight decks and small torpedo boats. They put up a furious fight against a vastly superior force of battleships and cruisers. They laid down smoke screens, hid in rain squalls, and sent small ships in on suicidal torpedo attacks. The Japanese heavy armor-piercing shells went right through the light American ships without exploding.

The Japanese believed the decoy plan had failed and they were facing the main American force. They withdrew. Actually, their ruse had worked to perfection, but what no one had counted on was the heroics of the small boys or "the very definite partiality of Almighty God," as Admiral Sprague put it.

4. WASHINGTON BEWILDERS CLINTON In 1781 George Washington decided to gamble. He was encamped across the water from New York when word came that a French fleet with reinforcements was arriving near Yorktown, Virginia, where a main arm of the British army was concentrated under Cornwallis. Washington decided that if he combined his army with the one already at Yorktown, he could overwhelm Cornwallis.

Success depended on surprise and on making the British think New York was his target. As he said later, "Much trouble was taken, and finesse used, to misguide and bewilder Sir Henry Clinton," the British general who held New York.

Washington ordered work parties to clear the roads approaching New York, but began to move his army secretly to Yorktown. Men were detailed to construct support facilities such as ovens for an invading army, not knowing it was a fake. "If we do not deceive our own men, we will never deceive the enemy," Washington said. Washington himself played a part. He went near the shore, asked a known Tory about the tides, and then, as if he had let something slip, said it was of no importance.

Clinton wrote Cornwallis that he couldn't fathom Washington's maneuvers. An American doctor wrote in his diary that "the menacing aspect of an attack on New York will be continued till time and circumstance shall remove the delusive veil from the eyes of Sir Henry Clinton, when it will probably be too late." It was. Clinton sailed to relieve Cornwallis on the day Cornwallis surrendered.

5. QUAKER GUNS STALL McCLELLAN Confederate General Magruder had fifteen thousand men to stall a ninety-thousand-man Union force headed up the peninsula to capture Richmond. Magruder, famous as an amateur actor, put up a theatrical defense. He marched thousands of men around within sight but out of range, giving General George McClellan the impression of a much superior force. He built elaborate earthworks with "Quaker guns"—big logs painted black. Phony notices appeared in the Richmond papers of units going to the front, duly reported to McClellan through the Union spy network. McClellan, normally slow to attack, was delayed so long that the Confederates were able to reinforce Richmond.

6. THE WORK OF A MADMAN During the Revolutionary War, a British force led by Barry St. Leger headed down the Mohawk Valley toward Albany with one thousand Iroquois allies. The American faced with fending them off was Benedict Arnold, who commanded only a small force but had access to a madman. The Indians believed that an insane Tory named Hon Yost Schuyler spoke with the voice of the Great Spirit. Arnold held Schuyler's brother captive. Through threats he forced him to get his mad brother to tell the Indians that an overwhelming American force was approaching. Suddenly the British found their Indian allies had melted away in the night. Arnold was able to turn back the invasion without firing a shot.

7. AN EMBARRASSED HAIR BUYER At the outset of the Revolution the British controlled the whole vast Ohio Valley, mainly through a strong fort at Vincennes commanded by Colonel Henry Hamilton, called the "hair buyer" because he paid Indians to bring in American scalps.

In the middle of the winter of 1778 George Rogers Clark led a daring raid on Vincennes with only 130 men. The two-hundred-mile march entailed incredible hardships, including wading for miles through ice-cold water, sometimes up to their shoulders. The British force was several times larger and entrenched in a strong fort, but Clark used boldness and bluff.

He approached from behind a low range of hills at dusk. The troops could not be seen, but two dozen flags and banners gave the impression of a larger army. The flags were flown from extra-long poles and carried by men who were marched around and around behind the same hillock. Only after dark did Clark let his outnumbered men near the fort.

He began shelling the fort at night. Shooting was spaced to make it seem as if his men were continually reinforced. After several days, Colonel Hamilton was intimidated into surrendering. When the conquering Americans entered the fort, Hamilton asked, "Colonel Clark, where is your army?" Chagrined when he realized the truth, Hamilton turned away with tears in his eyes.

Rivalry in the Military

1.   STEALING THE GLORY When the Sunday morning of July 3, 1898, dawned, all seemed quiet outside Santiago de Cuba where the U.S. Navy was blockading the harbor during the Spanish-American War. Admiral William Sampson decided to sail off on the battleship *New York* for a conference with General William Shafter, leaving his archrival, Commodore Winfield Schley, in charge.

Soon after Sampson left, the sailors on the American ships were on deck for a routine inspection before Divine Services when an alarm sounded. Incredibly, the Spanish fleet had chosen 9:30 that morning to try to bolt out of the harbor. Sampson was four miles away when he heard the guns. He turned the *New York* around and tried to race back, but by the time he caught up with the rest of his ships, the entire Spanish fleet had been sunk or destroyed.

Schley, who had seen Sampson promoted over him, tried to secure the glory by rushing a victory message to Washington. But Sampson's officers got to the cable station first and only allowed the admiral's report to be sent. It described a great victory and omitted any mention of Commodore Schley.

2.   DRINKING TEA WITH KINGS AND QUEENS General Douglas MacArthur's ego was hardly gratified when his former aide, Dwight Eisenhower, rose like a rocket to five-star general in World War II. Fortunately, the two headed up commands on opposite sides of the world, MacArthur in the Pacific and Eisenhower in Europe, where Ike showed his diplomatic prowess in dealing with world leaders. To MacArthur, however, Eisenhower "let his generals in the field fight the war for him. They were good and covered up for him. He drank tea with kings and queens. Just up Eisenhower's

In 1932 Major Dwight D. Eisenhower's uniform was without any of the decorations of his boss, General Douglas MacArthur (left), but in World War II, Ike caught up fast. The two are shown at the scene of the "Bonus Army," which besieged the Capitol during the Depression.
UPI/BETTMANN NEWSPHOTOS

alley." Eisenhower said of MacArthur, "I studied dramatics under him for five years . . ."

3. A SURPRISE ON A SURPRISE ATTACK The Revolutionary War was yet to begin when Ethan Allen, leader of the Green Mountain Boys, decided to lead an attack on the British at Fort Ticonderoga. About the same time, Benedict Arnold, from Massachusetts, got the same idea. The two met quite unexpectedly on the way to the fort and an immediate argument erupted as to who was in charge.

Arnold had written authority from Massachusetts and a nice new uniform, but he hadn't raised any troops yet. Allen had his unruly Green Mountain Boys. Allen threatened to put Arnold in irons. Finally both managed to calm down long enough to launch a joint attack. Arnold and Allen approached the fort side by side, but when they got close they began to race each other. In almost comic fashion they succeeded in a bloodless capture, since the British force was unprepared.

The Green Mountain Boys then proceeded to get drunk and take pot shots at Arnold. One threatened him with a loaded musket against his chest. Allen's lasting fame is in part due to the fact that he put down his experiences in a book. In it, he solved the problem of command by not mentioning Arnold.

4. NOT A BRILLIANT DISPLAY OF COURAGE One of the major unanswered questions about the Battle of Little Big Horn is whether Major Marcus Reno could have rescued Custer, a man he heartily disliked.

Flamboyant George Armstrong Custer, the "boy general" with the golden curls, was both idolized and hated. Major Reno's job at

Little Big Horn was to attack one end of the Indian encampment while Custer approached from the other side. Reno was repulsed and retreated to a hill. The Indians then concentrated their attack on Custer's force, wiping out his entire command.

Why didn't Reno make another foray to aid Custer? He claimèd the casualties he had suffered had made a rescue impossible. The question went before a court of inquiry, which concluded that although some subordinates outshone Reno "by brilliant displays of courage," there was nothing in his conduct that required "animadversion from this Court."

In 1926, on the fiftieth anniversary of the Little Big Horn Battle, a statue of Reno was unveiled. Custer's widow refused to attend and urged there be no memorial "to so great a coward as Major Reno."

5.   AN UNMENTIONED HERO At the Battle of Saratoga, Benedict Arnold was second in command to General Horatio Gates, a man he heartily disliked. Arnold was impulsive, a fighter who had no tolerance for the defensive strategy of "Granny Gates." He felt he was treated "like a cipher" and asked to go home. Gates, only too happy to oblige, relieved him of command. Then the battle broke out.

Benedict Arnold limped permanently as a result of his service to the American cause. At the Battle of Saratoga, his horse was shot out from under him and crushed his leg.
COURTESY OF THE NEW-YORK HIS-
TORICAL SOCIETY, NEW YORK CITY

Arnold had no command and no right to give orders, but he was unable to resist a fight. "No man shall keep me to my tent today," he cried. He raced off into battle and led a wild charge that carried a key redoubt. Arnold received a severe injury when his horse was shot and fell on his leg. He refused to have it amputated and was left with a permanent limp.

The defeated British commander, General Burgoyne, felt that Arnold's charge was the decisive factor in the battle. The American commander, however, gave him no credit. General Gates charged Arnold with disobeying orders and never mentioned his heroics when he reported this great victory to Congress.

Raising an Army

1. NO PROFIT FOR THE KING When King George III needed troops to put down rebellion in his colonies, he turned to German princes who were only too willing to make some money by renting out their armies. For every one of his soldiers killed, the German prince got an extra seven pounds, four shillings, and four and a half pence. Three wounded soldiers counted as one soldier killed.

For additional troops, George III turned to the German state of Hanover, which he also ruled. As king of England and elector of Hanover, he worked out an arrangement whereby he hired out troops to himself. "I do not mean to make one Sixpence by this," he explained.

2. NINETY-DAY SOLDIERS In the Revolutionary War, George Washington often faced the problem of a vanishing American army. The bulk of his soldiers came from state militias which generally had ninety-day enlistment periods. When the soldiers' stints were up, they went home, even if it was in the middle of a battle.

After Washington's famous December 26 attack on the Hessians at Trenton, he wanted to hold his army together for another battle, but most of the enlistments expired within forty-eight hours. To get the men to stay, the general promised those who fought for another six weeks a ten-dollar bounty plus a share in any goods captured.

A sergeant remembered that Washington, on a fine charger, "in the most affectionate manner entreated us to stay" and then rode off to one side. The drummer beat for volunteers. No man stepped forward. Washington then made a second and more impassioned plea, and finally most of the men agreed to fight, making the victory at Princeton possible.

3. $300 GOT YOU OUT When the Civil War broke out, both the North and the South thought the war would be fleeting, one or two battles at most. On April 15, 1861, President Abraham Lincoln issued a call for seventy-five thousand state volunteers to serve three months. Men signed up so rapidly that Secretary of War Simon

Cameron had to plead with the states to reduce the flow because the Union lacked the organization and equipment to handle large numbers of soldiers.

However, as the Civil War dragged on, volunteers quickly became scarce. In March 1863 a draft was begun for men twenty to forty-five, but it could be easily dodged. An affluent man could hire a substitute to fight in his stead or pay three hundred dollars—the equivalent of a year's wage for a common worker. Future President Grover Cleveland hired a substitute; future millionaires Andrew Carnegie and John D. Rockefeller paid the three hundred dollars. The money raised by the draft was used to pay bounties for enlistments. Some men worked the system and made a profit by enlisting and deserting repeatedly, collecting up to a one-thousand-dollar bounty with each new enrollment.

When substitutes became scarce, brokers emerged who would locate a substitute for a fee. Some states that needed to fill their quotas but were short of men to draft sent recruiting agents into occupied areas of the South to enlist freed slaves. The recruitment system hit further snags when unscrupulous doctors certified the physically and mentally unfit, thereby saddling the army with unqualified soldiers.

Despite these pitfalls, the North managed to raise huge armies, which proved decisive against the less populous South.

4. HORSELESS ROUGH RIDERS AND OTHER IRONIES OF WAR
When the war with Spain broke out in 1898, the Spanish had eighty thousand men in Cuba. The U.S. had a total of twenty-eight thousand men in its regular army. To raise sufficient troops the National Guard was called on, but the Guard posed a few problems. For one, its men still used rifles that fired black powder. These were considered useless in war because the cloud of black smoke gave away a soldier's position. Also, the Guard lacked equipment such as tents, blankets, and lightweight uniforms for the tropics. Its officers were chosen by popular vote and knew little about discipline or tactics. And its men flatly refused to fight under West Point graduates, the only trained officers available. New York's famous 7th Regiment voted not to participate in the war at all.

Only one volunteer regiment was allowed, and Theodore Roosevelt was delighted to leave his job as assistant secretary of the navy to help head it up. His volunteer cavalry regiment was composed of men ranging from the "harem-scarem rough riders of the West" to eastern socialites from the polo-playing set. They trained on a ranch in the West and were called the Rough Riders, but when they joined the war they fought on foot. It turned out there wasn't enough room on the ships to take the regiment's horses.

Fortunately for all soldiers involved, the Spanish-American War involved only one small land battle—the attack up the San Juan hills.

Lincoln's Generals—Four Losers and a Winner

When the Civil War began, Lincoln's first choice for command of the Union army, Robert E. Lee, turned him down. Lee was opposed to slavery and disunion but felt he could not fight against his native Virginia. Finding a man of Lee's stature kept Lincoln busy. He read books on military tactics and involved himself in strategic planning. He went through four commanders of the Army of the Potomac before he found the man he had confidence in—General Ulysses S. Grant.

1. GENERAL GEORGE McCLELLAN After the Battle of Bull Run in July 1861, the North realized it was in for a long fight. Lincoln turned to George McClellan, who assembled, drilled, and trained an impressive army but always found reasons why he could not move it into battle. He constantly felt he was outnumbered and needed more and more equipment, even though he had superior forces. Lincoln said he had "the slows" and once asked if he could borrow the army since McClellan wasn't using it.

McClellan tried to give the president the impression of rapid movement by marking his dispatches "Headquarters in the Saddle." "He has his headquarters where his hindquarters ought to be" was Lincoln's comment.

McClellan was soundly defeated outside Richmond by a smaller Southern army led by a man who thoroughly understood McClellan's personality—Robert E. Lee. Lincoln lost patience with McClellan and relieved him of the top command when he failed to pursue Lee's battered army after a bloody fight at Antietam in September 1862.

2. **GENERAL AMBROSE BURNSIDE** Burnside succeeded Mc-Clellan but really didn't believe he was qualified for the top job. He proceeded to fight a battle that proved he was right.

Lee's army was entrenched on heights above Fredericksburg, Virginia, and Burnside's job was to dislodge him. When circling tactics failed, Burnside decided to deceive Lee by charging up the heights. It did deceive Lee. He couldn't believe anyone would be so foolish. Southern General Longstreet said a chicken couldn't live out there. The bodies were soon three deep on Marye's Hill. The Northern army was shattered. When Burnside proposed sending troops back up the heights on the following day, his shocked commanders dissuaded him.

He asked to be relieved of the top command and Lincoln obliged him.

3. **GENERAL JOSEPH HOOKER** Hooker, chosen to fill Burnside's shoes, had earned the nickname "Fighting Joe" early in the war. He was determined to destroy Lee's army and at first it seemed as if he would succeed. However, at Chancellorsville, Confederate Generals Lee and Stonewall Jackson caught him off guard when they split their much smaller force and attacked Hooker from behind. It was a brilliant move and a total surprise. At a critical point in the battle, a shell landed near Hooker and he was stunned by a falling porch pillar. He lost his nerve and ordered a retreat.

Hooker also asked to be relieved of his command and Lincoln sent him to fight in the West.

4. **GENERAL GEORGE MEADE** As the war progressed, Lee launched an invasion of the North, hoping for a decisive victory that would win the war. The man Lincoln chose to counter this offensive was George Meade, his fourth commander. Meade won the great battle at Gettysburg, but when Lee's army was retreating across the swollen Potomac, Meade failed to pursue the Confederates and lost a chance to crush Lee and end the war in 1863—almost two years earlier than it did.

Lincoln, who desperately wanted the bloodshed to end, wrote Meade, "He was within your grasp, and to have closed upon him would . . . have ended the war," but, in typical Lincoln fashion, he thought it over and tore the letter up the next day. Perhaps, he said, if he had been through the fire and killing of Gettysburg, he too might not have pursued Lee. Shortly thereafter, Lincoln promoted Grant to overall command of all Union armies and Grant kept Meade on his staff.

5.   GENERAL ULYSSES S. GRANT Lincoln, impressed by Grant's victories in the West, made him a lieutenant general, a rank last held by George Washington, and summoned him to Washington, D.C. Grant's arrival was typically inconspicuous. Somehow the welcoming committee missed him at the train station. He checked in at Willard's Hotel, rumpled and travel-stained, a linen duster hiding much of his uniform. The writer Richard Henry Dana described him as "short, round-shouldered," and with a "rather scrubby look withal." A disinterested desk clerk gave him a room on the top floor. Then he saw the signature "U. S. Grant" on the register and immediately found him a second-floor suite.

That night he was escorted to the White House to meet the president. When Grant explained his plan of using all his forces to attack the South, Lincoln endorsed it immediately. It was what he'd wanted all along. As he put it in his frontier way, it was like a hog killing back home: "If a man can't skin he must hold a leg." Lincoln liked and trusted Grant. He had found the general who would take command and press the South on all sides at once until victory was won.

Battle Cries

1.   "DON'T GIVE UP THE SHIP." In the War of 1812, James Lawrence, captain of the *Chesapeake*, got a taunting note from a British ship blockading Boston to come out and fight. Lawrence took the bait. He ran up a flag with the motto "Free Trade and Sailors' Rights" and headed out for a fight which was witnessed by crowds thronging the Boston wharf and pleasure craft crowding the waters. The first volley left Lawrence mortally wounded. Dying, he gave his famous command. However, his men were soon forced to give up the ship, and when they did, the British towed the *Chesapeake* to Halifax, Canada, where Lawrence was buried with full military honors.

2.   "DON'T FIRE UNTIL YOU SEE THE WHITES OF THEIR EYES." The raw colonial militia entrenched at the Battle of Bunker Hill tended to get very nervous when columns of disciplined British Redcóats advanced toward them with gleaming bayonets. Even under the best of circumstances, their marksmanship was uneven because the muskets of the Revolutionary War were notoriously inaccurate ex-

cept at close range. Colonel William Prescott's famous order was a plea to make every bullet count. It did. The British ranks were decimated as they charged once and then twice up the hill. By their third bloody foray, the colonists were out of powder and had to surrender their position. British casualties numbered over one thousand. Four hundred Americans died or were wounded.

3. "WE'VE GOT THE DAMN YANKEES ON THE RUN." So cried Confederate General Joseph Wheeler—thirty years after the Civil War had ended. He'd been asked by President McKinley to fight in the Spanish-American War. At first Wheeler had declined because of age, but McKinley persisted because he wanted to show that the Civil War wounds had healed. At Las Guásimas in Cuba, Wheeler saw that the Cubans were retreating and excitedly let out a battle cry that had served him well decades before.

4. "I HAVE NOT YET BEGUN TO FIGHT." That was John Paul Jones replying to a British request for the surrender of the *Bonhomme Richard* in his famous 1779 sea battle. He enunciated every syllable emphatically, even though his battered ship had seen more than the beginnings of a fight. It had seven feet of water in the hold and was sinking. As Jones recalled later, it was "a tremendous scene of carnage, wreck and ruin."

Undaunted, he lashed the *Bonhomme Richard* to the superior British *Serapis* and his men swarmed across the decks. After three hours of bloody hand-to-hand combat, the British surrendered.

5. "DAMN THE TORPEDOES! FULL STEAM AHEAD." In the Civil War, the Confederates mined Mobile Bay at the mouth of the Mississippi River with "torpedoes." Union Admiral David Farragut was leading the sea attack on New Orleans when he saw a fellow Union ship, the *Tecumseh*, trigger a mine, explode, and sink within two minutes. Farragut was up on the rigging of his ship, the *Brooklyn*. Could his famous battle cry have been heard from that vantage point? Possibly, though it wasn't attributed to him for fourteen years. But whatever his words, he clearly sent down a command ordering his ship to steam boldly through the mined bay. Farragut's decision led to the capture of New Orleans, a city the Union troops held for the rest of the war.

6. "DON'T FIRE UNLESS FIRED ON, BUT IF THEY MEAN TO HAVE A WAR, LET IT BEGIN HERE." So said Captain James Parker on the nineteenth of April, 1775. He was standing on the village green in Lexington, Massachusetts, with some seventy-five men and

boys and no clear idea of what he was going to do when seven hundred crack British troops approached. "Disperse" was the order British Major Pitcairn gave to "ye dammned rebels," and the Americans were taking his advice when a shot from an unknown source rang out. More gunfire followed and the war did begin on Lexington Green with Captain Parker.

Famous Surprise Attacks

1.   'TWAS THE DAY AFTER CHRISTMAS In the early morning of December 26, 1776, Hessian commander Colonel Rall came to the window in his nightshirt and demanded to know what was happening. He had celebrated Christmas the night before in good German fashion and consequently was groggy.

Hired by the British to fight against the Americans, he had been left in charge of the Trenton outpost guarding the Delaware River. Lord Cornwallis, declaring the campaign over for the winter, had already gone back to New York to pack his bags for England. Suddenly Trenton was swarming with ragged American troops who had somehow crossed the ice-clogged river with 187 pieces of artillery. The surprise was so complete, only a few Hessians escaped. Washington took one thousand prisoners and lost only two men, neither of whom were victims of the British but of the freezing cold.

2.   DOOLITTLE DOES A LOT In the dark days following Pearl Harbor, the Japanese totally dominated the Pacific. For the U.S., striking back and attacking Japan seemed impossible because there was no safe place within flying range to launch planes.

Then General Jimmy Doolittle came up with the idea of outfitting an aircraft carrier with longer-range land-based B-25 bombers, something that wasn't thought to be possible. The Japanese certainly didn't think so. Their patrol planes sighted one of Doolittle's land-based bombers, but the report wasn't believed. The Japanese navy had been aware of the threat but wasn't alarmed enough to tell the army or the civil defense. When the American planes arrived over the Japanese coast, fishermen stood up and waved. The bomber crews roared over military bases, a crowded baseball stadium, playgrounds full of children, all without causing concern. Even the residents of the U.S. Embassy assumed the planes had to be Japanese. After dropping their bombs, most of the planes went on to land in China and Congress awarded Doolittle the Medal of Honor.

3. TAKING A CHANCE AT CHANCELLORSVILLE In May 1863, generals Robert E. Lee and Stonewall Jackson sat on a log and drew plans in the dirt with sticks. Jackson's idea was to take his troops and attack the right flank of Union General Joseph Hooker's army, which was discovered to be lightly defended. Lee was to make a decoy frontal attack.

The Union army numbered over a hundred thousand. Between them, the Confederates had only fifty thousand men. When Jackson proposed taking all but thirteen thousand troops with him, Lee said calmly, "Well, go on." Lee kept up a bluff attack on Hooker's front while Jackson made a long-forced march through back wilderness roads. He totally surprised the Union troops on the right flank. They were preparing supper and had their guns stacked when they heard the rebel yell and Jackson's men stormed out of the woods.

The victory at Chancellorsville was the greatest for the team of Jackson and Lee, but it was also their last. Jackson died from an infected arm wound. Lee wrote, "He has lost his left arm, but I have lost my right."

4. "MAGIC" DOESN'T SAVE PEARL HARBOR The Japanese attack on Hawaii was one of the great surprises that shouldn't have been. U.S. intelligence had intercepted Japanese messages and, through a system called Magic, decoded information that led them to believe a Japanese attack was likely. Two weeks before Pearl Harbor an alert had been sent to all Pacific bases. Then, on December 7, 1941, intelligence was received that the Japanese ambassador in Washington had been secretly instructed to break off diplomatic relations with the U.S. at precisely 1:00 P.M. Washington time.

Military communications were down so a warning of imminent war was sent via Western Union. It went out at 11:30 A.M. Washington time. In Honolulu, the telegram arrived an hour and a half before the dawn attack on Pearl Harbor and was given to Tadao Fuchikami, a Japanese-American messenger boy at Western Union. He pedaled off on his bicycle to Fort Shafter. When the bombs hit, he took refuge in a ditch. The Japanese surprise was complete. After the raid, Tadao Fuchikami arrived with his message—eight and a half hours after it was sent.

PART IV
Signposts of America's Past

Paper Chase: The Travels of the Declaration of Independence

1.   JULY 2, 1776 This was the day John Adams thought would go down in history "with pomp and parade, with shows, games, sports, guns, bells, bonfires and illuminations, from one end of this continent to the other, from this time forward forevermore." The vote for independence had been cast and Thomas Jefferson's draft of the declaration was submitted for debate.

2.   JULY 4, 1776 With one third of Jefferson's words changed, the Declaration of Independence was approved. It was signed by John Hancock and the Congress's clerk and turned over to the printer to be distributed as a handbill in the thirteen colonies.

3.   JULY 19, 1776 The Declaration's opening statement that "the 13 colonies unanimously declare" independence became a reality. No colony had actually voted against independence, but New York had abstained. Her delegates didn't have the proper authorization to cast such a ballot until the nineteenth of July. Hancock now ordered the unanimously approved Declaration "engrossed on parchment." He added the unusual suggestion that each man sign the final document, making it a pledging of "sacred honor," as Jefferson's words had stated.

4.   AUGUST 2, 1776 At the Philadelphia State House, which is now Independence Hall, the Continental Congress met to sign the parchment copy. The delegates were literally putting their lives on the line because if captured by the British, they would surely be hung for treason. Almost every signer suffered as a result of his participation.

John Hancock was the first to sign, with lettering bold enough that King George III could read it without his spectacles. Of the total of fifty-six who signed, some had not been present for the July 4 vote. Others who had cast their ballot for the Declaration never signed it. One delegate, George Read of Delaware, signed even though he had voted against the Declaration. He'd been a minority voice in his delegation. Probably fifty delegates signed at this time and others later as they became available. The last signature, that of Delaware's Thomas McKean, didn't come until the following year.

5.   1776 TO 1790 When the British invaded Philadelphia and forced Congress to run for its life, the Declaration was packed into a trunk along with other legislative papers and taken to such places as Lancaster and York, Pennsylvania, Annapolis, Maryland, and Trenton, New Jersey. After the war, Washington became president and decided the Declaration should be lodged in the office of the secretary of state, who also happened to be the document's author, Thomas Jefferson.

6.   1790 TO 1814 The Declaration was moved by ship with the U.S. capital from New York to Philadelphia and then to the new city of Washington. During the War of 1812, Secretary of State James Monroe had the Declaration and other important papers packed into linen sacks, loaded onto wagons, and sent to Virginia. While the British burned Washington in 1814, it was in hiding in a clergyman's home in Leesburg, Virginia.

7.   1814 TO 1876 After the war, the Declaration was returned to the ravaged capital and stored in various buildings until 1820, when it was moved to the headquarters of the Department of State. There it was kept rolled up like a scroll. In 1841, Secretary of State Daniel Webster thought the Declaration should be on view and so he ordered it unrolled, mounted, and framed. It was moved from his office to the new Patent Office, which was then a part of the Department of State, where it hung opposite a window, yellowing and fading, for thirty-five years.

8.   1876 TO 1877 The Declaration made the trip to and from Philadelphia for the Centennial Exposition. All the years of rolling and unrolling as well as fading had taken their toll. Many of the signatures were now so dim as to be unrecognizable.

9.   1877 The Declaration was moved from the Patent Office to the library of the Department of State, where it was displayed for another seventeen years. The move was providential as a few months later the Patent Office burned down.

10.   1894 TO 1921 The Declaration's deterioration caused so much concern that it was sealed between two plates of glass and locked away in a steel safe in the State, War and Navy Building. Only on rare occasions was it exhibited.

11.   1921 A Model T Ford mail truck brought the Declaration to the Library of Congress, which was thought to be a more appropriate home than the State Department. There it was given special care

and lighting and put back on display. A committee of experts formed to study the Declaration had decided that fading could not get much worse.

12.   1941 TO 1944 World War II made any building in the nation's capital dangerous, so on December 26, 1941, the Declaration was packed in a bronze container of a special design. Escorted by a Secret Service guard, it traveled in a Pullman compartment to Fort Knox, Kentucky, where it was stored in an underground vault at the Bullion Depository.

13.   1944 TO 1952 Even though peace had not been achieved, on October 1, 1944, it was considered safe enough to return the Declaration to the Library of Congress. It was sealed in insulating glass with the air expelled. Cellulose paper was put behind the aging parchment to absorb moisture and offset changes in temperature. New lighting was installed and it was put back on display. Guards from the army, navy, and marines stood watch on a rotating basis.

14.   1952 TO PRESENT On December 13, 1952, the Declaration was transported in an army armored personnel carrier and escorted by tanks, an army band, and troops with machine guns to the new Archives Building, its present home. Through modern sophisticated techniques, the Declaration has been restored and, along with the Constitution and the Bill of Rights, is displayed in a bullet-proof helium-filled display case. The outer glass case was smashed by a man with a claw hammer in 1986, but the inner case was undamaged. A push of a button sends the whole display down twenty-two feet through the floor into a fifty-five-ton vault built of steel and reinforced concrete for storage. Jefferson's Declaration has finally found a home.

Enshrining of Americana

1. MOVING THE ROCK Plymouth Rock was ignored for a century and a half before the Liberty Boys, fired up with patriotism at the time of the Revolution, decided it was a historic landmark. By this time the rock was partially buried in the middle of a roadway leading to a wharf and had to be dug out and hauled to the town square. In the course of several additional moves, the rock fell from a wagon and had to be cemented together. By 1920 tourists were

disconcerted when they found the rock was not at the water's edge, so for the three-hundredth-anniversary celebration of the arrival of the Mayflower, Plymouth Rock was moved to the shoreline and a Greek-style temple was erected over it. The rock has found a lasting home.

2.   COWS ON THE PORTICO After Thomas Jefferson died, Monticello and the surrounding land were sold to pay off his debts. Thirteen years later a visitor saw "nothing but ruin and change, rotting terraces, broken cabins, the lawn plowed up and cattle wandering among the Italian mouldering vases."

A wealthy U.S. Naval officer bought the property and made some improvements, but during the Civil War he was considered "an enemy alien" by the Confederacy so his estate was seized and sold off. Cows again rested in the shade of the portico and the parquet floor was covered with bins of grain. In 1878 a congressman reported that Monticello was all "Desolation and ruin . . . a standing monument to the ingratitude of the great Republic." It was not until 1923 that the Jefferson Memorial Foundation took up the task of restoring Jefferson's architectural masterpiece.

3.   FORD'S THEATRE CONFISCATED After John Wilkes Booth shot Abraham Lincoln during a performance of the play *Our American Cousin*, a mob wanted to burn down Ford's Theatre. Instead, the government confiscated it, giving John Ford $100,000. It was converted into an office and storage area.

On June 9, 1893, the day John Wilkes Booth's brother Edwin, a famous Shakespearean actor, was buried, three floors of the building collapsed, sending clerks, desks, and heavy file cabinets crashing down to the basement. Twenty people were killed and sixty-eight injured. The building was closed again.

In 1933 it was transferred to the control of the National Park Service, and on July 7, 1964, funds were finally voted to restore the building to the way it was on that fatal Good Friday in 1865. It now also serves as a working theater and a museum for displaying Lincoln memorabilia.

4.   A VISITOR'S SURPRISE Independence Hall was known as the Pennsylvania State House when it was completed in 1732. In 1774 it housed the First Continental Congress. It witnessed the birth of the Declaration of Independence and the Constitution. But its role in national history ended when the U.S. Capitol was moved from Philadelphia to Washington in 1790. Pennsylvania shifted its own

capitol from Philadelphia to Harrisburg and Independence Hall languished without a purpose.

In 1816 it was almost torn down to make way for building lots. From 1802 to 1827, parts of it were leased to the artist Charles Wilson Peale, who operated a museum. No one attached any particular importance to it until 1824, when the aging Lafayette made a nostalgic return to the United States and expressed surprise at the building's run-down condition. People took to calling it Independence Hall.

When the 1876 centennial came around, the chairs of the signers were brought back, gaslights added, and restorations made. Ever since, visitors have been able to imagine the history that transpired at Independence Hall.

5. A BIBLICAL INSCRIPTION In 1751 Pennsylvania celebrated its fiftieth birthday as a British province by ordering a bell from London. It was inscribed with a verse from the Bible: "Proclaim liberty throughout the land unto all the inhabitants thereof," a phrase now associated with the Revolution.

The bell was first rung hanging from a temporary stand in front of the unfinished State House. It cracked immediately. John Pass and Charles Stow were hired to melt it down and recast it. This second bell had such a harsh tone that it was compared to two coal scuttles, so it was melted down again. Finally, on the third try, a melodious bell was hung in the State House tower.

It was rung to celebrate good King George III's accession to the throne in 1761. It called the people out to hear the reading of the Declaration of Independence on July 8, 1776. When the British occupied Philadelphia during the Revolution, it was carted on a wagon and hidden in the basement of a church in Allentown, Pennsylvania, but it was returned in time to toll when the British surrendered at the end of the war. It rang when the Constitution was adopted in 1788 and on important occasions until July 8, 1835, when it cracked while tolling for the funeral of Chief Justice John Marshall.

In 1852 it was put on display in the State House, and in subsequent years it traveled to patriotic celebrations across the country. In 1915 it even made a trip to San Francisco when two hundred thousand schoolchildren signed a petition asking to see the Liberty Bell. On the return trip it cracked further, so an embargo was put on its travel. The Liberty Bell is now encased in a pavilion in front of Independence Hall.

6. A FORMER ROOT BEER STAND When the Capitol was first built, no one anticipated that the number of congressmen, which expanded with the nation's population, would exceed the number of seats in the chamber. But by 1857, the House of Representatives was forced to move to a new wing in the Capitol, abandoning its old home to "cobwebs" and "dust." One Representative lamented, "I look to see where Calhoun sat . . . and where Clay sat and I find a woman selling oranges and root beer."

In 1864 the old House chamber was cleared and converted into Statuary Hall, where each state was allowed to install two statues. However, as the Union added states, the number of statues became too much for the floor to hold up so some were moved out. The limit is now one per state, and plaques mark the places where Calhoun and Clay sat.

7. REMEMBERING THE ALAMO When the Texas defenders barricaded themselves inside the Alamo in 1836, they were actually fighting inside an old thick-walled 1718 Spanish mission. The convent was their barracks. The church, whose roof had caved in during the 1760s, was a battery.

In 1890 the Alamo's barracks housed Hugo & Schmeltzer's dry-goods store, which featured a new balcony and castlelike turrets. Texans could buy everything from whiskey to boots. DAUGHTERS OF THE REPUBLIC OF TEXAS LIBRARY AT THE ALAMO

After the Mexican victory, General Santa Anna's troops tried to burn down the ruins with little success. The Alamo languished as local residents helped themselves to its stones. In 1845, when Texas was annexed to the United States, the U.S. Army rented the Alamo from the Catholic Church and used it as a barracks. The army added the distinctive gable to the Alamo chapel.

In 1879 the army left and businessman Honore Grenet turned the Alamo into a grocery and mercantile store. He disguised the stone walls of its barracks with a two-story façade that included castlelike turrets and fake cannons. The chapel was his warehouse.

In 1883 Hugo and Schmeltzer took over the concern, which prospered for two decades. Then in 1905 a crisis occurred. The Daughters of the Republic of Texas wanted to buy the Alamo and restore it as a historic landmark, but a hotel syndicate was offering more money than they had—seventy-five thousand dollars—for an option on the site. The Texas legislature refused to match the hotel chain's offer. To the rescue came a twenty-two-year-old cattle heiress, Clara Driscoll. She paid the seventy-five thousand dollars outright and entrusted its restoration to the Daughters of the Texas Republic, its caretakers to this day.

8. "AY, TEAR HER TATTERED ENSIGN DOWN." In the War of 1812 the U.S.S. *Constitution* won the nickname "Old Ironsides" when sailors exclaimed how cannonballs bounced off her sides. She actually didn't have sides of iron but of wood—oak planks twenty-one inches thick. Her most famous battle was with the British frigate *Guerrière*, whose captain had sent a challenge to "any American frigate who dares to do battle." The *Constitution*'s Captain Isaac Hull accepted the dare, sunk the *Guerrière*, and returned to parades and celebrations. But when peace came, his ship was left to rot. By 1830 it was condemned as unseaworthy.

Newspapers took up the *Constitution*'s cause and a Harvard student named Oliver Wendell Holmes wrote a famous poem that began, "Ay, tear her tattered ensign down." As a result of the public outcry, America's most famous fighting ship was repaired and used as a training ship. In 1927 it again needed reconditioning. American schoolchildren raised the money, and on July 31, 1931, Old Ironsides was again seaworthy. Visitors may board it today in the Boston Navy Yard.

9. THE WALLS CAME CRUMBLING DOWN Star-shaped Fort Ticonderoga on Lake Champlain controlled the strategic waterway to Canada. Just before the Revolution, Ethan Allen and Benedict Arnold led a daring surprise attack and took it from the British. The captured cannons were hauled across the snow and used to drive the British out of Boston. Later in the war the fort was burned.

By the time peace came, walls were crumbling and farmers found it an easy source of stone for walls and cellars. Its owner, New York State, didn't mind the pilfering; neither did the local college it was donated to in 1790. In 1820 William Pell became intrigued by the fort and bought the land, but he lost interest in the fort when one of his sons' was blown up by a cannon on the property.

Gradually grass grew over the walls and cows grazed on its ruins.

Finally, in 1908, Stephen Pell, one of William Pell's descendants, decided to restore the fort. Pell had played on the walls as a boy and uncovered a Revolutionary War tinderbox, which inspired a fascination for the fort. In 1909 President Taft presided as the fort, its restoration still in the beginning stages, was officially opened to the public. Stone by stone it has been rebuilt without any government help. In 1931 the Pells donated the fort to the nonprofit Fort Ticonderoga Association, which maintains it as a museum.

What We Almost Got

1. A GREEK TEMPLE AT THE WASHINGTON MONUMENT The original proposal for a monument to George Washington was made by the Continental Congress in 1783. It called for a statue of Washington on horseback clad "in Roman dress, holding a truncheon in one hand and his head encircled by a laurel wreath." Washington objected to the cost and it was never built.

Congress kicked around the idea of a memorial for years but did nothing, so the Washington National Monument Society launched a design contest. The winning proposal by Robert Mills called for an unlikely combination of Greek, Roman, and Egyptian influences. The centerpiece of his design was the six-hundred-foot Egyptian obelisk that now sits on the Mall beyond the Capitol. It was to be encircled at the base with a colonnaded Greek temple, which was to be topped with a statue of George Washington in a Roman chariot driving four horses.

The society ran out of money in the course of building the obelisk. Gradually the idea of the Greek temple and Roman statue faded.

2. A HALF-NAKED WASHINGTON AT THE CAPITOL In 1832 Horatio Greenough received a five-thousand-dollar commission to make a statue for the rotunda of the Capitol. Greenough worked on it for eight years in Italy. It was ten and a half feet high, weighed twenty tons, and cost seventy-seven hundred dollars to ship to Washington. The Capitol entrance had to be widened to get it in. When the public saw it, a huge outcry ensued.

The statue showed George Washington naked to the waist, sitting on a throne with drapery flowing to his sandals. Capitol architect Charles Bulfinch feared it would "give the idea of entering or leaving a bath." Fortunately, it was discovered that the statue was too heavy for the rotunda floor. It was removed and given to the Smithsonian, where it resides today. Visitors now pass the toga-clad Washington on the second floor of the National Museum of American History.

3. FREEDOM IN THE NUDE "Freedom," who tops the Capitol dome, was first intended to take up her post without clothes. The ensuing public furor persuaded sculptor Thomas Crawford to drape her in a long, flowing buffalo robe. Even so, at nineteen and a half feet and fifteen thousand pounds, the statue's anatomy is prominent. "Freedom" has been described as "a big-bosomed, big-hipped" woman.

4. "HIS HIGH AND MIGHTINESS" The problem of how exactly to refer to the president was one of many faced by the young United States. John Adams thought he should be called "His Most Benign Highness." The Senate wanted a mouthful—"His Highness, the President of the United States of America and Protector of the Rights of the Same." Benjamin Franklin thought "His Mightiness" would do. George Washington didn't want any title. The House of Representatives agreed. They wanted only what the Constitution said— "President of the United States"—and that finally won out.

5. JEFFERSON GETS EDITED The truths which the Declaration of Independence refers to were not termed "self-evident" by Thomas Jefferson. He had originally written: "We hold these truths to be sacred and undeniable." The Congress changed that along with Jefferson's contention that "all men are created equal and independent, that from that equal creation they derive rights inherent and inalienable, among which are the preservation of life and liberty, and the pursuit of happiness."

The edited Declaration explained that "all men are created equal, that they are endowed by their Creator with certain unalienable Rights, that among these are Life, Liberty and the pursuit of Happiness." Altogether Congress cut out about five hundred words and made many other changes which Jefferson referred to as "mutilations."

6. A TOMB IN THE CAPITOL ROTUNDA For many years the rotunda floor under the dome of the Capitol had a gaping hole. This was intended to be a final resting place for George Washington where visitors could gaze down at his sarcophagus.

The problem was that the Capitol wasn't finished until long after George Washington died and was buried at Mount Vernon, as specified in his will. Martha had agreed to move the body, but she died before the rotunda was completed. Washington's heirs blocked reburial. The Capitol was left with a large, useless circular hole. Damp air rising from the crypt began to harm the paintings, so in 1828 it was covered up.

7.   MOSES ON THE GREAT SEAL On July 4, 1776, Congress set up a committee consisting of John Adams, Benjamin Franklin, and Thomas Jefferson to design an official seal for the new country. "Rebellion to tyrants is obedience to God" is the motto Benjamin Franklin wanted under the United States' Great Seal. As an illustration, he proposed Moses (with the face of George Washington) dividing the Red Sea and the Pharaoh (modeled after George III) flooded in his chariot.

Thomas Jefferson had an equally erudite proposal—the children of Israel guided through the wilderness by a cloud and a pillar of fire. On the reverse side he suggested the images of the Saxon chiefs, Hengist and Horsa.

Not to be outdone, John Adams proposed an allegory of virtue and vice—Hercules leaning on his club with Virtue attempting to lead him up the mountain trails and Sloth "wantonly reclining on the ground, displaying her charms . . . to seduce him into vice."

Congress rejected their report and went through two more committees before deciding on the present Great Seal. It has an eagle on one side holding a shield with thirteen stripes. In its beak is a scroll with "E Pluribus Unum," or "One from many." On the reverse side of the seal is another symbol of unity—a pyramid with thirteen layers of stone—plus an eye symbolizing Providence. Above the pyramid is "Annuit Coeptis," which means "He has favored our undertaking." Both faces of the Great Seal are shown on the one-dollar bill.

8.   MARKS AND QUINTS? The thirteen colonies used thirteen different monetary systems plus foreign coins such as the Spanish dollar, which was very popular. Congress appointed Robert Morris as superintendent of finance and asked him to come up with a uniform money system for the new country. Morris devised a system based on a unit that was $\frac{1}{1440}$ of the Spanish dollar—the smallest number the varied colonial systems would go into evenly. A mark equaled 1,000 of these units, a quint 500 units.

It may have been the most ingenious and complicated system ever devised, and by August 1784 Congress was ready to accept it. But Congress lacked funds to set up a mint due to "the tediousness of the states" in contributing funds to run the new government, as Morris complained.

Meanwhile, Thomas Jefferson became chairman of the currency committee and found Morris's system "inconvenient." An $80 horse, Jefferson pointed out, would be 115,200 units changed into marks, quints, cents, eights, and fives. It was thanks to Jefferson that Congress, on July 6, 1785, finally adopted a simple decimal system based on the dollar.

9. THE TURKEY LOST OUT It took six years of dispute before the bald eagle was chosen as our national emblem in 1789. Benjamin Franklin had been a strong opponent, calling the eagle a symbol of conquerers and accusing it of having "bad moral Character" and living by "sharping and robbing." Furthermore, he wrote, the eagle "is generally poor, and often very lousy." Franklin felt the turkey was a "much more respectable Bird and withal a true, original Native of America."

Congress rejected the turkey as a bluffer and a show-off and felt that the soaring bald eagle, also a bird native to the United States, was a more majestic symbol.

Memorable Markers

1. GUESTS FOR ETERNITY In Ridgefield, Connecticut, a plaque in the wall of the cemetery reads: "In defense of American independence at the Battle of Ridgefield, April 27th, 1777, died Eight Patriots who were laid in this ground, Companioned by Sixteen British Soldiers, Living, their enemies, Dying, their guests."

2. BOTH HERO AND TRAITOR At the Saratoga, New York, battlefield a monument is inscribed to the "most brilliant soldier of the Continental Army who was desperately wounded on this spot . . . winning for his countrymen the decisive battle of the American Revolution and for himself the rank of major-general." There is no name—only the left boot to symbolize the wounded leg and the epaulet of a major-general. When the monument was erected in 1887 no one could bear to write the name Benedict Arnold.

3. "UNCONQUERED IN SPIRIT" At Appomattox Court House, Virginia, the Daughters of the Confederacy erected this marker: "Here on Sunday April 9, 1865 After Four Years of Heroic Struggle in De-

fense of Principles Believed Fundamental To The Existence of Our Government Lee Surrendered 9000 Men The Remnant Of An Army Still Unconquered In Spirit To 118,000 men Under Grant."

4.   A TRAGIC LOSS Stonewall Jackson's greatest victory was at Chancellorsville, but it was also his last. At dusk he and his staff rode ahead of the Confederate lines to ascertain the position of Northern troops. In attempting to return to Confederate lines he was mistakenly shot by his own men. He received a ball in the palm of his right hand, one through the left wrist, and a third through the left arm above the elbow. His left arm was amputated and a Reverend Lacy took it to the Lacy farm about a mile away from the hospital, buried it near the house, and erected a marker indicating it was Jackson's arm. The marker is still there. Jackson died eight days later and was buried in Lexington, Virginia.

5.   NO BILLING FOR BOB FORD Jesse James was buried on his mother's farm in Kearney, Missouri. His tombstone reads:

Jesse W. James
Died April 3, 1882
Aged 34 years, 6 months, 28 days
Murdered by a traitor and a coward
whose name is not worthy to
appear here.

He was shot by Bob Ford, a member of his own gang who was eager to collect the ten-thousand-dollar price placed on Jesse James's head.

6.   DISOWNING A NATIVE SON Warren G. Harding graduated from Ohio Central College at seventeen and shortly thereafter started in the newspaper business at a salary of one dollar a week. He and two friends bought the *Marion Star* for three hundred dollars, and Harding was on his way to becoming a successful publisher. Gradually he entered politics. When he was inaugurated as president in 1921, the law school at Ohio Northern University was named the Warren G. Harding College of Law in a burst of state pride. Harding had read law for a short time but never became a lawyer. Nonetheless, his name was cut in a large stone slab over the library entrance.

Two years later Harding died in office and scandals about his administration and his personal life began to emerge. Gradually the Harding name was removed from the official stationery and from the university catalog. Finally, a trustee offered the law school fifty thousand dollars "if that name comes off." The stone slab over the library was removed and all traces of the former president were gone.

7. WHAT JEFFERSON VALUED MOST "All my wishes end where I hope my days will end, at Monticello" wrote Thomas Jefferson, who died there on July 4, 1826. Jefferson was buried in the graveyard he had designed years earlier. The tombstone he prescribed was a simple granite shaft with the following inscription:

Here was buried
Thomas Jefferson
Author of the Declaration of American Independence
Of the Statute of Virginia for religious freedom
& Father of the University of Virginia

It omits any mention of the fact that he was president or doubled the size of the country with the Louisiana Purchase.

Flags

1. A 200-POUND FLAG The flag that Francis Scott Key saw "by the dawn's early light" was hard to miss—forty-two by thirty feet. It had fifteen stripes instead of thirteen and each one was two feet wide. It cost $405.90, required more than four hundred yards of cloth, and weighed more than two hundred pounds.

Major Armistead, commander of Fort McHenry during the War of 1812, hoped the flag would be "so large that the British will have no difficulty in seeing it at a distance." They didn't. Even after an all-night bombardment of the fort, which guarded the Baltimore harbor, they could see that "our flag was still there."

2. LINCOLN WEEPS FOR A FRIEND From his window in the White House, Abraham Lincoln could see Confederate flags flying over Alexandria, Virginia. The Civil War had just begun and Lincoln feared for the security of Washington. He asked a man he considered a son, Elmer Ellsworth, to lead a Union action against Alexandria. All was quiet on the foggy morning of May 24, 1861, when Ellsworth and his men, a military division called the New York Fire Zouaves, took the city. Then they saw a Confederate flag flying over a hotel. Ellsworth decided to climb the stairs and pull it down himself. On his way down, the hotelkeeper shot him dead, one of the first casualties of the Civil War.

Ellsworth, who died at twenty-four, had worked in Lincoln's Illinois law office and lived for a while at the White House. Lincoln wept openly at the news of his death and ordered Ellsworth's body brought back to the White House for a military funeral. Mary Lincoln, to her horror, was presented with the blood-spattered Confederate flag that Ellsworth had taken down.

3. AN EXCEPTION IS MADE The War Department has flown its flag at half-staff upon the death of every secretary of war except one—Jefferson Davis. Ironically, Davis, who held the cabinet post from 1853 to 1857, was an extremely capable and inventive secretary. But when he died in 1889, the Civil War was too recent to honor the man who had also been president of the Confederate States of America.

4. UP AND DOWN THE FLAGPOLE On April 14, 1861, Major Robert Anderson hauled down the U.S. flag over Fort Sumter, surrendering the fort to the Confederacy in the first battle of the Civil War. Exactly four years later, April 14, 1865, Major Anderson, now General Anderson, returned to Sumter with the same flag. He had saved it for just such a day. It was raised again over Fort Sumter, a symbolic ending to the Civil War. When Anderson died the Sumter flag was draped over his coffin.

5. THIRTEEN STRIPES AND A RATTLESNAKE In 1778 the king of Naples opened his ports to American ships and asked U.S. representatives in Paris, Benjamin Franklin and John Adams, to give him a description of the flag for identification. They described the Stars and Stripes, but then admitted that some ships might be flying other flags such as "a pine tree" by the "State of Massachusetts Bay" and a "rattlesnake in the middle of the thirteen stripes" by South Carolina.

6. THE PRESIDENT SENSES SOMETHING IS WRONG President Lincoln was standing in front of the White House holding a flag in his hand. He was reviewing the Union troops marching on Pennsylvania Avenue when suddenly he became aware that something was interrupting the dignity of the occasion. Turning around, he saw his young son Tad waving a Confederate flag behind him. Lincoln gathered the flag and the boy up in his arms and gave them to an orderly.

7. DESIGN YOUR OWN FLAG The first flag adopted by the Continental Congress on June 14, 1777, had thirteen red and white stripes

and thirteen white stars in a blue field. The legislature left it to individual ingenuity to fit the stars in a pattern, to design the number of points on each star, and to figure out the proportions of the elements. It was not until June 24, 1912, that President Taft issued an executive order standardizing the flag's specifications. He was motivated by a report that showed there were no less than sixty-six different flags being flown by the federal government at that time.

8.   THE ARMY COMES ON BOARD The flying of the U.S. flag was essential for the navy because the nationality of ships at sea needed to be identified. However, the army rallied around regimental flags until 1834, when finally a General Regulation specified that garrison flags could still be used but the Stars and Stripes had to fly above them.

9.   THE IWO JIMA FLAG In World War II, the army classified thirty-three-year-old Joe Rosenthal as 4-F because he had one-twentieth normal vision, but he followed the fighting anyway as a war photographer. When the U.S. invaded the island of Iwo Jima under heavy Japanese fire, Rosenthal was there wearing his thick glasses and carrying two spare pairs.

Only three of the men who raised this flag on Iwo Jima during World War II would leave the island alive.
UPI/BETTMANN NEWSPHOTOS

At the top of Mount Suribachi he caught the greatest picture of the war—five marines and a navy corpsman raising the Stars and Stripes. Rosenthal became an immediate celebrity and his picture won the Pulitzer Prize. The flag-raising appeared on a three-cent stamp and broke all records for first-day-issue sales. On November 19, 1954, a seventy-five-feet-high sculpture of the raising was dedicated at Arlington National Cemetery. Three of the six men who had raised the flag died on Iwo Jima.

10.   WRONG FLAG The famous painting showing George Washington crossing the Delaware River is the masterpiece of Emmanuel Leutze, who had also been commissioned by Congress to paint a mural for the Capitol. The German artist painted Washington's crossing years after the event and used the Rhine as a model for the Delaware. The Stars and Stripes flag he depicted was not adopted until 1777, a year after the crossing on December 26, 1776.

11.   NOT MADE IN AMERICA For almost a century after the birth of the United States, all its flags were made overseas as no American company was set up to make bunting. Finally Congress put a duty of over 400 percent on imported bunting, and in 1866 a Lowell, Massachusetts, company presented the Senate with a flag made from U.S. bunting. It was flown over the Capitol.

12.   A BRITISH DIRTY TRICK The British held New York during almost the entire Revolution, and so reoccupying the city was a visible sign of victory and the end of the war.

Within hours after the last British troops left, George Washington entered the city in triumph. Riding a gray horse, he led some of his officers down through Harlem and the fields of upper Manhattan. They were joined by civilian officials and formed a procession. At Chatham and Pearl streets they halted to await the raising of the colors over Fort George on the Battery. The delay ended up being an hour long because it was discovered that the British had removed the halyard and cleats from the flagpole. Sailors tried climbing the pole, but the British had spread grease on it. Cleats were found in an ironmonger shop, and a volunteer tied the halyard around his waist and scaled the pole by driving in the new cleats one at a time. Finally the American flag fluttered, cannons boomed, and the procession continued down Broadway past the eight hundred troops who stood at attention.

13.   THE FORGOTTEN ALAMO FLAG At the battle of the Alamo, Colonel Travis and his fellow Texans flew a Mexican, not a Lone

Star, flag. It had red, white, and green stripes with "1824" embroidered at its center.

When the Texans first took up arms, they claimed that it was "in defense of the federal constitution of Mexico of 1824." They were fighting for fairer government, not independence. It was only after the Battle of the Alamo, a brutal fight in which all the Texans were killed, that independence was declared. From 1836 to 1845 the Lone Star flag flew over Texas. It was followed by the Stars and Stripes when the Republic of Texas became the twenty-eighth state.

14. A GIANT STEP FOR MANKIND The flag that flew on the moon in July 1969 was made of metal. It needed to withstand bombardment by rock and dust particles.

PART V

Mixed Media: Communication at Its Best

Anything for a Story

1. JEFFERSON DAVIS IN HOOP SKIRTS? After the Civil War ended, the federal cavalry chased the fleeing Confederate President Jefferson Davis. Seeing the troops outside his tent, he thought he might be able to escape in the confusion. He was caught wearing the shawl his wife had impulsively thrown over his head to ward off the early-morning cold. With this one detail, the rabid Northern press had a field day. JEFF DAVIS CAPTURED IN HOOP SKIRTS and JEFF IN PETTICOATS were headlines. The cartoonists went wild with the story and histories of the war repeated it for many years.

THE CONFEDERACY IN PETTICOATS.

"The Confederacy in Petticoats" was the Northern press's exaggerated version of Jefferson Davis's capture.
BOSTON PUBLIC LIBRARY PRINT COLLECTION

2. ANOTHER SCARE FOR THE LINDBERGHS After the death of his kidnapped son, Charles Lindbergh moved his family to his in-laws' estate, where guards could keep the public and the press away. Threats came continually and the Lindberghs feared for the safety of Jon, their second son. They had an informal agreement with the press that no closeup photographs of the child's face would be printed. But one day Jon was being driven to nursery school by his teacher when a black sedan forced the car off the road. Men jumped out and the teacher screamed in horror as they came toward her, cameras flashing. The men were news photographers. The next day Jon's face was on the front page. Shortly thereafter the Lindberghs left the U.S. to live in England.

3. A WOMAN DISHONORED? The Spanish-American War was brought about in large measure by New York's newspapers—the yellow press—trying to outdo each other in sensationalism. William

Randolph Hearst's *Journal* had a story about three young women who were searched for dispatches from Cuban rebels as they attempted to leave Havana on the U.S. steamship *Olivette*. The *Journal*'s headline was REFINED YOUNG WOMEN STRIPPED AND SEARCHED BY BRUTAL SPANIARDS. A drawing that took up half a page showed the naked girls, modestly trying to conceal themselves, surrounded by three Spanish men.

"War is a dreadful thing," the *Journal*'s copy ran, "but there are things more dreadful than even war, and one of them is dishonor." Women's groups rallied in anger and a congressman called for an investigation until the *World*, the *Journal*'s yellow-press rival, upset by missing a story, did some research and discovered that the ladies were searched by a police matron in the privacy of a stateroom.

4. THE PRESIDENT'S HONEYMOON When President Grover Cleveland married the young and attractive Frances Folsom in the White House, he had no idea that the country and the press would get so worked up about it. The press followed them to their honeymoon cottage and camped outside it, spying on them with field glasses. The president was enraged by such "colossal impertinence." After the honeymoon, when the press continued to hound his wife, Cleveland interrupted a prepared speech and with tears of indignation in his eyes castigated "those ghouls who would desecrate every sacred relation of private life."

5. INTERVIEWED IN THE RIVER In the summer months, President John Quincy Adams, an excellent swimmer, would arise early and walk down to the Potomac for some exercise. At the water's edge there was a large rock and a sycamore tree where he liked to undress.

One morning in 1828 a woman reporter, Anne Royall, followed him down to the river and said, "I am sitting on your clothes and you don't get them till I get the interview." The president pleaded for her to go behind some bushes so that he could dress first. But the reporter was adamant and Adams gave her the interview from the river.

6. A WOMAN'S DRESS WAS THE KEY TO HIS SUCCESS Six hundred women packed a San Francisco meeting hall in 1871 to hear feminist Elizabeth Cady Stanton's address on "Marriage and Motherhood." Men and reporters were banned, but one enterprising male journalist donned women's clothes and was able to report Stanton's answers to such questions from the audience as "How

can we follow your advice and keep from having babies?" and "What are we to do when men don't agree?" Stanton asserted, "The men must be educated up to the higher civilization as well as the women. The same force that governs the passions can be controlled and directed into brain power and result in great deeds."

The U.S. Versus Spain: The War the Newspapers Won

1. CREATING A WAR In 1898 the war that took top priority for newspaper magnate William Randolph Hearst was the battle between his New York *Journal* and Joseph Pulitzer's *World*. Eager for front-page material, Hearst sent artist Frederic Remington to Cuba to sketch the skirmishes. All seemed quiet and peaceful, so Remington asked to return. Hearst cabled his famous reply: "Please remain. You furnish the pictures and I'll furnish the war."

2. A REPORTER OUTWITS THE NAVY Rumors circulated wildly about Admiral George Dewey's crushing defeat of the Spanish fleet at Manila, but hard news was scarce. As a war measure, the underwater telegraph cables had been cut. The first official news was Dewey's own report, which he sat down to write after his victory. It took him five days. Then he dispatched it to the nearest cable station—in Hong Kong, a two-day trip.

The reporters with Dewey's fleet were given a lift to Hong Kong and they graciously agreed to let the navy account be cabled first. It was sent at the commercial rate of 60 cents a word. A smart newspaperman sent his story at the urgent rate of $9.90 a word. His story not only arrived first but, unlike Dewey's, did not have to be decoded. The result was that Secretary of the Navy John Long and President William McKinley were notified of Dewey's startling victory by the *Chicago Tribune*. Five hours later, Dewey's official report was shown to the president.

3. A "SECRET" MISSION IN THE HEADLINES The army leased an ancient side-wheel steamship with the improbable name *Gussie* for a secret mission to land arms and supplies to help Cuban rebels fighting the Spanish. The *Gussie* "blazed grandly with lights" and was accompanied by press boats as she headed toward her "secret" rendezvous with the Cuban guerrillas. When her two landing boats

neared the shore, the newspaper tugs came racing up with whistles blowing and crews gesticulating wildly. Since the newsmen often had the latest war reports, the landing boats halted. Across the water came the question, "What's the name of the man in the bow of the first boat?" The press was only interested in a good story. The mission proved to be a failure, a result Captain Dorst attributed to newspaper publicity.

4. A NEWSMAN SCOUTS FOR THE ROUGH RIDERS Bullets whizzed through the Cuban jungle as Theodore Roosevelt's Rough Riders toiled up a trail at Las Guásimas. They were on foot because there had not been enough room on the ships from Florida for their cavalry horses. The foliage was so thick they could not even see the enemy.

Fortunately, *Journal* star reporter Richard Harding Davis spotted the Spanish position with his binoculars and pointed them out to Colonel Roosevelt. The colonel turned his glasses in the direction Davis indicated, confirmed the finding, and then was able to direct the fire of his troops. The Spanish retreated and Roosevelt, as usual, came away with the headlines. However, he made sure to give Davis credit for his scouting.

5. "HOW DO YOU LIKE THE JOURNAL'S WAR?" That was the headline William Randolph Heast liked to run on page one. In the race for exclusive news, Hearst even chartered the tramp steamer *Sylvia* and headed to war himself. While covering the naval battle off Cuba, he became convinced that it would be "a glorious thing" to capture some Spanish prisoners.

His goal didn't prove difficult. Spanish survivors from the *Infanta Maria Teresa*, a ship destroyed by American shells, were huddled on the shore. The sailors were deathly afraid of capture by the Cubans and gladly accepted refuge with Hearst on the *Sylvia*. Hearst had the Spanish sailors kiss the American flag for the *Journal*'s photographer, then offered them to the navy. An officer on the battleship *Texas* refused to accept them: "We don't want any yellow fever on this ship." Finally, the commanding officer of the *Harvard* took them, Hearst insisting on a receipt.

Interviewed about the incident later in life, Hearst mused, "Ah, well, we were young. It was an adventure."

6. DAM THE SUEZ When the news broke that the Spanish were sending a fleet to reinforce their position in the Philippines, William Randolph Hearst decided to intervene personally. The battleships

were scheduled to sail via the Suez Canal, so he ordered his European representative to buy a "big English steamer" and sink it in the canal. However, before such a makeshift dam could be created, the Spanish changed their minds and their fleet was recalled.

7.   HE WAS UP ON THE ROOFTOP—AND WOULDN'T COME DOWN Sylvester Scovel, reporter for the New York *World*, knew that the highlight of any story on the surrender ceremonies between the United States and Spain would be the lowering of the Spanish flag and the raising of the Stars and Stripes. This was scheduled to take place at noon on July 17, 1898, in the main square in Santiago, Cuba. Officials, civil and military dignitaries, and thousands of onlookers would be there. So too would press photographers.

Scovel climbed to a palace rooftop and positioned himself so that pictures of the flag-raising would show a *World* reporter prominently in the foreground. When he refused to come down, General William Shafter, the portly American army commander, ordered him thrown off. Shafter was standing in the square ready to receive the Spanish surrender and he wanted ceremonies to proceed. Scovel descended, only to begin a loud argument with Shafter in front of the assembled dignitaries. The reporter became so incensed, he took a swing at the general, somehow missing his three-hundred-pound target. Shafter ordered him arrested and the surrender ceremonies began.

Signing Their Names

1.   A REVOLUTIONARY MOVE At the signing of the Declaration of Independence, delegate Dr. Benjamin Rush wrote of "the pensive and awful silence which pervaded the house when we were called up, one after another, to the table of the President of the Congress to subscribe what was believed by many at that time to be our own death warrants."

Delegate Charles Carroll certainly seconded Rush's thoughts. He was considered the richest man in America and didn't want anyone else to suffer harassment for his act. So he signed himself "Charles Carroll of Carrollton." There were many Carrolls in Maryland and more than one with the first name of Charles. Carroll was the only delegate to add an identifying phrase, the only Catholic to sign, and the last of the signers to die—in 1832 at the age of ninety-five.

2.   THE PROOF IS ON THE TREE Meriwether Lewis and William
Clark had made it to the Pacific Ocean, but it was by no means
certain that they'd survive the journey back across the Rocky Mountains and down the hazardous Missouri River to report the success
of their mission. With this in mind, Clark carved his name and the
date, December 3, 1805, on a pine tree by the Pacific, and added,
"By land from the U. States in 1804 & 1805."

3.   A WESTERN MYSTERY How Jim Bridger's name came to be
spelled out on 193-feet-tall Independence Rock, "great registry" of
the West, is unknown. Westward-bound pioneers would often stop
there to carve their names, but Jim Bridger, premier hunter, scout,
and mountain man for forty years, was not one of them. Illiterate,
he was unable to write his name with more than an X.

4.   AN IMMIGRANT'S PRIDE Constantino Brumidi said that his
one aim in life was "to make beautiful the Capitol of the one country on earth in which there is liberty." He was almost fifty when he
left Italy to escape political persecution in 1852. Two years later he
was assigned to work on the Capitol and continued working for a
quarter of a century until his death in 1880. He painted the ceiling
of the great dome of the rotunda and many of the frescoes of the
Capitol. He was so proud to be an American that he signed his
paintings "C. Brumidi, artist. Citizen of the U.S."

5.   FEMINISTS UNDER PRESSURE In 1848 it was a controversial
move to sign the Declaration of Rights and Sentiments, issued at
the first-ever women's-rights convention, which was held at Seneca
Falls, New York. The press responded to the document with a storm
of criticism. "A woman is a nobody. A wife is everything. . . . The
ladies of Philadelphia, therefore, under the influence of the most
serious, sober second thoughts, are resolved to maintain their rights
as Wives, Belles, Virgins, and Mothers, and not as Women," asserted the *Philadelphia Public Ledger and Daily Transcript*. Under such
pressures, many of the hundred or so signers withdrew their names,
including feminist Elizabeth Cady Stanton's sister, Harriet Eaton.
Her husband and her father objected.

6.   X MARKED THE SPOT In one of its most controversial pre–
Civil War decisions, the Supreme Court ruled that Dred Scott, a
slave, had to retain that status even though he had lived in an area
of the Missouri Compromise that Congress had declared forever free.
Scott was illiterate and said he didn't really understand what all the

fuss was about. His owner had been the one to initiate the court case. Scott had simply added his X to all the legal papers.

7.   HE SAW NO EVIL After his presidency, Ulysses S. Grant became a silent partner and investor in a banking firm called Grant and Ward. Ferdinand Ward, who actually ran the firm, was a master of manipulation. Every morning he put twenty-five excellent Havana cigars on Grant's desk. Minutes before the former president was to leave the office for a weekend at the shore, Ward would give him a pile of papers to sign, slipping any damaging letters in the middle. Grant had a habit of signing letters without reading them. When the firm failed, his reputation was ruined by certain damaging documents that he had carelessly approved.

8.   AN ENTERPRISING IDEA Wilford Woodruff noted that when his Mormon wagon train reached Independence Rock, "We examined the many names and lists of names of the trappers, traders, travellers and emigrants which are painted upon these rocks. Nearly all the names were put on with red, black and yellow paint." Paint or axle grease proved more lasting than carving in the soft rock. Sensing a profit-making opportunity, the Mormons, once established at Salt Lake City, sent two of their brothers back to put the names of "gentiles" on the rock for a fee.

9.   MOTHERLY ADVICE As a young assistant secretary of the navy in 1913, Franklin Roosevelt reported to his wife, Eleanor, "[I am] up to my ears. I must have signed three or four hundred papers today and am *beginning* to catch on." His mother wrote him about the same time admonishing, "try not to write your signature too small, as it gets a cramped look and is not distinct. So many public men have such awful signatures and so unreadable."

Signals, Codes, and Cues

1.   TAD'S KNOCK Abraham Lincoln's son Tad learned a secret code at the War Department. When he gave three quick raps on the door of Lincoln's office followed by two slow bangs, the president would always let him in no matter how important the meeting. To his visitors, he would explain simply, "I promised never to go back on the code."

2. GOBBLE, GOBBLE At the Battle of Saratoga during the Revolution, General Simon Fraser heard a weird turkey gobble as he led his British Advance Corps near the woods of Freeman's Farm. Then an unseen enemy picked off every officer in his advance. Hiding in the trees were American Commander Daniel Morgan's men, firing their frontiersmen's rifles from three hundred yards. Morgan was using the turkey gobble to signal orders to his men.

3. A RED FLAG Barricaded behind the Alamo's thick walls, Colonel Travis and his men saw the Mexicans raise a blood-red flag and knew they were in a fight to the death. The flag meant no quarter, or no mercy, and Mexican General Santa Anna showed none. The Texans who were taken prisoner were shot.

4. CANNON TALK After eight years of furious shovel wielding, the Erie Canal, the greatest engineering feat of its time, was completed, linking the Great Lakes to the Atlantic Ocean. At ten A.M. on October 26, 1825, four white horses came onto the Buffalo towpath and were hitched to the *Seneca Chief*, ready to pull the canal boat on its inaugural trip. This was the cue for a gunner to light the fuse to a thirty-two-pound cannon. In an age before the telephone or telegraph, news of his boom resounded in New York City within one hour and twenty minutes. It was transferred by additional cannons that were spaced all along the 415-mile route from Buffalo to New York City. When the sound of the first cannon reached the second cannoneer, he lit his fuse. In New York, the final cannon was the signal for a huge celebration to begin.

5. SOONER WAS SMARTER Envious eyes had been cast at the Indians' rich grasslands in Oklahoma, but the territory wasn't opened for settlement until April 22, 1889. On that morning, more than twenty thousand eager pioneers had to be held back by troops at the border. President Benjamin Harrison had declared that settlement could begin at noon, "and not before." When the clock struck twelve, a musket shot sounded and the Oklahoma Land Rush was on.

Within twenty-four hours, fifty thousand settlers had raced across the starting line. Oklahoma City became a city of ten thousand in a day. But some hadn't waited for the official musket shot. Called "Sooners," they'd hidden in the hills and grabbed the best lands.

6. CURTAILED PRAISE OF LIBERTY At the ceremony unveiling the Statue of Liberty in 1886, Senator William Evarts was in the midst of his dedication speech when all of a sudden he was inter-

rupted by steam whistles, foghorns, and cannons firing twenty-one-gun salutes.

The statue's sculptor, Frédéric Auguste Bartholdi, had mistaken applause during the senator's speech as the signal to yank the rope that released the French flags covering the statue's face. The unveiling of Miss Liberty was in turn a signal for the ships in the harbor to begin the celebration. Senator Evarts gamely continued with his speech, although most of it was totally inaudible.

7. SPEAKING IN TONGUES When Herbert Hoover and his wife, Lou, didn't want the White House servants to know what they were talking about, they spoke to each other in Chinese. Their honeymoon trip had been a voyage to China, where twenty-five-year-old Hoover was serving as chief mining engineer for the Chinese Imperial Bureau of Mines, a position he was to hold for roughly two years.

8. TRADING TIME Setting fire to the prairie was the customary signal used by fur traders to let the Indians know of their arrival and to get the chiefs to come in to bargain.

9. THE GOLDEN SPIKE WAS THE CUE For five years, two railroad crews, one working from the East and the other from the West, had been racing to lay the tracks for the first transcontinental railway. On the afternoon of May 10, 1869, the final connecting rail was to be laid at Promontory, Utah. Telegraph lines had been cleared so that the news could be relayed. A parade four miles long stood at the ready in Chicago. One hundred cannons were loaded in Omaha, waiting to be fired.

The cue everyone was waiting for was the hammering of the final, golden spike, an honor that belonged to Leland Stanford, the president of the Union Pacific Railroad. As Stanford lifted the silver-plated sledgehammer, the telegrapher tapped a message to the waiting nation: "All ready now. The last spike will soon be driven. The signal will be three dots for the commencement of the blows." Stanford swung. The telegrapher flashed the signal: dot, dot, dot. Stanford missed, but across the U.S. cannons fired, bells rung, and parades began.

10. THE EYES HAVE IT Senator Clair Engle didn't have the strength to say a word when his name was called for the historic vote to limit filibuster on the 1964 Civil Rights bill. Weak from terminal cancer, Engle had only been wheeled into the Senate chamber moments before. He knew his vote was crucial. Unable to speak, he

raised his hand and feebly pointed to his eye—three times. At last
the Senate clerk realized he was voting "aye." That day the longest
filibuster in the history of the Senate (534 hours, 1 minute, and 51
seconds) was legally curtailed—with four votes to spare. The historic Civil Rights bill was on its way to becoming law.

11.   SHE SUCKED HER FINGERS Sacagawea, Toussaint Charbon-
neau's wife, was an afterthought on the Lewis and Clark expedition, yet she turned out to be one of its most valuable assets. Having
a woman and baby along was a clear sign to the Indians that this
was not a war party.

Sacagawea was a Shoshone who had been captured by the Min-
netares when she was very young. She remembered very little of
her early life, but when the expedition reached the Shoshone homeland, she sucked her fingers—sign language that these were her
people. Her hopes of meeting up with her family were slim, since
there were many Shoshone tribes, but after listening to a Shoshone
chief for some time, she suddenly screamed and embraced him. It
was her brother.

12.   TWO IF BY SEA On the night of April 18, 1775, Paul Revere
was summoned "in great haste" by Dr. Joseph Warren, the Boston
patriot leader. The British were about to head out of Boston with a
force of seven hundred men to destroy the colonists' stockpile of
arms at Concord and to arrest Samuel Adams and John Hancock. It
had been agreed "that if the British went out by water, we should
shew two lanthorns in the North Church Steeple, and if by land,
one, as a signal." At Warren's bidding, Revere "called upon a friend
and desired him to make the signals"—two lanterns. Then Revere
set out on his famous ride.

In Henry Wadsworth Longfellow's famous poem, the logistics of
Revere's task were much easier. The poet's line, "One if by land
and two if by sea; and I on the opposite shore will be," placed
Revere across the harbor in Charleston. But actually, Revere began
his journey in Boston. Like the British, he headed out by sea and
was rowed across to Charleston by two friends. They used a borrowed petticoat to muffle the oars as they had to pass a British
warship in the darkness.

The Art of Shaking Hands

1.   UNTOUCHABLE GEORGE At presidential receptions, George Washington was austere and aloof. He avoided physical contact and greeted his guests by bowing. To thwart those angling for a handshake, he rested one hand on the hilt of a dress sword; in his other he held a special hat that only consisted of a false front and feathers.

2.   JEFFERSON REACHES OUT TO THE PEOPLE John Adams bowed to Washington's tradition of greeting guests, but the third president, Thomas Jefferson, instituted what he felt was a more democratic custom—shaking hands. To him, bowing smacked of monarchy. He also began the tradition of throwing open the White House doors on New Year's Day and personally shaking the hand of anyone who came by. From that day until 1930, all presidents welcomed the new year by greeting their public. When Herbert Hoover was president, he felt that the number of visitors, which had grown into the thousands, was too unwieldly, so he ended Jefferson's tradition.

3.   A HERO'S WELCOME When the Marquis de Lafayette made his triumphal return to America almost half a century after the Revolution, he was met with an outpouring of adulation and affection. At City Hall in New York he was met by the mayor, and then he greeted admirers for two hours. For the next five days he allotted two hours each morning to shaking hands with the thousands who came to see him.

4.   ALL SHOOK OUT President-elect William Henry Harrison had a notice put in the papers that there would be no handshaking during or after his inaugural ceremonies as his arm and hand were already sore from greeting the public at prepresidential celebrations.

5.   DODGING THE GRIPPERS President James K. Polk did not like shaking hands. He was frail and sickly and he worried that muscular types coming along the receiving line would have a painful grip. But he found he could deflect a strong man's grasp "by being a little quicker . . . and seizing him by the top of his fingers, giving him a hearty shake."

6. A GENERAL'S KINDNESS A wounded Union soldier at Gettysburg saw General Robert E. Lee passing on horseback. With an
effort, he raised himself up and shouted, "Hurrah for the Union."
To his amazement he saw Lee stop, get off his horse, and come
toward him. He thought the Confederate leader meant to kill him,
but he saw that Lee's expression showed only sadness. Lee shook
the soldier's hand, looked him in the eye, and said, "My son, I
hope you will soon be well."

7. PROCLAMATION PROBLEMS Three hours of handshaking
could leave Abraham Lincoln's hand, as he said, "swollen like a
poisoned pup." So on New Year's Day, 1863, he knew he would
have a problem. Not only did he have to face the traditional handshaking ceremonies with the public but January 1 was the day Lincoln had promised to issue his famous Emancipation Proclamation.
If his signature were shaky, people might think he had hesitated.
Just before the historic moment, he commented, "I have been shaking hands since nine o'clock this morning and my right arm is almost paralyzed." Yet, with a conscious effort he managed to sign
with a firm hand.

8. GRANT TAKES A STAND In February 1864, Congress revived
the rank of lieutenant general, which George Washington had held,
and Abraham Lincoln awarded it to Ulysses S. Grant. Everyone was
eager to meet the new hero, and when Grant came to a White House
reception unannounced, he created a sensation. Lincoln persuaded
him to stand on a sofa so that those who couldn't shake his hand
immediately could at least get a better look at him.

9. A FIRST LADY'S FIRSTS Frances Folsom Cleveland, President
Grover Cleveland's new twenty-two-year-old bride, shook an estimated nine thousand hands at her first public reception.

10. MOVING RIGHT ALONG One of the most effective handshaking techniques was developed by President William McKinley.
He would smile, grab the guest's right hand, and squeeze it quickly
before his own hand got squeezed. By holding the guest's elbow
with his left hand, he could pull him along and turn to smile at the
next person in line.

11. A BANNER YEAR Theodore Roosevelt was a champion at
handshaking. On New Year's Day, 1902, he shook hands with eighty-
one hundred callers at the White House's traditional open house.

12. HIS WEAK POINT President Woodrow Wilson's handshake "felt like a ten-cent pickled mackerel in brown paper—irresponsive and lifeless" to newspaper editor William Allen White. Wilson's right hand had been weakened by a stroke in 1896.

13. THEY BOTH LOVED IT When told that handshaking took up too much of his time, President Warren G. Harding said, "I *love* to meet people. It is the most pleasant thing I do; it is really the only fun I have." He continued to be available every noon to all who wanted to come by and shake his hand. Mrs. Harding felt the same way. After more than two hours of handshaking at a New Year's Day reception, a friend offered sympathy but Florence Harding said, "Oh, now, my hand is good for two hours yet." When the reception was over, she'd shaken 6,756 hands. Her own was swollen for days.

14. FIFTY-FIVE HANDS PER MINUTE Just before lunch, Calvin Coolidge liked to throw open the White House doors to the public. "On one occasion I shook hands with nineteen hundred in thirty-four minutes," he recalled. Obviously there was little chatting with Silent Cal.

Tokens of Appreciation

1. IT'S YOUR BULLET In 1813 Andrew Jackson got into a brawl with Thomas Benton and his brother Jesse. A bullet shattered Jackson's shoulder, becoming embedded in the bone, and he was carried to the Nashville Inn where a doctor ordered amputation of the arm. A grim Jackson said, "I'll keep my arm." He also kept the bullet, which caused him increasing pain for nineteen years. By then Jackson was president, Thomas Hart Benton was senator and the two had become friends again. A doctor told Jackson he thought he could remove the bullet. Jackson sat down in a chair, gripped the back, and told the doctor to go ahead, which he did without anesthetic. The bullet popped out on the floor. A friend decided to send it to Benton as a gift, but Benton refused it since Jackson had "acquired clear title to it in common law by twenty years peaceable possession."

2. THE KEY TO THE BASTILLE "A tribute which I owe as a son to my adopted father, as an aide-de-camp to my general, as a mis-

sionary of liberty to its patriarch" was how Lafayette described his sending "the main key of the fortress of despotism" to George Washington. The general thanked him and sent a return gift. He wrote, "Not for the value of the thing, my dear Marquis, but as a memorial, and because they are of the manufacture of this city, I send you herewith a pair of shoe-buckles."

3. CHRISTMAS, 1905 A drawing of a five-story house showing smoke curling from the chimney was a gift from Sara Delano Roosevelt to her son Franklin and his young bride, Eleanor. She noted that the number and street were "not quite decided." It developed that she was purchasing two town houses and moving in next door. Eleanor discovered that the dining and drawing rooms on the upper floors connected, providing easy access for her strong-willed mother-in-law, who had intensely opposed FDR's marriage to her in the first place.

4. THE SPOILS OF WAR Though General Ulysses S. Grant had unified America's divided house, he didn't have a home to call his own after the Civil War. Citizens of Galena, Illinois, Philadelphia, and Washington, D.C., responded by offering him a house in each city, but he chose New York when it gave him a check for $105,000.

5. FARMER'S BOUNTY As president, Dwight Eisenhower accepted more than forty thousand dollars in tractors, livestock, and gifts for his Gettysburg, Pennsylvania, farm. Because of a furor in the press, Eisenhower called a news conference on July 31, 1957 and explained, "The conflict of interest law does not apply to me." However, he added that the farm would one day become public property anyway. Six years after leaving office he deeded it to the U.S.

6. A PAIR OF GRIZZLIES Explorer Zebulon Pike bought a pair of grizzly bear cubs from a "Savage" in Spanish New Mexico and made his men "carry them in their laps on Horse back." They became "extremely Docile" and followed the men about camp like dogs. Pike wrote President Jefferson that he was making him a gift of "a pair of Grisly Bears-mail and femail." Although pleased, Jefferson off-loaded them on a Philadelphia museum, where they ended up getting shot and mounted after one broke out and terrorized the neighborhood.

7. INDIAN GIVING Columbus was impressed by the generosity of the natives he met, who invited him to share anything they pos-

sessed and would "show as much love as if their hearts went with it." The natives, called Indians by Columbus, were pleased by the gifts he gave them: glass beads, red caps, and small hawks' bells, which had a pleasant tinkle. In fact, the Indians were so delighted, they paddled out to the Santa Maria waggling their fingers and calling, "Chuq! Chuq!" They wanted more bells.

8. THE POPE'S STONE Funds for building the Washington Monument were so scarce that the sponsors came up with the idea of donating stones—individuals, states, schools, all contributed. But one stone—called the Pope's Stone—caused a problem. It was donated by Pope Pius IX and came from the Temple of Concord in Rome. This roused strong anti-Catholic sentiment, particularly among a political party called the Know Nothings, who denounced the "papist gift." On March 5, 1854, masked men attacked a watchman at the monument construction site and stole the Pope's Stone. It was never seen again and the controversy delayed construction further.

9. ANONYMOUS GIFTS George Washington Carver, one of the first blacks at Simpson College in Iowa, lived in a small shack and survived on the money he earned by doing laundry for his fellow students. He had only boxes for furniture. Students took up a collection and bought a table, chairs, and a bed and, while Carver was away, placed the furniture in his shack. He also received money and concert tickets that were slipped under the door, but no one ever let him know where the gifts came from.

10. A ROYAL JACKASS George Washington was a progressive farmer interested in animal breeding. He tried to obtain "a good Spanish jack whose abilities for getting Colts can be ensured," but Spanish authorities would not allow male donkeys to be exported. The king of Spain heard about Washington's problem and in 1785 sent him two male and two female mules as a gift. One jack died. Washington named the other Royal Gift and ran an ad in a Philadelphia paper: "Royal Gift—A Jack Ass of the first race in the Kingdom of Spain will cover mares and jennies at Mount Vernon the ensueing [sic] spring."

11. NIXON'S GIFT A month after the Watergate scandal forced Richard Nixon to resign from the presidency, President Gerald Ford sent Benton Becker to see Nixon and negotiate terms for a pardon. Becker found the ex-President slouched in his desk chair, his jowls loose and flabby, his shirt collar too big for his neck, looking aged

and shrunken. "It was almost as if he had lost the will to live," Becker said.

Though without a pardon Nixon faced years of trial and possibly prison, he showed no interest in the subject. Instead he asked about the Washington Redskins football team. When Becker was about to leave, Nixon said, "I want to give you something. But look around the office. I don't have anything anymore. They took it all away from me."

Finally he sent his wife, Pat, to his jewelry box and gave Becker a pair of cuff links and a tiepin.

Twenty-one-gun and Other Salutes

1. FOR THE BIRDS Two years after the Civil War ended, Navy Commander Reynolds sailed to lonely Midway Island in the mid-Pacific. He called all hands on deck, fired off a twenty-one-gun salute that startled the birds—the island's sole inhabitants—and declared Midway Island U.S. territory. The U.S. claimed several other uninhabited islands during the 1800s.

2. AN ENEMY NO MORE When news of George Washington's death reached England in 1799, the British fleet in the English Channel fired a twenty-gun salute.

3. AN UNNECESSARY APOLOGY During the 1898 Spanish-American War, a U.S. convoy en route to the Philippines stopped off at Guam, a Spanish island, and began bombarding the fort that was guarding the harbor. There was no reply. After the shelling stopped, a Spanish official came out in a rowboat and apologized for not returning the American salute. He was told that it wasn't a salute, he was being attacked, that Spain and the U.S. were at war, and that he was a prisoner. Guam became U.S. territory at the end of the war.

4. A TRAGIC SALUTE When Union Major Robert Anderson surrendered Fort Sumter to the Confederates on Sunday, April 14, 1861, the opening battle of the Civil War was over. During the surrender ceremony Anderson was asked if he would order a thirty-four-gun salute since there were thirty-four states in the Union counting the Confederate States, a sore point. Instead, Anderson ordered a one-hundred-gun salute, saying it was "scarcely enough."

Troops were standing at attention on the parade ground as the salute was being fired and the Stars and Stripes was slowly lowered. Suddenly a cannon exploded, killing Private Daniel Hough, the first casualty of the Civil War. In the shelling of Fort Sumter, Confederate and Union forces had fired four thousand shots at each other without killing anyone. The salute was cut to fifty guns, Private Hough was buried in the parade ground, and Union troops boarded waiting transports for New York.

5. A CELEBRATION WASN'T IN ORDER When the news of Robert E. Lee's surrender at Appomattox Court House reached Union lines, the soldiers began firing a one-hundred-gun salute. They knew that the South had finally been defeated. General Ulysses S. Grant immediately sent word to have it stopped. "The Confederates are our countrymen again," he said.

PART VI

Morality and Immorality, Ethics and Beliefs

Never a Dull Sunday

1. FIGHTING WITH THE LORD'S BLESSING Confederate General Stonewall Jackson knew two books cover to cover: a study of the eighty-eight campaigns of Napoleon and the Bible. He was a deeply religious man and spent camp Sundays during the Civil War going to church and handing out religious tracts to his men.

Religion came to the Civil War soldiers in the field in the form of makeshift services, such as this Union mass. However, few observed the Sabbath as earnestly as Stonewall Jackson, who wouldn't even write a letter on Sunday.
BOSTON PUBLIC LIBRARY PRINT COLLECTION

On Sunday, March 23, 1862, he fought the Northern forces at Kernstown in the Shenandoah Valley only after wrestling with his conscience. When his wife heard about it, she wrote to him saying that she was distressed, particularly since he had been the attacker. Jackson, who would not read or write a letter on the Lord's Day, replied, "Had I fought the battle on Monday instead of Sunday, I fear our cause would have suffered." Since he won the battle, Jackson took it as a sign of the Lord's favor and wrote, "So far as I can see, my course was a wise one."

2. SWORN IN TWICE March 4, 1877, Inauguration Day, fell on a Sunday, so the swearing in of the president was postponed until Monday. However, just who the president would be wasn't decided until four A.M. on Friday, March 2.

The eventual victor, Rutherford B. Hayes, had left his home in Ohio for Washington good-humoredly remarking that he might be back immediately. His opponent, Samuel J. Tilden, had actually won the popular vote but had been short one electoral vote. Rumors flew that Tilden would be sworn in on Sunday. Labor unrest and financial turmoil abounded. It was not a good time to be without a president for twenty-four hours, even technically.

Outgoing President Ulysses S. Grant came up with a scheme. On the last Saturday of his term, he honored Hayes with an elaborate White House banquet. Before dinner the president and the president-elect stole away from the assembled guests. They took a circuitous route to the Red Room, where the chief justice, who had been ushered in unseen, stood before the fireplace.

Everything was carefully planned. Mrs. Grant had ordered the room filled with flowers. But when the moment to take the oath came, everyone realized that one thing was missing—the Bible. Since guests could be heard in the hall, Hayes was sworn in without it, the first such ceremony held in the White House. On Monday he took the oath again, this time publicly at the Capitol.

3.   UNFINISHED BUSINESS When Samoset, the Pilgrims' first Indian friend, showed up at Plymouth with five braves bearing deer skins and beaver furs to trade, the Pilgrims were put in a very awkward position. It was the Sabbath and, though they were eager to obtain furs to send to England in exchange for more supplies, they had to ask the Indians to come back another day. Being good hosts, they first offered their new friends food (Samoset loved butter, cheese, biscuits, and pudding), which inspired another breach of Sunday etiquette: The braves broke into a wild dance of thanks.

4.   A DELAYED HERO'S WELCOME The great French hero of the Revolution, the Marquis de Lafayette, was invited to return to America in 1824 to receive the honors of a grateful nation. When his ship, the *Cadmus*, sailed into New York harbor on August 15, Lafayette expected a reception would be waiting for him in Manhattan. Instead, a welcoming delegation came aboard and urged him to delay his arrival in the city. He was invited to spend the night on Staten Island at the home of Vice-President Daniel Tompkins. The marquis was astounded to learn that since it was Sunday there could be no reception, nor could anyone legally be out on the streets except to go to church.

5.   HE TURNED PALE IN HIS PEW April 2, 1865, dawned bright and beautiful in Richmond, Virginia, the capital of the Confederate government. At 10:45, Confederate President Jefferson Davis began a leisurely walk to church intending to take holy communion. Federal forces were at nearby Petersburg and for safety's sake Davis had sent his wife and children farther south, but nobody expected to have to evacuate Richmond suddenly. Davis took his seat in his pew, wearing what his Secretary of the Navy Stephen Mallory called his usual "cold, stern face."

The service had no sooner begun than there was a disturbance in the rear. A soldier had entered and demanded to see the president. The sexton walked rapidly down the aisle and handed Davis a telegram. Constance Cary, sitting nearby, plainly noted "a gray sort of pallor creep over his face." The president left; others departed with him. The rector came to the altar rail and begged those present to remain and finish the service. After the service they learned that Union troops had broken General Robert E. Lee's lines and Davis had ordered an immediate withdrawal of the government from Richmond.

6. A SLAVE FOR SALE IN BROOKLYN Just after the closing hymn on Sunday, June 1, 1856, Henry Ward Beecher, America's foremost preacher, told his congregation he was about to do something unexpected—hold a slave auction, an unusual move for the abolitionist brother of Harriet Beecher Stowe. A slave trader in Richmond wanted to set a girl free but had raised only $100 of her $600 purchase price. Beecher agreed to help collect the rest. Dramatically, he introduced the girl to his stunned congregation by saying, "Come here, Sarah, and let us see you." Then he asked, "May she read her liberty in your eyes? Shall she go free?" As Sarah watched, an emotional congregation donated $738 plus jewelry to buy her freedom.

Infidelity

1. FRIENDLY COUPLES Warren G. Harding and his wife, Florence, were good friends with Jim and Carrie Phillips. They went on picnics and cruises together and socialized in Marion, Ohio. One of the bonds that held the couples together was the fact that Harding and Carrie Phillips were having a passionate affair. It took almost fifteen years for their respective spouses to find out and even longer for the public to catch on. When reporters were digging for information at the time of Harding's presidential campaign, close friends didn't reveal a thing. Conveniently, Jim and Carrie Phillips were away on an around-the-world trip while Harding was in office, the money provided by Republican national chairman Will Hays.

After two and a half years as president, Harding died and his secret lay buried until the 1960s, when a Harding biographer, Francis Russell, found a cache of 250 love letters that Harding had written Carrie Phillips from 1909 until the year he was elected president, 1920. The letters had been in the possession of a Marion, Ohio, lawyer who had handled Mrs. Phillips's affairs before she died a recluse in 1960.

2. ADULTERY WAS THE HEART OF THE MATTER James Reynolds was an unsavory character who had deserted his wife. Or so said beautiful, penniless Maria Reynolds when she appealed to Secretary of the Treasury Alexander Hamilton for help. Hamilton was entirely taken with her and began a passionate liaison, which he continued even after Reynolds suddenly reappeared.

Maria confessed the affair to her husband and Hamilton found himself getting into deeper and deeper water. First Reynolds asked for one thousand dollars in blackmail to keep news of the adulterous affair from Mrs. Hamilton. Then he leaked false information to several congressmen, including Senator James Monroe, that Hamilton was misusing his position and partaking in illegal speculations. The congressmen confronted Hamilton, who astonished them by frankly admitting that his problem was actually adultery.

Hamilton had caught on to the fact that Reynolds was a dangerous character and saved documents which he proceeded to show the embarrassed congressmen. These included passionate letters from Maria. With apologies and vows of gentlemanly discretion, the congressmen retired and agreed to say no more about the affair. However, the story soon leaked out.

3. INTERCEPTED LOVE LETTERS In 1918 Franklin D. Roosevelt became ill with pneumonia. His wife, Eleanor, was sorting his mail for him and found love letters to FDR from Lucy Mercer, her social secretary. A marital storm resulted and Eleanor agreed not to sue for divorce if the relationship was cut off. In 1920 Lucy married Wintie Rutherfurd. She and FDR continued to correspond as friends. After her husband died in the 1930s and Roosevelt was president, they sometimes dined together at the White House when Eleanor was away, always in the company of others. A close personal friend of Lucy's said, "I've always been convinced that their romance was never a sexual thing." By coincidence, Lucy Rutherfurd and an artist friend who was painting a portrait of FDR were visiting him at Warm Springs, Georgia, when he died. They discreetly left before Eleanor arrived from Washington.

4   THE PRESIDENT DEFENDS VIRTUE Andrew Jackson's Secretary of War John Eaton confided to the president that he was wor-

ried about the reputation of the woman he'd been seeing. Peggy O'Neale was the daughter of a Georgetown tavern-keeper and the widow of a sailor who had committed suicide at sea. Jackson advised him, "Well, your marrying her will disprove these charges, and restore Peggy's good name."

It did nothing of the kind. Washington society refused to receive Peggy and the wives of cabinet members declined to call on her. Jackson's dander was up and he called one of the strangest cabinet meetings ever to "examine evidence having to do with the private lives of Secretary and Mrs. Eaton." Clergymen who were critical of the Eatons were invited to testify. They claimed that Peggy and then-Senator Eaton had visited a New York hotel together while Peggy's sailor husband was at sea. Jackson called such talk slander and declared Peggy a vindicated woman. "She is chaste as a virgin," he said angrily. The ladies of Washington continued to boycott White House receptions where "Pothouse Peg," as they called Mrs. Eaton, was present. Jackson reorganized his whole cabinet to exclude Peggy's detractors.

5.   DID HE OR DIDN'T HE? *Harper's Weekly* called Henry Ward Beecher "the most brilliant preacher who has ever appeared in this country." Brother to Harriet Beecher Stowe, Beecher was a pillar of Victorian morality. When he was charged with adultery in July 1874, it was a public sensation.

Did Reverend Henry Ward Beecher seduce his parishioner, pretty Mrs. Elizabeth Tilton? The press had a field day with the scandal. Strangely enough, Mrs. Tilton was among those undecided about the Reverend's guilt.
COURTESY OF THE NEW-YORK HISTORICAL SOCIETY, NEW YORK CITY

The charge came from his longtime admirer, protégé, and parishioner Theodore Tilton, whose wife, Elizabeth, confessed to having an affair with her minister. When Beecher's lawyers apologized for consulting him on Sunday, the minister replied: "We have it on good authority that it is lawful to pull an ass out of the pit on the Sabbath day. Well, there was never a bigger ass, or a deeper pit." The public and the press wallowed in sensationalism for six months as Mrs. Tilton changed her mind about the reverend's guilt at least five times while Beecher consistently denied the charges. He was not convicted because the confused jury failed to reach a verdict.

6.   ADULTERY AT EIGHTY? When Alexander Hamilton died in a duel, the coroner's inquest found "a verdict of willful murder by Aaron Burr, Vice-President of the United States." Burr was never brought to trial, but his reputation remained sullied. On July 1, 1833, Burr made headlines again when, at the age of seventy-seven, he married Eliza Bowen Jumel, a former prostitute who at fifty-eight was said to be the wealthiest woman in the U.S. The public responded with ribald songs and Burr responded by using his male prerogative to squander his new wife's money. Eliza filed for divorce only a year after the wedding, charging Burr with adultery with "one Jane McManus . . . and other females." The divorce became final on September 14, 1836, the day Aaron Burr died at the age of eighty.

Invoking the Almighty

1.   DIVINE AUTHORITY Harriet Beecher Stowe felt that she did not write Uncle Tom's Cabin. "God wrote it," she said. "I merely did his dictation."

2.   PREDESTINATION "God ordained that I should be the next President of the United States," said Woodrow Wilson on becoming president. The son of a minister, his sincere belief in predestination may have been something of a surprise to those who organized his campaign and got him the Democratic nomination on the forty-sixth ballot.

3.   THE LORD'S BUSINESS In 1902 the average wage in the coal mines was three hundred dollars a year. Breaker boys, who sorted coal, started working at age ten for thirty-five cents a day. Lost limbs, cave-ins, and black lung disease were a way of life. Fed up, the miners went on strike. George Baer, spokesman for the mine owners, would not negotiate with the workers' union, explaining that

the workers were cared for by "the Christian men to whom God in his infinite wisdom has given the control of the property interests of this country."

4.   SEDUCED BY THE DEVIL When former Confederate President Jefferson Davis was indicted for treason in federal court in May 1866, Judge Underwood described him as a "yeoman" and charged that Davis had been "seduced by the institution of the devil" and that he did not have "the fear of God before his eyes."

5.   BATHTUB PIETY Lincoln's Secretary of the Treasury Salmon P. Chase was known for being pious. He attended church three times on Sunday, quoted psalms in the bathtub, and saw to it that "In God We Trust" was put on U.S. coins.

6.   HEAVEN-SENT BULLET Armed troops ringed the Virginia to-bacco barn where John Wilkes Booth had taken refuge in his flight south after killing President Lincoln. Booth refused to come out and so the barn was set on fire. He was visible through the slats and, silhouetted against the flames, was an easy target. But the troops had strict orders to bring Booth in alive. Suddenly a shot rang out, hitting Booth in the head. He died within hours, leaving many questions about the assassination conspiracy forever unanswered. The man who admitted to shooting Booth was Sergeant Boston Corbett. When asked why he disobeyed orders, he said God had directed him to do it.

7.   RELIGIOUS BUSINESS According to Calvin Coolidge, "The man who builds a factory builds a temple" and "The man who works there worships there."

8.   DOING UNTO OTHERS "I do believe, with all my heart and mind and spirit, that I, not as President but as the humble servant of God, will receive justice without mercy if I fail to show mercy," said President Gerald Ford on his reasons for pardoning Richard Nixon after the Watergate cover-up.

9.   FREE THINKING Accused by his political opponents of being an atheist, Thomas Jefferson responded: "I have sworn upon the altar of God, eternal hostility against any form of tyranny over the mind of man."

10.   WINNER BY A PRAYER The 1824 electoral college was dead-locked, so on February 9, 1825, the House of Representatives met to name the next president. Each state had a single vote and a pre-

liminary tally showed that John Quincy Adams was one vote shy of a majority. New York's vote could put him over the top, but its representatives were evenly split, with General Stephen Van Rensselaer undecided. Both sides bombarded the aging general with arguments and he became confused. While awaiting his turn to vote, he closed his eyes and prayed. When he opened them, he saw a ballot on the floor with the name John Quincy Adams on it. Believing it to be a sign from God, he voted for Adams, who then carried New York and became president.

Prayer

1.   LAND HO! It was with good reason that on the night of October 11, 1492, Christopher Columbus "prayed mightily to the Lord." The captains of the *Niña* and *Pinta* had pulled him over and begged him to return to Spain. Their crews were close to mutiny. Columbus had miscalculated the size of the "Sea of Gloom." It was twice as big as he had thought. But his logbook, which had fake entries minimizing the distance traveled from Spain, calmed the other captains. Columbus promised that if they didn't sight land in forty-eight hours he would turn back. Fortunately, the next day his prayers were answered and San Salvador, which he maintained was Asia, appeared.

2.   "A LOAD OF HAY" On becoming president at the death of Franklin D. Roosevelt, Harry S Truman told reporters, "Boys, if you ever pray, pray for me now. I don't know whether you fellows ever had a load of hay fall on you, but when they told me yesterday what had happened, I felt like the moon, the stars and all the planets had fallen on me."

3.   GRACE UNDER PRESSURE As a youth, Ben Franklin avoided attending public worship whenever he could because he preferred to devote his time to studying. However, there didn't seem to be any way out of family prayers at mealtime. Once he tried to convince his father, after he had helped salt and store their winter's provision of meat, to say grace over the whole cask right then, once and for all. That ploy failed but Ben found a way to interest himself during morning and afternoon prayers. Since the dining room had a wall with large maps, he taught himself geography.

4. LEAVING INTERVENTION TO THE LORD With the Civil War imminent, President James Buchanan could not wait to leave office. Yet during his last months, South Carolina commissioners pressed Buchanan to withdraw Union troops from Fort Sumter in Charleston harbor. "Mr. Barnwell," the president complained, "you are pressing me too importunately; you don't give me time to consider; you don't give me time to say my prayers. I always say my prayers when required to act upon any great State affair." The president managed to pray long enough so that Fort Sumter became Abraham Lincoln's problem.

5. A GOOD QUESTION After Woodrow Wilson suffered a paralytic stroke during his last year as president, a committee of senators called on him. Senator Albert Fall, a political opponent, entered the darkened room and said to Wilson, "We have all been praying for you, Mr. President."

"Which way, Senator?" was Wilson's answer.

6. DOING IT WITHOUT DIVINE HELP At the Constitutional Convention, Benjamin Franklin proposed that all sessions be started with a prayer because without divine help they would do no better "than the Builders of Babel." But the delegates were not enthusiastic. Their concerns included the lack of funds to hire a chaplain. Franklin's motion died.

7. A MIDNIGHT PRAYER "Your daddy may have started World War III," an upset Lyndon Johnson told his daughter Luci on June 29, 1966. She had come home late from a date and found him pacing the White House floor, worrying about a bombing raid he'd ordered on Vietnam. Luci told her father that whenever she needed consolation she visited St. Dominic's Catholic Church. LBJ agreed to go with her even though it was midnight. The monks opened the church so the president could pray. Johnson complained that the unpadded benches were hard to kneel on, but he continued to visit St. Dominic's when he needed solace.

8. A MATTER OF LIFE AND DEATH Susannah Dickinson, her baby Angelina, a Mexican nurse, and a Negro boy were among the few survivors of the Alamo. Mexican General Santa Anna had killed all the Texans, including Mrs. Dickinson's husband. Mrs. Dickinson was in the sacristy of the Alamo church when she found she was spared. She had fled there amid approaching screams and shots and fallen to her knees in prayer. Four Mexican soldiers had burst in, shot and killed Jacob Walker, a gunner, and took him out hoisted

on their bayonets. A Mexican officer appeared and said, "Is Mrs. Dickinson here? Speak out! It's a matter of life and death." When she answered yes, he said, "If you want to save your life, follow me." She did. Santa Anna gave her two dollars and a blanket and sent her to Gonzales to spread the word of the Mexican success.

Do's *and* Don'ts

1. NO MASTERLESS WOMEN Colonial taverns in New England were forbidden to "knowingly harbor . . . any rogues, vagabonds, thieves, sturdy beggars, masterless men or women."

2. VICTUALING WAS THE RULE In Colonial times Massachusetts required that each town have a tavern or "common victually-ing house" or pay twenty shillings a week fine.

3. THE PRICE FOR DICE John Adams recorded the rules for a student at Harvard: a five-shilling fine if caught telling a lie, entering a saloon, fighting, swearing, disturbing classmates with noise, or getting drunk. If caught playing with cards or gambling with dice, the fine went up to twenty shillings.

4. BEHAVING ON THE SABBATH John Quincy Adams's political opponents accused him of "traveling through Rhode Island and Massachusetts on the Sabbath," which they felt was a "shocking impiety."

5. ONLY GAMES OF DIVERSION George Washington issued a proclamation on May 8, 1777, stating that "the Commander-in-Chief, in the most pointed and explicit terms, forbids all officers and soldiers playing at cards, dice, or at any games, except those of exercise or diversion."

6. ON MY HONOR, I SWEAR . . . When hiring riders, the Pony Express specified a preference for a "Young skinny wiry fellow, not over 18" who was "willing to risk death daily." He had to memorize and recite aloud, with his hand pressed against an open Bible: "While I am in the employ of Russell, Majors & Waddell, I agree not to use profane language, not to get drunk, not to gamble, not to treat animals cruelly, and not to do anything incompatible with the conduct of a gentleman."

7.   KEEPING UP APPEARANCES Robert Fulton's *Clermont* started the steamboat era. Fulton also started the trend of steamboat elegance by setting strict rules: "It is not permitted for any persons to lie down in a berth with their boots or shoes on, under a penalty of a dollar and half, and a half a dollar for every half hour they may offend against this rule. . . . As the steamboat has been fitted up in an elegant style . . . gentlemen will therefore please to observe cleanliness . . . no one must sit on a table under the penalty of half a dollar each time. . . ."

8.   TAMING SPRING FEVER "I want the brethren to be ready, for meeting to-morrow at the time appointed, instead of rambling off, and hiding in their waggons at play cards, etc.," announced Brigham Young to his Mormon followers. In their trek west in search of the promised land, discipline weakened as they neared what is now the Nebraska-Wyoming line. It was spring, and playing cards, checkers, and dominoes as well as fiddling and dancing had become a problem. "I think it will be good for us . . . to humble ourselves and turn to the Lord and He will forgive us," added Young.

Lies and Other Mistruths

1.   NOTHING TO HIDE When Warren G. Harding was finally called to the proverbial smoke-filled room and told he was the party's choice for president, he was cautioned that "before acting finally, we think you should tell us, on your conscience and before God, whether there is anything that might be brought up against you that would embarrass the party, any impediment that might disqualify you or make you inexpedient, either as a candidate or as President."

A stunned Harding asked for time to respond. He needed to consider the consequences of an extramarital affair with Nan Britton, who had just born his child. She had extremely explicit love letters in her possession, as did Carrie Phillips, the wife of a close friend, with whom Harding had been having an affair for the past fifteen years. After ten minutes Harding returned and said that there was no impediment. His infidelities didn't come to light until after his death.

2.   COLOR BLINDNESS AT "OLE MISS" In 1961 James Meredith applied to the all-white University of Mississippi, stating that he

was an "American-Mississippi-Negro citizen." When he was denied admission, he took his case to court.

Registrar Robert Ellis of Ole Miss testified that he was "shocked, surprised and disappointed" that Meredith would think he was rejected solely because of his "race and color." Asked if he had ever seen a black student at Ole Miss, the registrar hedged: "I have seen students with varying degrees of darkness of skin but I can't tell you whether any of them were of the Negro race or not." A Supreme Court decision and twenty-five thousand soldiers and U.S. marshals sent in by President Kennedy finally enabled James Meredith to enroll. From that time on, Registrar Ellis would be able to say for sure that there were blacks at the University of Mississippi.

3. A PRESIDENT GETS RICH "I don't have any interest in government-regulated industries of any kind and never had," President Lyndon Johnson stated at a 1964 press conference. Johnson was under fire for his holdings in an FCC-regulated Austin, Texas, radio-TV station. Lyndon Johnson was one of the wealthiest U.S. presidents. Since his days in the Senate, his net worth increased to an estimated $14 million, thanks largely to the TV-station stock, which was in the names of his wife and his daughter. His interests were put in a blind trust when he became president.

4. FALSE WAS TRUE Columbus kept two logs of his voyage—one was a true log and the other understated the distance traveled. He used the second log to show the crew so they would think they were closer to Spain and less likely to fall off the end of the earth. Ironically, Columbus miscalculated his speed and the false log was closer to being correct.

5. A DAMNED LIE At eighty-one, Cornelius Vanderbilt became ill and some newspapers reported he had died. Reporters came to the door of the Vanderbilt mansion to find out if the stories were true. The servant wouldn't let them in, but Vanderbilt heard them at the door and shouted downstairs, "It's a damned lie." There was no mistaking the old man's roar—the reporters left satisfied.

6. A LAWYER'S SLIP When John D. Rockefeller was called to testify about his involvement in the South Improvement Company, a notorious 1872 oil-refining scam, he astonished the court.

"Was there a Southern Improvement Company?" John D. Rockefeller was asked under oath.

"I have heard of such a company," Rockefeller replied.

"Were you not in it?" he was asked.

"I was not." There was a gasp as it seemed that Rockefeller had committed perjury. But he had not since his questioner had mistakenly used *Southern* for *South*.

7. NOT A CRIPPLE "As a matter of fact, I don't use a wheelchair at all," said President Franklin Roosevelt, "except a little kitchen chair on wheels to get about my room while dressing . . . and solely for the purpose of saving time." Though his legs were paralyzed, FDR was unwilling to have the public think of him as a cripple. In his mind, he was able to deny using a wheelchair because the one he relied on was built, at his specifications, around a straight-backed kitchen chair. It had no arms so that he could shift into a regular chair more easily. His wheelchair almost never made public appearances.

Photographs of FDR in his wheelchair were strictly off limits. One rare exception was this shot of the president with little Ruthie Bie and Fala at Hyde Park, New York.
FRANKLIN D. ROOSEVELT LIBRARY

8. TEAPOT DOME FALLOUT President Harding's Secretary of the Interior Albert Fall leased out government-owned oil reserves at Teapot Dome and Elk Hills to oilmen Harry Sinclair and Edward L. Doheny. He then retired from his $12,000-a-year post to his run-down Arizona ranch, which he transformed with new livestock, expensive repairs, and a $124,500 addition of land. His sudden wealth came, he said, from $100,000 he had received from a friend, Edward B. McLean. He hadn't gotten "one cent on account of any oil lease or upon any other account whatsoever."

A Senate Committee investigating the Teapot Dome scandal tried to reach his friend Edward B. McLean at Palm Beach, Florida. McLean admitted he had lent Fall $100,000 but said he was too ill to come to Washington to testify. A member of the committee, Senator Walsh, designated himself a subcommittee of one and took the train to Palm Beach. He asked where the $100,000 checks were. McLean, now under oath, admitted that Fall "returned them to me." The checks had been a ruse. Fall had indeed received payoffs in return for the coveted oil leases. The former secretary of the interior became the first cabinet member to be sent to jail.

9.   THE YEAR THE FOURTH OF JULY CAME EARLY Eighty-three-year-old Thomas Jefferson did not expect to live through the summer of 1826 but valiantly hoped to last until the Fourth of July, the fiftieth anniversary of the adoption of his Declaration of Independence.

On July 2 he was clearly fading. On July 3 he lapsed in and out of consciousness, awaking to ask, "Is this the Fourth?" Nicholas Trist, who tended Jefferson through the night, had to answer no each time. "My eyes were constantly turning from his face to the clock in the corner," he said. About an hour before midnight Jefferson awakened and said, "This is the 4th?" Trist tried to pretend he hadn't heard, but when Jefferson repeated the question, he nodded. "Ah," murmured Jefferson as he sank back to sleep relieved. He roused himself only once more and, on the afternoon of the Fourth, quietly passed away.

Through Indian Eyes

1.   HIS ACHILLES' HEEL Roman Nose, a statuesque Cheyenne chief, prided himself on an impressive feathered bonnet that he believed was his secret to immortality—provided no other hands but his touched it. After the massacre of the Cheyennes at Sand Creek in 1864, Roman Nose donned his war bonnet and led a series of successful attacks—until September 16, 1868, when a squaw, unaware of the taboo, touched his bonnet. The next day he was wounded in the side and carried from the field. On September 18 he died.

2.   ROPING THE IRON HORSE To halt the advance of the transcontinental railroad, four braves, not understanding the nature of steam power, decided to try to capture the "iron horse." They took forty feet of rope that had been infused with potent magic by a medicine man and laid it across the track, waiting for the engine. When the train was only a few yards away, they leaped up and

strained against the rope. The two closest to the track were swept under the wheels. The remaining two retreated, badly bruised.

3. COUP STICK COURAGE In Sioux language the word for *peace* meant being idle. The Sioux loved to fight and valued courage, which they measured by the number of coups a brave had. Coups were scored when a brave vanquished an enemy in close combat and then touched him with his coup stick. Without coups a man had no standing in the tribe.

Sioux Indians who fought in World War I and were members of the American Legion were denied admission to the tribal order of Old Warriors. Shooting an enemy at long range was not the same as scoring coups.

4. FORGET DOING IT THE ARMY WAY In the Revolutionary War the Stockbridge Indians were recruited to fight on the American side, but they rebelled at the drilling and training that were part of the white man's army. One said, "Brothers, one thing I ask of you, that you will let me fight in my own Indian way. . . . Only point out to me where your enemies keep, and that is all I shall want to know."

5. THEY DIDN'T BELIEVE HIS SKIN WAS BLACK Lewis and Clark spent their first winter en route to the Pacific encamped on the banks of the Missouri River. The nearby Mandan Indians were astounded when the explorers set up a portable blacksmith's forge, complete with bellows. They called it "Big Medicine."

But most amazing to the Indians was York, William Clark's good-natured slave. The Mandans had never seen a black and found it hard to believe his skin was really black. Occasionally a daring brave would spit on his thumb and try to rub the black off, thinking it was paint covering light skin. York's hair also dazzled the Mandans. They considered it a real treat to be allowed to run their fingers through his curly locks and would offer him a favor such as a squaw for the night in return for the privilege. Afterward they were anxious to learn the details. York had busy nights all winter.

To Err Is Human

1. A SHOT IN THE TAIL On the way home from his Pacific journey with William Clark, Meriwether Lewis went off hunting. He

was looking for a wounded elk when he was shot "across the hinder part of the right thye," as he put it. The bullet came from Peter Cruzatte. Blind in one eye and nearsighted in the other, Cruzatte had mistaken his boss for an elk because Lewis had been wearing brown leather. The wound made it difficult for Lewis to sit down for a while, but it was not serious.

2. SO SORRY In 1842 Commodore Thomas Ap Catesby Jones heard a false report that war had broken out between Mexico and the U.S. He raced his ships from Peru up to California. At Monterey he heroically demanded that an astonished Governor Alvarado surrender. Since Alvardo had no troops, he signed the articles of capitulation and Jones landed 150 marines and sailors. The Mexican flag was lowered, the U.S. flag raised.

It took thirty hours to convince the commodore of his error. When he finally realized that there was no war, he said, "This change in the aspect of international affairs called for prompt action on my part." The flags were reversed, Jones apologized profusely, and he had his ships fire a salute of honor. The apology was accepted. Jones was entertained with a rodeo and Indian dancing. A formal ball was given for the American naval officers and the Mexicans asked for a set of musical instruments for their band as reparations.

3. RUNAWAY STAGE The highlight of Buffalo Bill's Wild West Show was always the Indian attack on the Deadwood stage. In 1883, when the show played near Columbus, Nebraska, the mayor and the town councilmen were offered a chance to ride in the stage. What they didn't know was that they were being driven by a team of barely broken wild mules.

This was in the early days of the show, and Buffalo Bill had outfitted the stage just as it would have been in the real West. When the Indians ambushed the stage, the jittery mules bolted. Then Buffalo Bill and the cowboy rescue party appeared. The mules began to stampede around the ring and the Indians, delighted at the success of their ambush, forgot their cue to retire.

"Stop: Hell: stop—let us out," shouted the purple-faced mayor. He didn't have a prayer of escaping the runaway stage until the mules had been tired out enough to be reined in.

4. MOVING TOO FAST When the Civil War began, President Lincoln appointed the popular and politically well-connected John C. Frémont as military commander of the Department of the West. One of the first things Frémont did was free the captured slaves

with an emancipation proclamation that anticipated Lincoln's by several months. His move greatly embarrassed Lincoln, who was trying to keep slave-holding border states like Kentucky in the Union. Frémont had to rescind his proclamation and was relieved of his command after only one hundred days.

5.   NO EXIT Henry Ford finished his first car late on the night of June 4, 1896, and seized an ax. In his inventive fever, he hadn't realized that the shed behind his Detroit house had a door large enough to bring the parts in but too small for a five-hundred-pound automobile to be pushed out. Undaunted, Ford hacked away at the doorframe and knocked out enough bricks to free his quadricycle, so named because the car looked like a baby carriage with four bicycle wheels.

6.   THE LOADED GUN Brigham Young's best horse was accidentally shot to death on the long westward trek to Salt Lake City. A Morman herdsman named Holman had attempted to prod the animal with the butt of his rifle, but the trigger, which caught in his clothing, fired. Young issued a recommendation that his fellow brothers not carry guns loaded "with caps upon their tubes."

7.   A TOUGH WITHOUT CUFFS When the Senate pointed out that J. Edgar Hoover had never actually apprehended a criminal, the FBI chief decided to arrest personally Alvin Karpis, public enemy number one in 1936. The FBI tracked the bank robber and kidnapper to New Orleans, where he was surrounded in front of his apartment. Hoover came over and ordered Karpis handcuffed. The agents looked at each other aghast. That was the very item they had forgotten. Karpis's hands were bound with an agent's necktie.

8.   THE MISSING BABY Abraham Lincoln had periods of absent-minded abstraction that were very trying to his wife. When they were newly married in Springfield, Illinois, Mary would go to church while Lincoln minded the baby. One day he bundled the baby up and put him in a wagon. He then began to read a book while pulling the wagon back and forth in front of their house. When Mary returned, she found that the baby had fallen out and was squalling on the ground. Lincoln, obliviously absorbed in his reading, was pulling an empty wagon.

PART VII
Life-styles

Living Wages

1.   The salary for the Revolutionary War soldier was set at $6.66 a month. He also was supposed to receive a daily ration of one pound of beef or twelve ounces of pork and one pound of salt fish plus one pound of bread or flour. His beverages were one pint of milk and one quart of spruce beer. Vegetables were included at weekly intervals.

2.   Irishmen made the best diggers on the Erie Canal. They were paid thirty-seven and a half to fifty cents a day. They put in twelve- to fourteen-hour days and received a fringe benefit called "grog time." This occurred a dozen or more times a day when a boy called the jigger boss brought rations of whiskey. The total amounted to almost a quart of whiskey per day for each worker.

3.   In 1833 Abraham Lincoln made fifty dollars a year as village postmaster of New Salem, Illinois.

4.   Wages for a cowhand on the Chisholm Trail in the 1860s were thirty dollars a month plus expenses and one month's pay for the return trip.

5.   As marshal of Abilene, Kansas, Wild Bill Hickok was paid $150 a month plus 25 percent of all the money he collected in fines.

6.   Bloody Knife was General George Armstrong Custer's favorite scout and he died with Custer at the Battle of Little Big Horn. She Owl, Bloody Knife's widow, put in a claim for wages owed her husband up to the time of his death. Five years after the battle, the government allotted "said widow, She Owl, $91.66."

7.   A millinery worker in New York City in the 1880s made one dollar a week. The fine for being five minutes late was twenty-five cents.

8.   In 1894 an electrical engineer who was an honor graduate from Massachusetts Institute of Technology received twelve and a half cents an hour on his first job. The work week had just been shortened to fifty-six hours.

9.   The Census Bureau estimated that the wage for the average worker in 1905 was $523.12 a year.

10.   In 1914 the average wage was $2.40 a day. Henry Ford set the minimum for every worker in his factory at $5 a day. The Model T

Ford cost $850. Twelve years later the average wage was $10 a day and the Model T cost $350.

Schooling

1.   BLAB SCHOOL The autumn that Abraham Lincoln was fifteen he knew his alphabet, but he hadn't learned the art of "cipherin' " until he attended what was called a blab school—where all the children recited their lessons out loud at once. It was run by an itinerant teacher, Azel Dorsey. Early each morning Lincoln and his sister Sarah would walk four miles to the schoolhouse, a windowless cabin with split logs for seats. Paper was precious, so the students wrote on boards with charcoal sticks. The blab school lasted only briefly. Lincoln's formal schooling was to total about twelve months. The rest of his education, including studying law, was accomplished on his own.

2.   EXTRACURRICULAR ACTIVITY When emancipation came, young Booker T. Washington, born a slave in 1856, desperately wanted an education. However, his impoverished family needed him to work and bring home an income. They reached a compromise. Booker got a job packing salt into barrels and worked from four A.M. until nine A.M. Then he went to school, after which he returned to the salt mine and worked for another two hours.

3.   AN ADDLED INVENTOR Sam Edison was convinced that his son, Thomas Alva, was stupid. The local schoolmaster agreed and described young Edison's mind as "addled." Overhearing this, the boy ran back home from school and refused to return. His formal schooling was over after only three months. His mother, a former teacher, educated him at home.

4.   SIGN-LANGUAGE LESSONS When William F. "Buffalo Bill" Cody was a boy, the schoolmaster "wore out several armfuls of hazel switches" on him. Cody only submitted to school because his mother forced him to. But years later, on the plains, his attitude toward his education changed. He would sit for hours and watch Kit Carson, the legendary scout, "talk to Indians in sign language. Without a sound they would carry on long and interesting conversations." Buffalo Bill said he was not only willing but anxious to

learn this "mysterious medium of speech, and began my education on it with far more interest than I had given to the 'three R's' back at Salt Creek."

5. FAME FROM THE PEANUT George Washington Carver was fourteen when Mariah Watkins found him asleep on her woodpile in 1878. The young black had set off to make his way in the world with his few possessions tied in a bandana. Mariah took him in. He attended Lincoln School, a fourteen-by-sixteen-foot room with seventy-five students. During recess, he'd go through the yard to Mariah's house to do chores and study. Carver learned as much as he could and then wandered off, taking odd jobs and picking up schooling where he could. At twenty-five he was accepted at Highland University, but the school quickly changed its mind when he showed up. "We don't take Negroes here," he was told.

Finally, at age thirty, Carver was accepted at all-white Simpson College in Indianola, Iowa, but the twelve-dollar tuition took all his savings. After he paid it, he had ten cents left. He got through school by taking in laundry, washed in two tubs he'd bought on credit. When he graduated, Carver went on to teach at Iowa State College and Tuskegee Institute. He began experimenting with the lowly peanut and eventually came up with 300 peanut products, ranging from soap to ink. He made 118 products from the sweet potato, 75 from the pecan, and won international fame as a scientist.

6. THE RIGHT TO LEARN Mary Antin, one of thousands of Russian-Jewish immigrants in the 1890s, recalled her discovery of the meaning of freedom of education. When she had been in America for two days, a young neighbor child offered to bring her to school. Her benefactor was a child who "had never seen us till yesterday, who could not pronounce our names, who was not much better dressed than we, was able to offer us the freedom of the schools of Boston! No application made, no questions asked, no examinations, rulings, exclusions; no machinations, no fees. The doors stood open for every one of us. The smallest child could show us the way."

7. BECOMING HEALTHY, WEALTHY, AND WISE "I was put to the grammar school at eight years of age," recalled Benjamin Franklin. By the age of ten he had to help in his father's business and his schooling was ended. But Franklin believed that "the doors of wisdom are never shut." He went on to teach himself French, Italian, Spanish, Latin, algebra, geometry, navigation, and physical sciences, becoming one of the best-educated men of his time.

Traveling in Style

1. THIRTY CARTLOADS OF BAGGAGE British General Burgoyne, known as "Gentleman Johnny," was a dandy, gambler, and drinker. He devised a plan to divide the colonies by leading an attack south from Canada. His men had to hack their way through thick woods and cross terrain that the Americans had made even more hazardous by felling trees across paths, filling ravines, and blocking streams to flood low areas. Nevertheless, Gentleman Johnny traveled with thirty carts for his baggage, which contained his own silver plate, choice wines, and an extensive wardrobe for himself and his mistress.

2. A SILVER CHAMBER POT President of Mexico and General-in-Chief Antonio Lopez de Santa Anna arrived at the battle of the Alamo with monogrammed china, crystal decanters with gold stoppers, a striped marquee for his tent, and a silver chamber pot.

3. MAKING AN ENTRANCE Baron Friedrich von Steuben, the German general who is credited with drilling the raw American militia into disciplined troops, arrived at General Washington's grim winter camp at Valley Forge in a new sleigh trailed by a carriage and riders, five grooms and drivers, a military secretary, two French aides, and three servants.

4. MISTRESSES AND OTHER "USELESS STUFF" In the spring of 1777, the British decided to abandon Philadelphia and concentrate their forces in New York. The army marched across New Jersey with a supply train of fifteen hundred wagons stretching out at the rear. As British commander Sir Henry Clinton admitted, the supply train was "wantonly enormous" and included loot, "mistresses and every other kind of useless stuff."

5. THAT FRESH-FACED LOOK Apache warriors, even when they served as U.S. army scouts, never traveled without a personal kit that included a knife, an awl for sewing moccasins, and tweezers for plucking facial hair—the Indians' answer to shaving.

6. THE NECESSITIES OF AN OCEAN VOYAGE In 1778 during the Revolution, sugar and chocolate were scarce, but somehow Abigail Adams managed to procure those plus Indian meal, hasty pudding, five bushels of corn, six live chickens for eggs, and even a

ten-gallon keg of rum for her husband and son, who were traveling to France, where John Adams was assigned to woo Louis XVI's support in the war. The voyage took six weeks and they needed to bring all the food they would eat, plus their own mattresses, sheets, and blankets. The first night Adams reported that he and young John Quincy "lay very comfortable, slept very well" in their cabin, despite a violent storm.

The Tobacco Habit

1. TWENTY CIGARS A DAY The Northern press, after Ulysses S. Grant's early victories in the West, played up the fact that he smoked cigars. Grant said many people concluded that "tobacco was my chief solace," and he soon received "as many as ten thousand" cigars.

Four days after this picture was taken, Ulysses S. Grant, a cigar smoker, would be dead from throat cancer. Still, he donned a dress suit, silk scarf, top hat, and slippers to sit on the veranda of his Mount McGregor cottage. Cocaine helped ease his suffering, but talking was so painful he communicated with notes.
LIBRARY OF CONGRESS

He gave a lot of them away, but "having such a quantity on hand I naturally smoked more than I would have done under ordinary circumstances and I have continued the habit ever since." He liked to smoke twenty cigars a day. Grant died of cancer of the throat.

2. BURIED TREASURE On their way back from the Pacific, the men of the Lewis and Clark expedition retrieved a cache of supplies that they had hidden near the Jefferson River on their way west. The most welcome portion was the plugs of chewing tobacco.

3. TRIAL WITHOUT SMOKE Temperance advocate Carry Nation was violently opposed to both liquor and tobacco and expressed her views by destroying saloons with rocks or a hatchet. In Wichita,

where she was charged with wrecking the city's finest bar, the arraigning judge asked the fifty-four-year-old Mrs. Nation if she was ready to stand trial. Her empatic answer was that she would not have anything to do with the court until the county attorney got rid of his cigar. "It's rotten and the smell of it poisons me," she added. The county attorney, an avowed antifeminist, got up in a rage and hurled his cigar into the spittoon.

4.   SETTING AN EXAMPLE Before being photographed, President William McKinley was always careful to put away his cigar. He said, "We must not let the young men of this country see their President smoking."

5.   THROUGH SICKNESS AND HEALTH Racked by fits of coughing so severe that he spat blood, Andrew Jackson canceled the presidential farewell address he had planned to deliver to Congress. Yet he resolutely refused to relinquish his pipe, his chewing tobacco, or one of his favorite curatives—strong gin and water.

6.   A PRESIDENTIAL BAROMETER? Was FDR's signature cigarette holder aimed up, ahead, or to the side? The savvy claimed that his mood—or feelings on a proposition—could be determined

Bonnie Parker was upset when this photo hit the papers. She claimed that the idea of her seriously smoking cigars was "bunk."
UPI/BETTMANN NEWSPHOTOS

by the direction of his cigarette holder. For the wheelchair-bound Roosevelt, smoking, combined with the optimistic upward thrusting of his jaw, was a power gesture. He was consistently having to look up to others who were able to stand, and his smoking was a tool he used to give himself a larger presence.

7. THE PICTURE LIED Bonnie Parker and Clyde Barrow liked to shoot more than guns. They often aimed cameras at each other and struck gangster poses. In one, high-heeled and gun-toting Bonnie mimicked the true tough with a cigar clenched in her teeth. The snapshot hit the newspapers when the police uncovered it—and not the outlaws—in a raid. Conscious of her image, Bonnie later told one of her hostages, police chief Percy Boyd: "Tell the public I don't smoke cigars. It's the bunk."

Oh, How They Danced

1. WASHINGTON HAS "A PRETTY LITTLE FRISK" During the Revolution, General Washington's officers held a dance in March 1779 at his headquarters in Middlebrook, New Jersey. Since Martha seldom danced, George took pretty twenty-five-year-old Kitty Greene as his partner. She was the wife of General Nathanael Greene, who was older and had a stiff knee but enjoyed the show. Greene wrote an account of the affair to Colonel Jeremiah Wadsworth: "His Excellency and Mrs. Greene danced upwards of three hours without once sitting down. . . . We had a pretty little frisk."

2. MRS. POLK IS NOT AMUSED First Lady Sarah Polk curtailed liquor at the White House and forbade dancing. When a young lady called on her and pleaded, "Oh, Mrs. Polk, why will you not let us dance?" she replied, "Would you dance in so public a place as this? I would not. . . . How indecorous it would seem for dancing to be going on in one apartment, while in another we are conversing with dignitaries of the republic or ministers of the gospel. This unseemly juxtaposition would be likely to occur at anytime, were such amusements permitted."

3. WITH SPURS JANGLING In Abilene, Kansas, in the 1860s, cowboys celebrated the end of a cattle drive by taking their girls to the dance halls. They fast-stepped with their wide-brimmed Stetsons tilted at a jaunty angle, "spurs jangling at every step or mo-

tion," and "revolvers flopping up and down like a retreating sheep's tail." When the dance was over the cowboy was supposed to buy a drink for his partner and himself, which he was delighted to do at fifty cents a clip.

4.   A ROYAL CHOICE President Gerald Ford's guest of honor at a White House party was Queen Elizabeth II of England. Just as Ford took the queen out on the dance floor, the orchestra struck up "The Lady Is a Tramp."

5.   THE PRESIDENT'S BUCK-AND-WING During his second term, widowed Woodrow Wilson married Edith Galt on December 18, 1915, and boarded a special train for a honeymoon in Hot Springs, Virginia. The following morning Secret Service agent Starling entered their private railway car and was astonished to see the ebullient president all dressed up in a high silk hat and cutaway dancing a buck-and-wing while singing "O What a Beautiful Doll" at the top of his lungs.

6.   WALTZING THROUGH WORK In the 1920s, executive lunches at Henry Ford's engineering lab sometimes included a waltz. Guests would find themselves spirited down the hall to the dancing area, complete with a special wooden floor. There, Ford's own dancing master would explain the intricacies of folk steps and even the minuet. Ford's evening dances, which featured a four-piece orchestra, were command performances for senior company executives.

7.   NIXON GOES PUBLIC "My parents were Quakers. They didn't believe in this sort of thing," said Richard Nixon as he danced with his wife at their daughter Tricia's 1971 Rose Garden wedding. It was the first time President Nixon had danced in public and the wedding guests applauded. He danced with Tricia to "Thank Heaven for Little Girls."

8.   GOOD-NIGHT, LBJ President Lyndon Johnson loved dancing and even did the frug with his teenage daughter Luci. When he was campaigning in 1964, he would try to dance with every woman in the room so she could tell her friends, "I danced with the President."

When one White House party went on until three A.M., his talent for twirling pretty woman after pretty woman began to try Lady Bird Johnson's nerves. Finally she asked the band to play "Goodnight, Sweetheart," a signal for guests to leave. LBJ responded by stopping in the middle of the dance floor, glaring at the pianist, and sticking out his tongue. The pianist stuck to his good-bye tune and the party broke up.

Bed Times

1.   A CHIEF-SIZED BED Pilgrims Edward Winslow and Stephen Hopkins ought to have slept well. They'd just trekked forty miles to meet with Chief Massasoit about an urgent problem. Friendly Indians had been descending upon Plymouth in such numbers that the fledgling colonists were in danger of being eaten out of their new homes.

The Pilgrims presented Massasoit with a red horseman's coat and trinkets. He agreed to curtail his tribe's visits and in a gesture of royal hospitality invited the Pilgrims to share his bed, which consisted of a thin mat on planks in his lice- and flea-infested wigwam. Other bedmates included Massasoit's wife and two of his men, who kept the Pilgrims awake by their habit of singing themselves to sleep.

2.   WASHINGTON AND THE BEDBUGS George Washington was sixteen years old when he first crossed the Blue Ridge Mountains on a surveying expedition and was green behind the ears about the backwoods. "I, not being as good a woodsman as the rest of my company," he wrote, "stripped myself very orderly and went in to ye Bed as they called it, when to my Surprize, I found it to be nothing but a Little Straw—Matted together without Sheets or anything else, but only one thread Bear blanket with double its Weight of Vermin, such as Lice, Fleas, etc." Washington quickly put his clothes back on and lay down on the cabin floor with his companions.

3.   HE SLEPT WITH LINCOLN Everything Abraham Lincoln owned was stowed in the saddlebags of his borrowed horse when he arrived in Springfield, Illinois, in 1837. He was eleven hundred dollars in debt due to the failure of the store he had operated in nearby New Salem. Lincoln's first order of business included buying bedclothes for a single bedstead, which Joshua Speed, the general-store owner, priced at seventeen dollars. "Cheap as it is, I have not the money to pay," said Lincoln. "But if you will credit me until Christmas, and my experiment here as a lawyer is a success, I will pay you then. If I fail in that, I will probably never pay you at all."

Speed thought that he'd never seen "so gloomy and melancholy a face in my life." He offered Lincoln free lodging in his room over the general store. A friendship began and for the next five years Lincoln and Speed shared a double bed.

4.   BELL AND THE DEATH KNELL Bedridden President James A. Garfield held on to life by a thread. He'd been shot in the back in a railway station and physicians were unable to operate for the most frustrating of reasons: They simply could not locate the bullet. While the nation's medical experts conferred, Alexander Graham Bell volunteered to bring in his new electromagnetic invention. He ordered that all metal be removed from the president's bedroom. The attendants, however, didn't understand the nature of the experiment and failed to take away Garfield's mattress with its metal springs. The experiment failed. Eighty days after he was wounded, the president finally died.

5.   A PRESIDENT WITHOUT A BED The invitation to visit the United States was gracious, and Albert, Prince of Wales and son of Queen Victoria, accepted. However, his host, President James Buchanan, had no suitable guest room for the prince in the White House, which in 1860 was decidedly cramped. Buchanan solved the problem by giving the prince his own bed and sleeping on a cot in an anteroom to his office.

6.   SURPRISED DURING A SIESTA Smarting from a Texan defeat at the Alamo, Sam Houston's army managed to take the Mexicans by surprise at San Jacinto. General Antonio Lopez de Santa Anna, caught totally off guard, was taking a siesta in his bed. During the ensuing confusion, he managed to escape but was soon found hiding in tall grass under a blanket.

The general and president of Mexico was wearing a blue jacket and white cotton trousers and was trying to pass himself off as a private. His disguise, however, had little credence when he entered the prison compound to murmurs of "El Presidente." Santa Anna feared for his life, as the Texans were hungry for revenge after the Alamo. But Sam Houston wanted the general alive, not dead, so he could use him as leverage to gain recognition for Texas's independence.

Houston ordered the Mexican's elaborate tent and luxuries, such as silver teapots and decanters with gold stoppers, brought to the prison camp and set up for Santa Anna. His champagne was turned over to Houston's men, who got drunk. But that night they slept on the ground as usual while Santa Anna dozed off in his traveling bed in the very spot the Texans had found him earlier.

7.   PALLET ON THE FLOOR "I cannot remember having slept in a bed until after our family was declared free by the Emancipation Proclamation," wrote Booker T. Washington in his 1900 *Up from Slavery*. "Three children—John, my older brother, Amanda, my sister, and myself—had a pallet on the dirt floor, or to be more correct, we slept in and on a bundle of filthy rags laid upon the dirt floor." Their cabin, fourteen by sixteen feet, was also the kitchen of the plantation.

8.   A DICKENS OF A SITUATION When novelist Charles Dickens was touring the new United States in the early 1800s, he traveled by canal boat, a favorite mode of transportation at the time. Sleeping arrangements were makeshift. The dining cabin became a men's dormitory at night, when collapsible berths made of wood and canvas were set up in tiers. Dickens described how the travelers gathered around the tables to draw lots for the berths "with all the anxieties and passions of gamesters." They then undressed and crawled into bed. "The rapidity with which an agitated gambler subsided into snoring slumber," wrote Dickens, "was one of the most singular effects I have ever witnessed."

9.   WHAT SHE SUFFERED FOR SUFFRAGE By the time feminist Elizabeth Cady Stanton, a native New Yorker, felt a mouse run over her head as she lay in a Kansas pioneer cabin, her romantic notions of frontier life had already faded. In 1867 she was campaigning in untamed Kansas for the first-ever state referendum on women's suffrage. Her diet sometimes narrowed to dried herring, crackers, slippery elm, and gum arabic. She slept in rustic cabins wherever there was a spare mattress. When she encountered the mouse, her hostess, bedded down in another corner, commented, "Well, I should not wonder. I heard such a squeaking from that corner during the past week that I told sister there must be a mouse nest in that bed." Mice proved to be the least of Stanton's setbacks. The referendum failed.

10.   TOO TALL FOR HIS DEATH BED From Ford's Theatre, dying Abraham Lincoln was carried across the street to a boardinghouse. He was taken to a small room under the stairs at the end of a hall. Too tall for the bed, he had to be laid crosswise on it. His wounded head was supported by two pillows and his feet were left to dangle off the end.

Man and His Dog

1.   AN INTERNATIONAL YELP On April 27, 1964, President Lyndon Johnson inadvertently created an international news story—he picked up his favorite beagle, Him, by the ears. Him yelped. Since it happened just outside the Oval Office with a swarm of reporters and photographers present, the story went worldwide. Johnson tried explaining that pulling dogs by the ears was good for them. Experts from all over were questioned by the media, but the chairman of the Canine Defense League in London was one of the very few who defended President Johnson's theory.

Lyndon Johnson's persistence in pulling his beagle's ears became a pet peeve of America's dog lovers. Here the president holds a bottle of dog vitamins in his left hand.
UPI/BETTMANN NEWSPHOTOS

2.   NO FLEAS OR BUGS The Kennedys were given a dog called Pushinka by Soviet leader Khrushchev. Pushinka was the daughter of the Russian space dog Strelka, but in the cold war era Pushinka had to be checked for internal bugs to be sure that he wasn't a "spy dog" before Caroline and John-John could play with her.

3.   "THE INFORMER" During World War II, the Secret Service attempted to keep FDR's train travels a secret. However, the presi-

dent's famous Scotty was often a giveaway. Like most dogs, he'd insist on being let out for a walk when the train stopped. Fala, with a Secret Service agent in tow, was a big clue as to FDR's presence, especially when the dog was being walked beside a closed train parked at a siding and guarded by military sentries. The Secret Service code name for Fala was "The Informer."

4. THE CHINOOKS WANTED HIM FOR SUPPER Meriwether Lewis brought Scannon, a 160-pound Newfoundland dog, on the expedition overland to the Pacific. Scannon endured the hardships and dangers of the expedition just like the men. He guarded the camp at night and probably saved his master's life by scaring off a charging buffalo. But his most dangerous moment came when Chinook Indians stole him. The Indians were chased by the men of the expedition, who finally forced the Indians to abandon Scannon and flee, saving Scannon from becoming stew.

5. HE POCKETED A PUPPY "I have a dog for you!" President Franklin Pierce told his Secretary of War Jefferson Davis. Pierce had just received a tiny "sleeve dog" from the Orient, one of the many exotic presents brought back by Commodore Matthew Perry from his historic 1855 voyage to open Japan to trade. The tiny dog's name was Bonin and, wrote Mrs. Davis, "he was a little creature with a head like a bird with a blunt beak, eyes large and popped, and a body like a new-born puppy of the smallest kind." Little Bonin was so tiny that "a coffee saucer made an ample scampering ground for him." Davis loved him and rode about Washington with his sleeve dog in his pocket.

What's in a Name?

1. "UNCONDITIONAL SURRENDER" GRANT For six weeks Hannah Simpson Grant didn't bother to name her first child. Finally relatives and friends formed a lottery and wrote out names on slips of paper. The winner was "Hiram Ulysses Grant." But Hannah skipped the "Hiram" and called the boy "Lyss." Young Grant kept Ulysses as his first name because he didn't like the initials H.U.G.

At West Point, he lost Hiram altogether when the congressman sponsoring his application mistakenly wrote down his middle name as Simpson, his mother's family name. The cadets called him "Sam," taking his initials, U.S., for Uncle Sam. When Grant won the first great Northern victory in the Civil War, his initials became short for "Unconditional Surrender," the stunning demand he made at Fort Donelson. It was a nickname that took him to the White House.

2. HE NEEDED A LAST NAME Born a slave, Booker T. Washington was always known simply as Booker. When emancipation came and he went to school for the first time, he heard the other students respond to the roll with two names. Suddenly he realized that he needed a last name and picked Washington because it was the grandest name he could think of. Later he learned that his mother had given him Taliaferro as his last name, so he used it as a middle name.

3. "TOMMY THE TURKEY" Woodrow Wilson was born Thomas Woodrow Wilson and called Tommy by family and friends until 1881. Then, at age twenty-four, he decided Woodrow was more dignified. "It's Tommy the turkey and Tommy the cat and Tommy the gardener." So he dropped it.

4. "MOLLY PITCHER" Mary Hayes was her real name. Her husband was a gunner in the 1st Pennsylvania Artillery and Molly followed him to the army's winter camp at Valley Forge, making herself useful by doing washing and cooking.

The next summer she marched with the army into New Jersey and was with her husband at the Battle of Monmouth on June 28, 1778. The temperature got up to 100 degrees. Molly brought water from a nearby spring amid cries from the soldiers of "Molly, the pitcher." Her nickname was born. When her husband dropped from heat stroke, she took his place, swabbing and loading his cannon under fire. "Sergeant Molly" smoked a pipe, chewed tobacco, and swore like the trooper she was. In 1822 the Pennsylvania state legislature rewarded Molly Pitcher for her efforts with a yearly pension of forty dollars.

5. "OLD ROUGH AND READY" In the 1848 Mexican War, General Zachary Taylor won a series of victories against vastly superior armies, accounting for half of the nickname he came away with: He proved he was ready.

That he was rough there is little doubt. His typical uniform consisted of baggy pants, a plain coat with no insignia, and a farmer's wide-brimmed straw hat. He had a large head but short legs—hardly an imposing figure. There were times when he was mistaken for a hick farmer instead of the commanding general. When he became president he liked to sit in his office with his feet up on a chair and a good wad of tobacco in his mouth. The cuspidor was nearby and Old Rough and Ready was known as a sure shot.

6. "A LUCY STONER" Miss Lucy Stone was not afraid to create a stir. Like many of her feminist friends, she adopted the bloomer costume in the 1840s and was ridiculed, though some conceded that pants suited her figure better than they did most women. In her mid-thirties she fell in love with Henry Blackwell, a women's rights supporter ten years her junior. At her wedding she agreed to love and cherish but not obey him. Afterward she made the radical move of refusing to take her husband's name. The public didn't know what to call her and finally settled on Mrs. Stone. Women who kept their maiden names became "Lucy Stoners."

7. "BUFFALO BILL" William F. Cody, the man behind the legendary Wild West Show, earned his nickname as a buffalo hunter who provided meat for railroad work gangs. He is said to have killed 120 buffalo in 40 minutes and 6,000 in 60 days.

He served as an army scout but was just another frontier unknown until he met writer Ned Buntline, who gave him star billing in a dime novel. According to Buntline's romantic prose, Buffalo Bill advocated temperance and saved a beautiful white girl from renegade Indians, killing their leader, Tall Bull. This surprised Buffalo Bill Cody since he was a man who liked his liquor. He'd also missed the raid where Tall Bull was killed and a nondescript German woman captive was released. But Buffalo Bill was on his way to fame.

8. "OLD HICKORY" That Andrew Jackson was tough as a hickory stick there can be little doubt. In a duel with Charles Dickinson he took a bullet next to the heart and then stood firm and shot his opponent dead. In a brawl with Jesse and Thomas Hart Benton he was shot twice, one bullet shattering his shoulder. He refused to have his arm amputated.

He seems to have received his nickname during the War of 1812 when he led twenty-five hundred Tennessee militiamen to New Orleans to fight the British. They got as far as Natchez, Mississippi, when the War Department called off the expedition and ordered Jackson to disband his troops on the spot "with thanks."

This would have left his troops five hundred miles from home without pay, food, or transportation. Jackson was furious and flatly refused. He issued a proclamation saying he would march his militiamen home "on my own means and responsibility." He not only bore the expense but also the privations and the hard work. One soldier remarked, "He's as tough as hickory," and the name stuck.

9. "LANDSLIDE LYNDON" When Lyndon Johnson ran for senator in the Texas Democratic primary, he appeared to be losing by a hair. Then in Jim Wells County there was a recount, and 202 votes suddenly appeared, all in alphabetical order in the same handwriting and same ink. Every one was for Lyndon Baines Johnson. His opponent, former Governor Coke R. Stevenson, charged fraud, but Johnson was declared the winner by 87 votes. He went to the U.S. Senate with the tongue-in-cheek nickname "Landslide Lyndon."

10. "STONEWALL JACKSON" Though dubbed "Stonewall" in the Civil War, Confederate General Thomas Jonathan Jackson was famous for movement. In his lengendary Shenandoah Valley campaign he marched his army four hundred miles in six weeks, during which they fought five battles, terrified Washington, D.C., with the threat of invasion, beat off three armies, captured half of another, and still had time to join Robert E. Lee for a key battle for Richmond. Jackson's nickname of Stonewall came when, at the first Battle of Bull Run, a fellow Confederate officer, General Barnard Bee, encouraged his own men by shouting, "There is Jackson standing like a stone wall."

When General Dwight D. Eisenhower came back from World War II, I LIKE IKE *bedecked everything, from stores to buttons. Soon he was running for president in the 1952 elections with a button of his own.*
UPI/BETTMANN NEWSPHOTOS

11. "IKE" WAS A GOOD NAME President Dwight D. Eisenhower was born "David Dwight" on October 14, 1890. Later, his mother reversed his names—partly to avoid confusion with his father, whose name was also David, and partly because she didn't

like nicknames. She figured that Dwight could not be shortened. She was right, but in World War II, G.I.'s in Europe invented their own nickname for him—"Ike." Eisenhower thought that "was one of the luckiest things that could have happened. A soldier always likes a good name for his officers," he explained. "Ike was a good name. When they called me Uncle Ike, or during the war, just plain Ike, I knew everything was going well."

12.   THEY CALLED HIM "SCARFACE" The three jagged scars on the left side of Al Capone's face were hard to miss, even though he tried to disguise them with talcum powder. When asked to explain their origin, he'd say he was wounded by shrapnel while fighting in France with the "Lost Battalion." Actually, he'd been on the wrong end of a stiletto when he was a bouncer and bartender at a brothel with the unlikely name of Harvard Inn. Capone had made the mistake of passing derogatory remarks about one of the girls within earshot of her brother, who leaped over the bar and knifed him. In an unexpected move, Scarface never exacted revenge. He later hired his attacker as a bodyguard for one hundred dollars a week.

13.   GERRY FORD'S FIRST MAJOR SHOCK On July 14, 1913, future President Leslie L. King, Jr., was born. His mother divorced his father shortly afterward and married Gerald R. Ford. Young Leslie King was renamed Gerald R. Ford, Jr. He didn't learn about his real father until he was twelve, and never saw him until one day in the spring of 1930, when he got the "first major shock of my life." He was in high school and working part time in a restaurant when a stranger came up to him and said, "I'm Leslie King, your father. Can I take you to lunch?"

After lunch King drove his son back to South High and gave him twenty-five dollars. That night in bed, Gerry Ford broke down and cried.

Dressed for the Occasion

1.   HIS SUNDAY BEST Orville Wright made the first powered flight lying face down on the wing and wearing a dark suit, starched collar, and tie.

2.   DIAMOND-STUDDED SHOE BUCKLES For his second inaugural, on March 4, 1793, George Washington wore a black velvet suit trimmed with silver lace, an embroidered white satin vest, black

silk stockings, diamond-studded knee and shoe buckles, and yellow kid gloves. Over his powdered hair he wore a cocked hat, and he carried a dress sword with a jeweled hilt sheathed in a white leather scabbard. He arrived at the Philadelphia State House in a cream-colored coach with cherubs painted on the door panels and drawn by six pure-white horses.

3. UNDERDRESSED FOR SUCCESS Benjamin Franklin went to Paris during the Revolution to represent the new United States and found himself an instant hero. Crowds followed him everywhere and he was given a château to live in free of charge. Franklin was fond of finery and expensive clothes but sensed that the French saw him as a rustic philosopher, a "natural man," so he altered his wardrobe.

When he was presented at court among silk-clad nobles in powdered wigs, he wore humble clothes and his dreadfully unfashionable spectacles. He became famous in Paris for his long staff and the frontier-style fur cap that artists often show him wearing.

4. GOING DOWN IN STYLE In 1912, when the *Titanic* hit an iceberg and started to sink, multimillionaire Benjamin Guggenheim was helped into a life vest by a solicitous steward. The steward insisted on pulling a heavy sweater over the mining king as it would be cold in the lifeboat. When it became apparent that there would be no lifeboats left for the men—women and children came first—Guggenheim and his secretary changed into evening clothes. "We've dressed in our best and are prepared to go down like gentlemen," he said.

5. A MAN OF THE PEOPLE The British minister complained that when he called at the White House, President Thomas Jefferson received him with his hair loose instead of neatly tied in a queue and wearing heelless carpet slippers and an old brown coat.

6. SWORDSMANSHIP Robert E. Lee met Ulysses S. Grant at the Civil War surrender ceremony at Appomattox Court House wearing a new uniform with a sash and dress sword, high boots with red silk stitching, and gold spurs at the heels. Grant had on an unbuttoned and dusty fatigue jacket and rumpled trousers that were tucked into mud-spattered boots.

When it came to the terms, Grant, who had earned the nickname "Unconditional Surrender," was generous. Arms were required to be turned in and stacked, but Grant wrote that this "will not embrace the side arms of officers." Lee would not have to suffer the indignity of handing over his fine sword.

7. A SHIRT THAT FELT LIKE CHESTNUT BURRS "The most trying ordeal that I was forced to endure as a slave boy, however, was the wearing of a flax shirt," wrote Booker T. Washington in his 1900 *Up from Slavery*. Made from the roughest and cheapest flax, the shirt, when new, felt like "a dozen or more chestnut burrs, or a hundred small pin-points," in contact with his flesh. His brother John "performed one of the most generous acts" by breaking in a new flax shirt for him.

8. A LAWMAN'S VANITY Marshall "Wild Bill" Hickok walked the streets of Abilene, Kansas, wearing a Prince Albert coat, checkered trousers, and a silk vest embroidered with floral designs. Over his shoulder he had a cape with a flowered silk lining, and about his waist, pearl-handled pistols.

9. OUT OF UNIFORM In the war with Mexico, the invading American army found the weather so hot that General Zachary Taylor ordered the men to march in their underwear.

10. TALLOW STIFFENED THEIR CURLS Comfort and practicality were not the hallmarks of British uniforms during the Revolution. The regulars wore heavy greatcoats with sleeves as "tight as stockings" in winter *and* in summer. Their tight waistcoats had high stiff collars which forced them to keep their heads up. The knee britches were skintight, and coverings for the lower legs were put on wet so they would shrink for a snug fit.

They carried bayonet scabbards that knocked against the legs and cartridge boxes attached to a broad belt worn over the shoulder and across the chest. On their backs were haversacks with extra clothing, a brush and blackball to keep shoes gleaming, blankets, rations, and tent equipment.

When the British charged up Bunker Hill, each soldier was carrying 120 pounds of equipment. It could take three hours to dress for parade. Brass buttons had to be polished and facings whitened with pipe clay. Finally, tallow had to be applied to the hair to shape the required stiff curls.

11. SHOWING HIS ANKLES President James Monroe went to his inauguration wearing an old-fashioned wig, broadcloth coat, knee britches, silk stockings, and shoes with silver buckles. He was the

last of the Revolutionary War hero-presidents, and the last president to wear knee britches.

12.   IN PRAISE OF BLOOMERS When feminist Elizabeth Cady Stanton was first introduced to Susan B. Anthony on a street corner in Seneca Falls, New York, she was wearing bloomers. The radical outfit—short pants under a knee-length skirt—was something she loved because it "makes it easier to do all these things—running from cradle to writing desk, from kitchen to drawing room, singing lullabies at one moment in the nursery and dear old Tom Moores ditties the next moment on the piano stool. If I had long skirts, how could I accomplish all this?" Her husband didn't disapprove of her exposed limbs, but her sons pleaded with with her not to visit them at school "in costume." Eventually the dress detracted from the acceptance of her feminist ideas and she gave it up.

13.   FLOUR FOR THEIR HAIR The day the British surrendered at Yorktown, ending the Revolutionary War, our French allies were resplendent in white uniforms bordered with bright colors, plumed hats, and black leg coverings. In order not to be shamed by the French, Washington had ordered his ragtag men to "look as neat and respectable as possible" and to "take care to be well-shaven." To improve their impression, Washington had ordered flour issued for powdering their hair.

14.   IN PARIS WITHOUT A TOOTHBRUSH "To avoid extra weight," wrote Charles Lindbergh, "I had carried no unnecessary items with me in the *Spirit of St. Louis,* not a razor or a tooth brush. I had even trimmed the margins of my maps to save a few ounces." That meant that Lindbergh had arrived in Paris in his flying clothes, which were "hardly adequate" for all the ceremonies he faced. A friend was able to lend him "a business suit that came close to fitting me. It was a little baggy around the shoulders and a bit short in the pants, but it would do for the moment." A tailor was soon found to make several suits and a tailcoat.

Insights on Eyesight

1.   DOUBLE VISION Benjamin Franklin lamented the fact that he had to keep changing his spectacles as "the glasses that serve me best at the table to see what I eat" weren't good for seeing "the

faces of those on the other side of the table." So he came up with the idea of having his glasses cut and putting "half of each kind associated in the same circle," thus inventing bifocals.

2.   A WHOLE NEW WORLD Theodore Roosevelt was thirteen years old when he noticed that the boys he was playing with could read an advertisement in large letters on a distant billboard. Young Theodore "realized that something was the matter, for not only was I unable to read the sign, but I could not even see the letters." He spoke to his father about it and soon had his first pair of spectacles. "I had no idea how beautiful the world was," TR wrote. When he set out for Cuba in the Spanish-American War, he carried twelve extra pairs stored in various places, including his hat lining.

3.   "FLAT EYEBALLS" In 1889 a young Harry Truman enjoyed the noise of the Fourth of July fireworks but paid no attention to the brilliant visual display. Something was wrong. His mother drove him fifteen miles into Kansas City in a buggy for an eye exam. The doctor discovered he had "flat eyeballs." Truman could read the large type of the Bible but couldn't see anything at a distance. The thick glasses he had to wear changed his life—he couldn't partici- pate in games or sports so he turned to the books he loved. His poor eyesight kept him out of West Point but didn't prevent him from becoming a captain in World War I.

4.   AN UNCONSCIOUS FLIRT Short, stocky Zachary Taylor could survey a battlefield with confidence, but in reading commands, the general often had trouble focusing. Imbalanced eye muscles con- tributed to double vision, a condition he counteracted by closing one eye tightly. At parties ladies were sometimes flustered because it looked as if Taylor were winking at them.

5.   READING COULD BECOME A PAIN Abraham Lincoln's vi- sion problems began with a weak muscle in the left eye and most likely were complicated by a boyhood injury—a kick from a horse that left him with a permanent dent in the forehead. As a result, reading was tiring and painful. Lincoln learned to speed read and to memorize lengthy law texts rather than face rereading them.

6.   CROSS-EYED JULIA Near the end of Ulysses Grant's first term, the president found his wife, her bags packed, ready to head to New York for an operation that would remedy her crossed eyes. Grant protested, "I met you and fell in love with you the way you are and, anyway, I'm not such a handsome fellow myself." Julia

Grant declined the operation. Her vision, however, was so distorted that she had to turn her head sideways and gaze out the corners of her eyes to see across a room. To avoid bumping into furniture she developed a crablike side-to-side walk. At presidential parties, she usually stood in place unless escorted by a guiding arm. Photographs almost always show her in profile.

7. BLIND DEVOTION Encamped at New Windsor, New York, awaiting the peace treaty that would end the Revolutionary War, General George Washington faced the serious threat of a military coup by his own officers. They had not been paid for a long time and were so angry at the ineptness of the Continental Congress that they proposed going to Philadelphia and taking over. Washington was appalled. He gathered his officers together in a building called the Temple. His speech did little to change their minds. They had been through too much frustration. Then Washington wanted to read them a letter, halted, and fumbled for a pair of spectacles, then uttered the words that averted a coup and moved some officers to tears: "Gentlemen, I have grown gray in your service, and now I am going blind."

Napping on the Job

1. EDISON NODS OUT Teenaged Thomas A. Edison worked as a telegraph operator on the Grand Trunk Railway all night from 7:00 P.M. to 7:00 A.M. In order to have time for his chemistry experiments during the day, he took catnaps throughout the night. Since few messages came through during his shift, his job mostly involved sending a signal of dots and dashes at specified times to show that he was alert and at his post.

Edison, eager to nap, devised a clockwork mechanism that tapped out the message for him. His system worked for a while, but the company operator got suspicious when he couldn't reach Edison after his automatic message was sent. Nearly fired, the young inventor was transferred to another job.

2. STAYING AWAKE WAS A LOSING BATTLE General Winfield Scott was seventy-five years old, had dropsy, and was commanding general of the army when Abraham Lincoln became president. The first battle of the Civil War was at Bull Run in Virginia. Scott exer-

cised his overall command from an office in the War Department. But the fighting was close enough to Washington for Lincoln to be able to hear the cannons booming.

When the telegrams from the front indicated a Southern victory, Lincoln rushed over to the War Department to find out what was happening. He discovered the general asleep and had to wake him up. Scott pulled himself upright with a rope attached to a pulley on the ceiling. He looked at the telegrams, assured Lincoln there was nothing to worry about, and went back to sleep. Soon Union troops were streaming back into Washington. The first great battle of the war was a disaster for the North.

3. SNORING IN CHURCH William Howard Taft could drop off to sleep anytime, anywhere. His wife, Helen, called him her "Sleeping Beauty." He slept sitting up in the presidential automobile, his 355-pound hulk swaying from side to side. He slept at cabinet meetings. Once he went to sleep when House speaker Joe Cannon was talking to him.

An aide, Archie Butt, used to sit alongside him and cough loudly when he sensed the president was about to doze off. Coughing, however, was indiscreet in church. So one time when Taft nodded off during a service and started to snore, Butt poked him. Taft awoke "with such a start as to attract the attention of everybody around him." The presidential aide decided to abandon that technique.

4. NEWSPAPERMEN PUT LBJ TO SLEEP It was no news that Lyndon Johnson liked to take a nap every day after lunch, but what did surprise top newsmen is that a few of them were invited to interview the president right up until he fell asleep.

Such occasions usually began with an impromptu invitation to lunch in the family quarters. LBJ would give an off-the-record talk right through the meal, which usually ended with diet tapioca pudding. Then he'd signal the reporters to follow him up to his bedroom, where he'd change for his nap, talking all the while. When the president fell asleep, they'd rush off to the press room and often telephone in a story that began, "A high administration source said today . . ."

5. PRESIDENTIAL IMPOSTOR "Bill, how would you like to be President for a while?" FDR asked a Secret Service agent on a train trip. Positioned by the window, the man was fitted out with FDR's prince-nez glasses, shown how to wave with a cigarette holder, and given a primer on smiling. "Fine! Just fine! Now every time we pass

a town, sit there and wave. I'm going to take a nap," said Roosevelt.

6.   ASLEEP UP AGAINST A TREE General Irwin McDowell led the untrained Northern troops south to Bull Run in Virginia, where he suffered the first in a series of Northern defeats. Retreating from Bull Run after an exhausting all-day battle, McDowell reached Fairfax Court House, Virginia, that night and sat on the ground up against a tree to begin writing a dispatch. He was so tired he fell asleep in the middle of a sentence, his pencil in hand. His adjutant found him, woke him up, and the general finished his dispatch before resuming his weary ride back to Washington, D.C.

7.   CAUGHT NAPPING Charles Dawes, newly elected as vice-president under Calvin Coolidge, liked to take a nap in the afternoon and normally his job didn't present much of an obstacle. His only constitutional duty, presiding over the Senate, could be left to someone else, but he had to be present if there was a tie so that he could cast the deciding vote. Dawes's services looked like they might be necessary when Coolidge's appointment of Charles B. Warren as attorney general ran into trouble. But Republicans and Democrats were squabbling endlessly and Dawes believed that the wrangling would go for hours, so he left for his hotel room and a nap.

Suddenly the issue was brought to a vote and it was tied 40 to 40. The Republicans tried to stall while Dawes was rushed back to the Senate in a taxi. He sprinted down the halls to the Senate chamber, but he was too late. A vote had been switched and the appointment rejected.

Price Tags

1.   In 1778 in Boonesboro, the frontier town founded by Daniel Boone, a bushel of salt was worth a cow and a half.

2.   In the last full year of Washington's administration, it cost $5,727,000 to run the entire federal government.

3.   A ride on the Erie Canal in 1825 cost a cent and a half a mile, and passengers traveled at a mile and a half an hour.

4.   In the California gold rush, claims at an area called Rich Bar were so lucrative that they were limited to ten square feet. A pailful

of dirt might reap $1,500 to $2,000 in gold. The record reported was $2,900 in one pail. Four men took in $50,000 in a day.

5.   At age forty-six, Abraham Lincoln stopped off in a Springfield, Illinois, jewelry store and bought his first pair of eyeglasses for thirty-seven and a half cents.

6.   When the Butterfield Overland stage opened in 1859, the passenger fare from St. Louis to San Francisco was two hundred dollars, or, for lesser distances, ten cents per mile traveled. Forty pounds of luggage was the limit.

7.   Julia Ward Howe sold her "Battle Hymn of the Republic" to the *Atlantic Monthly* for four dollars.

8.   Mail on the Pony Express cost five dollars per half ounce, but a letter was guaranteed to go from St. Joseph, Missouri, to Sacramento, California, in under ten days.

9.   In 1867, Secretary of State William Seward negotiated a treaty to buy the islands of St. Thomas and St. John from Denmark for $7.5 million, which was more than he had just paid for the vast Alaskan territory. Congress opposed the purchase but in 1917 agreed to pay Denmark $25 million for the two islands and St. Croix plus about fifty islets.

10.   In May 1904, steerage rates for immigrants sailing from Europe to America were cut to ten dollars.

11.   In the early 1900s, sweaters were advertised to sell for 8 cents and a sofa cost $9.98. Eggs were 21 cents a dozen, gold fillings, 75 cents; haircuts, 15 cents; and a live-in maid, $10 a month.

12.   The Wright brothers built their first airplane for less than one thousand dollars.

13.   Charles A. Lindbergh's plane, *The Spirit of St. Louis*, was built in San Diego to Lindbergh's specifications at a cost of $10,585. He navigated to New York with railroad maps that he had bought in a drugstore for 50 cents each.

PART VIII
Words and Wisdom

Toasts

1. Dolley Madison had just fled from the White House when British Admiral Sir George Cockburn broke in during the War of 1812. He and his men found the table set for dinner in the State Dining Room. Cockburn sat down, poured himself some wine, and drank a toast to "Jemmy's health." President James Madison was "Jemmy" to his close friends. The admiral then ordered the White House burned.

2. When President John Kennedy gave a dinner where guests included forty-nine Nobel Prize winners, he offered this toast: "I think this is the most extraordinary collection of talent, of human knowledge, that has ever been gathered together at the White House— with the possible exception of when Thomas Jefferson dined alone."

3. After the presidency, Theodore Roosevelt went to Africa to hunt. J. P. Morgan, no Roosevelt fan, toasted, "Let every lion do his duty."

4. Just before the Revolution, the Sons of Liberty held a dinner which began with forty-five toasts to celebrate the forty-fifth issue of a patriot paper. They offered salutes to the king, and then touched more Revolutionary themes, including "the speedy removal of all task-masters" and "the abolition of all craft and low cunning in Church and State." John Adams noted that "To the honor of the Sons, I did not see one person intoxicated, or near it."

5. At the end of the Revolutionary War, George Washington bid an emotional farewell to his officers. There wasn't a dry eye as he lifted his wine glass and said, "With a heart full of love and gratitude, I now take leave of you. I most devoutly wish that your latter days may be as prosperous and happy as your former ones have been glorious and honorable."

6. On April 13, 1830, a Democratic dinner honoring Thomas Jefferson's birthday fell in the middle of a political controversy over South Carolina's right to nullify any law deemed unconstitutional and to secede from the Union. John C. Calhoun planned to use the dinner to defend nullification and put the president on the spot.

After twenty-four regular toasts, the toastmaster called on President Andrew Jackson as the guest of honor to give the first voluntary toast. Looking at Calhoun, Jackson deliberately and emphatically toasted: "Our Union! It must be preserved!" There was silence.

Jackson raised his glass, a signal that the toast should be drunk standing. Calhoun was unnerved; toasting the Union was the antithesis of what he had in mind. As he drank his hand trembled so that drops of wine trickled down the side of his glass.

7.   After a bloody fight for independence from Mexico, Texas President Sam Houston sent William Wharton to Washington to plead for U.S. recognition of his Lone Star Republic. President Andrew Jackson was for it, but Northerners opposed the idea of a huge new slave-holding neighbor and Mexico threatened war over the issue. Finally, on Jackson's last day in office, Congress voted to recognize the Republic of Texas. Just before midnight in the dismantled study of the White House, while slaves carried out the last of the president's possessions, Wharton and Jackson met and drank a toast to the Lone Star Republic of Texas.

8.   Commodore Stephen Decatur, hero of the war against the Barbary pirates, attended a banquet in his honor in 1816. His toast ended in the words that he has made famous: "Our country: In her intercourse with foreign nations may she always be in the right; but our country, right or wrong."

9.   Major Robert Anderson, who had surrendered Fort Sumter in Charleston harbor to the Confederates in the Civil War's first clash, came back to reclaim it at the end of the war. That night, April 14, 1865, at a dinner in Charleston, he proposed a toast to President Abraham Lincoln: "I beg you, now, that you will join me in drinking the health of . . . a man who now can travel all over our country with millions of hands and hearts to sustain him." At that moment Lincoln was at Ford's Theatre and had only hours to live.

10.   Fifty years after fighting in the Revolution, Lafayette returned to the country he had helped create and received a hero's welcome everywhere he went. At a banquet in his honor he responded to a series of laudatory toasts with: "To the perpetual union of the United States. It has always saved us in times of storm, one day it will save the world."

11.   In 1826, ninety-one-year-old John Adams was too ill to attend the Quincy, Massachusetts, Fourth of July ceremonies, but he did agree to provide a toast. "Independence forever" was his terse salute. The local orator, the Reverend Mr. Whitney, tried to persuade the former president to come up with something more eloquent.

Adams snapped that he would add "not a word." On the day the toast was given, Adams quietly died.

Oh, Hell

1. "I never gave them hell, I just tell the truth and they think it's hell," said Harry Truman.

2. "Hell, men, I been clean t'the Pacific Ocean!" reported Jim Bridger, who actually had not been quite that far at the time. He'd just discovered Great Salt Lake and spit out a mouthful of salt water in disgust.

3. At the Battle of Buena Vista, a bullet cut through Zachary Taylor's sleeve and another ripped his coat lining. He still sounded casual as he ordered his artillery to "double-shot your guns and give 'em hell."

4. "It is only those who have neither fired a shot or heard the shrieks and groans of the wounded who cry aloud for blood, more vengeance, more desolation. War is hell."—Civil War General William T. Sherman

5. "General Ethan Allen died and went to Hell this day." This was the president of Yale's entry in his diary in 1789 on learning of the death of the free-thinking, hard-drinking leader of the Green Mountain Boys.

6. Calvin Coolidge was presiding at a Massachusetts legislative session which he was attempting to adjourn. A senator kept interrupting, intent on getting a bill for his district introduced, and Coolidge kept putting him off. Finally, the irate senator snapped at Coolidge, "You can go to hell." "Senator," Coolidge replied, "I've looked up the law and I find I don't have to."

7. Stephen A. Douglas tried to give a speech before a hostile Irish crowd in Chicago, but the audience kept interrupting him with catcalls and hisses. It was a Saturday night and finally, after four hours, Douglas lost his temper, exchanged insults with his audience, then stalked off in a rage, shaking his fist and shouting, "It's now Sunday morning; I'll go to church. And you can go to hell."

8. John Dillinger and his gang had guns aimed at the employees of the Central National Bank in Greencastle, Indiana, while they

quietly scooped up $75,346—their biggest take ever. An elderly for-
eign-born woman, unruffled by the situation, started out the back
door. When the armed lookout told her gently, "Better go back inside, lady," she brushed his gun aside and snapped, "I go to Pen-
ney's and you go to hell." She proceeded down the street unharmed.

Last Words

1.   William Henry Harrison was the first president to die in office.
He served only one month, but it was a month of constant hound-
ing by office-seekers. His final words were, "I can't stand it. . . .
Don't trouble me. . . . These applications, will they never
cease . . . ?"

2.   John Wilkes Booth, shot in a tobacco barn in Virginia after mur-
dering Abraham Lincoln, asked that his hands be raised so that he
could see them. He murmured, "Useless! Useless!" as he died.

3.   "Strike the tent."—Robert E. Lee

4.   As Daniel Webster lay dying, he heard the doctor say, "Give
him a spoonful of brandy in fifteen minutes, another in half an hour,
and another in three quarters of an hour, if he still lives." The directions were followed until it came to the third dose, when the
attendants had trouble deciding if he was still alive. Webster raised
his head and said feebly, "I still live." They were his last words.
He got the brandy.

5.   President Warren G. Harding was in a San Francisco hotel bed
recovering from a heart attack. He was worried and upset about the
corruption in his administration. His wife was reading aloud from
the *Saturday Evening Post*'s profile of Harding, entitled "A Calm View
of a Calm Man." He said, "That's good. Go on; read some more,"
and fell back dead.

6.   "So little done, so much to do."—Alexander Graham Bell

7.   Thomas A. Edison, when asked if he was suffering, murmured,
"No, just waiting." He looked toward the window and said, "It's
very beautiful over there."

8.   "Mr. Adams is dying!" cried a congressman, while another
caught the stricken John Quincy Adams as he slumped from his
seat at the House of Representatives. The eighty-year-old former

president turned congressman was laid on the speaker's table. He was carried on a sofa to the Capitol rotunda, then the east portico, and finally to the speaker's chamber, where he died two days later. "Thank the officers of the House. This is the last of earth: I am content," were Adams's last words.

9. "Let us cross over the river and rest under the shade of the trees."—Thomas Jonathan (Stonewall) Jackson

10. "I think I'll sleep now."—George Washington Carver

11. "I have always done my duty. I am ready to die. My only regret is for the friends I leave behind me."—Zachary Taylor

12. "I have tried so hard to do right."—Grover Cleveland

13. Eighty-year-old Aaron Burr, the former vice-president, didn't belong to any church, a situation several clergymen were anxious to remedy. He curtly rejected them all except the Reverend Dr. P. J. Van Pelt, who used the subtler approach of discussing theology in general. As Burr began to fail, Van Pelt made a strenuous effort to get him to accept God. Burr's last words, said with a humorous glint in his eyes, were, "On that subject I am coy."

14. "I die hard, but I am not afraid to go. . . . Let me go quietly."—George Washington

Matters of Semantics

1. TWEEDLEDEE OR TWEEDLEDUM? Coal was king in 1901— the major fuel for heating and cooking. A strike of coal miners brought on severe shortages and a major national crisis. To resolve it, President Theodore Roosevelt pressured the mine operators into accepting arbitration by an impartial commission. They agreed it could include "a man of prominence such as a sociologist," but not a union man. They would not "meet with a criminal" and it appeared that the talks would collapse.

At last it began to dawn on TR that the owners would accept a union representative provided he wasn't called that. So he immediately appointed the grand chief of the Order of Railway Conductors as the "eminent sociologist" and the crisis ended. Roosevelt's comment afterward was: "The mighty brains of these captains of industry would rather have anarchy than tweedledum, but if I used the word tweedledee, they would all hail it as meaning peace."

2. ALL IN A POINT OF VIEW Temperance advocate Carry Nation was brought into Judge O. D. Kirk's Wichita City Court for destroying the city's finest saloon, which she had shattered with rocks and an iron bar. She referred to the judge as "Your Dishonor," and when she heard the charge was "malicious destruction of property," she immediately demanded that it be changed to "destruction of malicious property."

3. NO MR. WASHINGTON On Sunday, July 14, 1776, British Lieutenant Philip Brown of the Royal Navy set out in a barge from Staten Island flying a flag of truce. American Colonel Reed rowed out from Manhattan to meet him in the middle of the harbor. Brown stood up in his boat, bowed, removed his hat, and said he had a letter from Lord Howe to Mr. Washington. The American asked how the letter was addressed and was told, "George Washington, Esq." "Sir," replied Reed stiffly, "we have no person in our army with that address." The British could not bring themselves to address Washington as *General*. So Lieutenant Brown bowed once more and left. Later the British tried again with "George Washington, Esq., etc., etc., etc." but without the title *General* the Americans refused to accept it.

4. A THIEF IS NOT A HOODLUM "I'm no hood." That's what public enemy number one, Alvin Karpis, told J. Edgar Hoover, director of the FBI, who had personally arrested him in 1936. "I'm a thief," he said. When Hoover persisted in referring to him as a hoodlum, Karpis protested that he was not part of organized crime. "You don't understand. I was offered a job as a hoodlum and I turned it down cold. A thief is anybody who gets out and works for a living, like robbing a bank or breaking into a place and stealing stuff, or kidnapping somebody." Karpis had done all that and more—and it landed him a life sentence at Alcatraz.

5. BAFFLING THE NAZIS Surrounded by the Germans at the Battle of the Bulge in December, 1944, Brigadier General Anthony McAuliffe of the 101st Airborne Division was asked to surrender. His reply was: "To the German Commander: Nuts! From the American Commander." Even after translation, the German commander had to ask what it meant.

The Indian Speaks

1. CRAZY HORSE OF THE OGLALA SIOUX "Now, you tell us to work for a living, but the Great Spirit did not make us to work, but to live by hunting. You white men can work if you want to. We do not interfere with you, and again you say, why do you not become civilized? We do not want your civilization! We would live as our fathers did, and their fathers before them."

2. CHIEF JOSEPH OF THE NEZ PERCE "I am tired of fighting. Our chiefs are killed. Looking Glass is dead. The old men are all killed. . . . The little children are freezing to death. . . . I want time to look for my children and see how many of them I can find. Hear me, my Chiefs, I am tired; my heart is sick and sad. From where the sun now stands, I will fight no more forever."

3. TECUMSEH OF THE SHAWNEES "My heart is a stone: heavy with sadness for my people; cold with the knowledge that no treaty will keep the whites out of our lands; hard with determination to resist as long as I live and breathe."

4. SITTING BULL OF THE HUNKPAPA SIOUX "Where are our lands? Who owns them? . . . What law have I broken? Is it wrong for me to love my own? Is it wicked for me because my skin is red? Because I am a Sioux; because I was born where my father lived; because I would die for my people and my country?"

5. CHIEF CADETTE OF THE NAVAHOS "Give us like weapons and turn us loose, we will fight you again; but we are worn-out. . . . You have driven us from our last and best stronghold, and we have no more heart. Do with us as may seem good to you, but do not forget we are men and braves."

6. BIG EAGLE OF THE SANTEE SIOUX "The whites are always trying to make the Indians give up their life and live like white men—to farming, work hard and do as they did. . . . If the Indians had tried to make the whites like them, the whites would have resisted, and it was the same with many Indians."

7. RED CLOUD OF THE OGLALA SIOUX "Whose voice first sounded on this land? The voice of the red people who had but bows and arrows. . . . When the white man comes in my country he leaves a trail of blood behind him."

8. BEAR TOOTH OF THE CROWS "Fathers, fathers, fathers, hear me well. Call back your young men from the mountains of the big-horn sheep . . . your young men have devastated the country and killed my animals, the elk, the deer, the antelope, my buffalo. They do not kill them to eat them; they leave them to rot where they fall. *Fathers, if I went into your country to kill your animals, what would you say?*"

9. SANTANA OF THE KIOWAS "I have heard that you intend to settle us on a reservation near the mountains. I don't want to settle. I love to roam over the prairies. There I feel free and happy, but when we settle down we grow pale and die."

10. BLACK KETTLE OF THE CHEYENNES Shortly before he was killed at the Sand Creek Massacre, he said: "We have come with our eyes shut. . . . All we ask is that we may have peace with the whites. We want to hold you by the hand. You are our father. We have been traveling through a cloud. The sky has been dark ever since the war began. . . . I have not come here with a little wolf bark, but have come to talk plain with you."

11. BLACK ELK OF THE OGLALA SIOUX "I did not know then how much was ended. When I look back now from this high hill of my old age, I can still see the butchered women and children lying heaped and scattered all along the crooked gulch [at Wounded Knee] as plain as when I saw them with eyes still young. And now I can see that something else died there in the bloody mud, and was buried in the blizzard. A people's dream died there. It was a beautiful dream . . . the nation's hoop is broken and scattered. There is no center any longer, and the sacred tree is dead."

Advice

1. DON'T SMILE President Calvin Coolidge, nicknamed Silent Cal, advised in-coming president Herbert Hoover on how to handle White House visitors: "Nine-tenths of them want something they ought not to have. If you keep dead still they will run down in three or four minutes. If you even cough or smile they will start up all over again."

2. HOW NOT TO BE "A SLOVEN OR SLUT" Thomas Jefferson, writing to his young daughter Martha in 1783: "Do not fancy you

must wear your clothes until the dirt is visible to the eye. You will be the last one who will be sensible of this. Some ladies think they may, under the privilege of dishabille, be loose and negligent of their dress in the morning. But be you, from the moment you rise until you go to bed, as cleanly and properly dressed as at the hours of dinner or tea. A lady who has been seen as a sloven or slut in the morning will never efface the impression she has made with all the dress and pagentry she can afterwards involve herself in. Nothing is so disgusting to our sex as want of cleanliness and delicacy in yours."

3.   CUTTING CAMPAIGN COSTS Joseph Kennedy wired his son Jack, who was running for reelection as senator in 1958: "Don't buy a single vote more than is necessary—I'll be damned if I'm going to pay for a landslide."

4.   THE SECRETS TO GOOD HEALTH At Thomas Jefferson's bidding, Meriwether Lewis consulted with Benjamin Rush, the preeminent doctor of his day, about medical precautions for his pioneering trip west with William Clark. Rush wrote "a few short directions" which were mostly disregarded. "Flannel should be worn constantly next to the skin, especially in wet weather," he insisted. "Also fasting and diluting drinks a day or two will generally prevent an attack of fever. . . . Washing the feet every morning in *cold* water, will conduce very much to fortify them against the action of cold."

5.   HOW TO GET TO THE WHITE HOUSE Powerful Senator Boise Penrose helped get Warren G. Harding nominated in 1920 and then warned Republican leaders: "Keep Warren at home. Don't let him make any speeches. If he goes out on a tour somebody's sure to ask him questions, and Warren's just the sort of damned fool that will try to answer them."

6.   THE THINGS WE SHOULDN'T DO FOR LOVE "Love is a mighty pretty thing . . . but too dainty a food to live upon alone," George Washington wrote his about-to-be married granddaughter. He told her to marry someone with "good sense, good disposition and the means of supporting you in the way you have been brought up . . ." Good advice from a man who had little money of his own but who married one of the richest widows in Virginia.

7.   ON NOT GETTING BURNED When Assistant Secretary of the Navy Franklin Roosevelt left for an official inspection tour of Haiti

in January 1917, his indomitable mother wrote that she hoped he'd take "dark glasses and a pith hat for I know how you feel the tropical sun."

8.   BEAUTY TIPS FOR A TALL, THIN MAN Grace Bedell, a young girl living in Westfield, New York, saw a picture of Abraham Lincoln in 1860 and wrote him suggesting that ". . . if you will let your whiskers grow . . . you would look a great deal better for your face is so thin." Lincoln wrote a reply asking her if she didn't think it would be "a piece of silly affectation" at this point to start growing a beard. But he did take her advice. En route to his inauguration from Springfield, Illinois, he remembered Grace as his train stopped at Westfield. When he called her from the crowd, she timidly approached Lincoln and he showed her the new whiskers. Then he bent down and kissed her.

9.   THE IMPORTANCE OF TAKING IT EASY In his last year at Harvard, Theodore Roosevelt was told by the college physician that his heart, strained by asthmatic heavings, was weak and that he should avoid all strenuous exercise, even climbing stairs at a fast clip.

"Doctor," replied TR, "I am going to do all the things you tell me not to do. If I've got to live the sort of life you have described, I don't care how short it is." The following year, 1881, Roosevelt went off to Europe with his new wife, Alice, and climbed the fifteen-thousand-feet-high Matterhorn, a feat accomplished by few amateurs.

10.   STAGECOACH ETIQUETTE Travelers on the Concord stage to California were advised, "Don't keep the stage waiting. Don't smoke a strong pipe inside the coach. Spit on the leeward side. If you have anything to drink in a bottle pass it around."

Good Replies

1.   When told that Samuel Morse's new telegraph would now make it possible for Maine to talk to Florida, Ralph Waldo Emerson said, "Yes, but has Maine anything to *say* to Florida?"

2.   At the Battle of New Orleans in January 1815, General Andrew Jackson was told that long-awaited reinforcements of Kentucky militia had arrived but only a few of them had guns. Jackson said, "I

don't believe it. I have never seen a Kentuckian without a gun and a pack of cards and a bottle of whiskey in my life."

3.   The battle that won independence for Texas—San Jacinto—was fought across a farm belonging to Mrs. McCormick. She came to Sam Houston complaining about the dead Mexicans that were littering her land. Houston told her, "Madam, your land will be famed in history as the classic spot upon which the glorious victory of San Jacinto was gained."

"To the *devil* with your glorious history. Take off your stinking Mexicans," Mrs. McCormick answered.

4.   On Black Friday, September 24, 1869, Jay Gould's scheme to corner the gold market of the United States collapsed. The ever-nimble Gould got out with a profit but many were ruined, including Gould's partner, Henry N. Smith. When Smith ran into Gould on the street, he said, "I'll live to see the day, sir, when you have to earn your living by going around this street with a hand organ and a monkey."

"Maybe you will, Henry," Gould replied, "maybe you will. And when I want a monkey, Henry, I'll send for you."

5.   Charles A. Lindbergh supervised the building of his plane, *The Spirit of St. Louis*, with a care for every detail. When a mechanic dropped a wrench on an air-cooling fin on the motor and cracked it, Lindbergh demanded that it be replaced. The mechanic asked why since it shouldn't affect the running of the engine. Lindbergh said simply, "I don't swim so well."

6.   "What have you done with your children?" was a question Elizabeth Cady Stanton received after her 1854 address on women's

Mother of seven, feminist Elizabeth Cady Stanton was quick to defend her abilities as both lecturer and child raiser.
BOSTON PUBLIC LIBRARY PRINT COLLECTION

rights, given to the New York State legislature. The questioner was a woman. Stanton replied, ". . . it takes me no longer to speak than you to listen; what have you done with your children the two hours you have been sitting here?" Stanton's children were with "a faithful nurse" at a nearby hotel.

7. When Benjamin Franklin was in Paris during the American Revolution, he learned that Englishman Edward Gibbon, the author of *The Decline and Fall of the Roman Empire*, was visiting Paris. He invited Gibbon to dine with him but received a frosty reply saying that he would not share a dinner table with a rebel. Franklin sent a pleasant reply saying how sorry he was and that when Gibbon came to write *The Decline and Fall of the British Empire* to let him know as he could furnish him with a great deal of material.

8. A supporter of presidential candidate Henry Clay accosted Andrew Jackson and said, "I want you to understand that I am not going to vote for you." Jackson's reply was: "Sir, I have given much of my life to my country, and it was that you might have this privilege!"

9. "General Miles is your friend," an interpreter told Geronimo as surrender between the Apaches and the U.S. Army was being negotiated in 1886. Geronimo and his defiant band of Indians had bolted from the reservation and been pursued by troops which numbered at times five thousand. "I have been in need of friends," Geronimo told the general's interpreter, "Why has he not been with me?"

10. President Lyndon Johnson was headed toward a row of helicopters when he was stopped by a young officer who said, "That's your helicopter over there, sir."

"Son, they are all my helicopters," replied Johnson.

11. In 1966, Ronald Reagan, with a lifetime career of acting behind him, ran for governor of California. A reporter asked him what kind of a governor he would be. "I don't know," Reagan answered, "I've never played a governor."

"Trubel" with the Three R's

1. A PIONEER SPELLER In 1796 Daniel Boone applied for a job working on the Wilderness Trail, the pathway west across the Ap-

palachians. He explained that he felt "intitled to the ofer of the Buisness as I first Marked out that Rode in March 1775 and never rec'd anything for my trubel."

2. HE SHOULD KNOW "Money," wrote millionaire Henry Ford, is "the Root of all Eval."

Henry Ford liked to carry a notebook with him to record thoughts, which included his feelings about money when not "used for good purpus."
HENRY FORD MUSEUM AND GREEN-FIELD VILLAGE

3. THE PROFESSOR AND THE POET PASS JUDGMENT At his last cabinet meeting, Woodrow Wilson, former president of Princeton University, commented on the man who would soon be stepping into the Oval Office, Warren G. Harding: "There will be one very difficult thing for me, however, to stand, and that is Mr. Harding's English." The poet e. e. cummings wrote that Harding was "the only man, woman, or child/who wrote a simple declarative sentence/with seven grammatical errors."

4. HARVARD SLIPS UP John Quincy Adams, a Harvard graduate, was appalled when his alma mater decided to give President Andrew Jackson an honorary degree. "I would not be present to witness her disgrace in conferring her highest literary honors upon a barbarian who could not write a sentence of grammar and hardly could spell his own name."

5. SHAKESPEARE IN THE WILDERNESS Jim Bridger, the famous trapper and western scout, couldn't read or write so he traded $125 worth of cattle for a book of Shakespeare and hired a wagon boy at $40 a month to read it to him. But when Richard III was mean enough to kill his mother, Bridger gave up in disgust.

6.   YORK, THE "TURRIBAL" When Arikara women and children gathered around York, William Clark's slave, the huge black had some fun by telling the Indians he had been a wild animal until Clark caught and tamed him. But when York let out a roar, the scared Indian children fled screaming. Clark's journal noted that York "made himself more turribal than we wished him to doe."

7.   WRONG MATCH FOR THE DANDY Andrew Jackson picked Martin Van Buren to succeed him as president. Since Van Buren was an eastern dandy, Jackson wanted the ticket to include Richard M. Johnson, a frontiersman and Indian fighter, as vice-president. Johnson was unmarried but had two beautiful mulatto daughters from his slave mistress and insisted on introducing them and his newest black mistress to Washington society. When Van Buren ran for a second term in 1840, Jackson agreed to drop Johnson from the ticket as he would be "dead wait."

8.   HOW TC SPELL MONKEY Abraham Lincoln's attitude toward his beloved son Tad was, "Let him run. There's time enough yet for him to learn his letters and get poky." When Tad was twelve, he still could not read or write, preferring to fly a kite than sit with his tutors. After Lincoln's assassination, Mary tried to help Tad spell, but her son resisted. "A-P-E," he insisted, spelled *monkey* because he'd seen a small woodcut illustrating an ape and it looked just like a monkey to him. Tad argued that he'd seen many a monkey in the streets with organ grinders and that he knew more about the subject than his mother. He continued a spirited resistance, but eventually Tad did learn his letters, as Lincoln knew he would.

PART IX

The Political Process

Speeches

1. A NEAR KILLER OF A SPEECH At 8,578 words, William Henry Harrison's inaugural address was the longest ever. Initially it had been even wordier, but Daniel Webster had edited it down, eliminating flowery classical allusions. Webster said his pen killed "seventeen Roman proconsuls as dead as smelts, every one of them." Still, the speech may have caused the death of the sixty-eight-year-old Harrison. He read it on a cold, raw Inauguration Day, refusing to wear either hat or coat. He then led the inaugural parade to the White House and attended three balls. The cold he caught that day turned into pneumonia. He died one month later.

2. ONLY 120 SECONDS "Is that all?" a reporter asked Abraham Lincoln as he sat down from his two-minute-long Gettysburg Address. "Yes, for the present," was Lincoln's answer. His speech had followed a two-hour oration by the famed speaker of the day, Edward Everett, a veteran crowd pleaser. The *Chicago Times* ridiculed Lincoln's words as "the silly, flat, and dishwatery utterances of the man who has to be pointed out to intelligent foreigners as the President of the United States." Everett, however, wrote Lincoln, "I would be glad if I could flatter myself that I came as near the central idea of the occasion in two hours as you did in two minutes."

3. LESS IS MORE "I rise only to say I do not intend to say anything. I thank you for your kind words and your hearty welcome." That was Ulysses S. Grant's complete speech at a New York dinner when he was the Republican candidate for president in 1868. It was to become his standard speech as he intensely disliked public speaking.

4. PROMISES, PROMISES Franklin D. Roosevelt opened his first campaign for the presidency in Pittsburgh in 1932 with a speech that advocated a balanced budget and reduced federal spending. Four years later, after huge deficits and unprecedented peacetime spending, he decided to return to Pittsburgh to launch his reelection campaign at exactly the same spot. FDR's opponents were charging that he had gone back on his promises, so the president asked speechwriter Sam Rosenman to work out "a good and convincing explanation." Rosenman studied the first speech, then returned to the president and told him there was only one way to do it. "Fine," said FDR, "what sort of explanation would you make?" "Mr. President," Rosenman replied, "the only thing you can say

about that 1932 speech is to deny categorically that you ever made it!"

5. "GOOD-BYE" Even though President Truman relieved Douglas MacArthur of his command during the Korean War, the general was still a hero. When he left his headquarters in Japan in April 1951, he was given an emotional farewell unique for a soldier who had conquered the country only a half dozen years earlier. On his way to the airport, a quarter of a million Japanese lined the twelve-mile route. In San Francisco, it took him two hours to get through a half million well-wishers. When he came to Congress to address a joint session, he received a standing ovation.

Applause interrupted his thirty-four-minute address thirty times. His speech ended with these famous lines: "The world has turned over many times since I took the oath on the Plain at West Point, and the hopes and dreams have long since vanished. But I still remember the refrain of one of the most popular barrack ballads of that day, which proclaimed, most proudly, that 'Old soldiers never die. They just fade away.' And like the soldier of the ballad, I now close my military career and just fade away—an old soldier who tried to do his duty as God gave him the light to see that duty." Then came a hushed "Good-bye."

Vice-presidential candidate Richard Nixon rubs noses with Checkers, the cocker spaniel whose fame helped to keep Nixon on the 1952 ticket.
UPI/BETTMANN NEWSPHOTOS

There was pandemonium and sobbing in the House chamber. President Truman heard it on TV and commented, "A hundred percent bullshit."

6. PLAYING WITH CHECKERS Presidential candidate Dwight Eisenhower was on the verge of dumping his running mate, Richard Nixon, who had been charged with using an eighteen-thousand-dollar annual fund collected by California businessmen for his own personal purposes. To clear his name, Nixon went on national television along with his wife and dog. He denied accepting any such gifts for his personal use except for a little black and white cocker spaniel that his six-year-old daughter had named Checkers. "And you know, the kids love the dog, and I just want to say this right now, that regardless of what they say about it, we're gonna keep it." In living rooms across American people wept. Eisenhower decided to keep Nixon on his ticket.

7. RAW EGGS AND BRANDY Ailing Congressman Thaddeus Stevens hated Andrew Johnson with a passion. His dying wish seemed to be to witness the president's impeachment. Stevens's health held out long enough for him to lead the impeachment proceedings and give a speech denouncing Johnson. It was the shortest of any speech either for or against the president, but it was still too long for Stevens's feeble body. He read it in a voice so low it could only be heard by those near him. He fortified himself by sips of a mixture of raw eggs and brandy, but after twenty minutes he was forced to ask his colleague Benjamin Butler to finish reading the speech for him. Stevens died only three months after the impeachment vote failed in the Senate.

8. A TWICE-TOLD TALE On July 1, 1776, the Continental Congress was trying to decide whether to vote for independence. The task of summing up the reasons for revolution fell to John Adams. He stood and explained that he had not the talents of Pericles and the ancient orators and went on to make one of the most brilliant speeches of his career. Then the New Jersey delegates walked in.

They asked to have the case for independence restated as they were not quite decided on how to vote. Adams protested that he was not a gladiator or an actor, but finally consented to recapitulate his speech. Afterward, delegate Richard Stockton of New Jersey wrote, "the man to whom the country is most indebted for the great measure of independency is Mr. John Adams of Boston. I call him the Atlas of American independence."

9. A SILVER TONGUE CAPTURES A GOLDEN OPPORTUNITY
Presidential candidate William Jennings Bryan had a compelling voice
which filled the far corners of the Democratic Convention hall. He
was thirty-six years old and not a front-runner for the nomination
in 1876. But when he gave his famous "Cross of Gold" speech,
which was a cry against the gold standard believed to be hurting
farmers, "the audience seemed to rise and sit down as one man,"
he recalled. Bryan noted the look of inspiration in their faces and
compared them to a trained choir. "In fact, I thought of a choir as I
noted how instantaneously and in unison they responded." He closed
with words found to be successful previously and saved for this
occasion: "You shall not press down upon the brow of labor this
crown of thorns, you shall not crucify mankind upon a cross of
gold!" The result was pandemonium on the convention floor and
Bryan's subsequent nomination.

*When Martin Luther
King, Jr., was address-
ing this massive civil
rights demonstration, he
suddenly decided to dis-
pense with his prepared
text. "I have a dream,"
he improvised. It was
his greatest speech.*
UPI/BETTMANN NEWSPHOTOS

10. "I HAVE A DREAM." The gathering was the largest Washington, D.C., had seen. On August 28, 1963, more than one hundred
thousand people marched to the Mall in support of civil rights. Joan
Baez, Paul Newman, Marlon Brando, and others spoke. Then it was
Martin Luther King, Jr.'s turn. He began a prepared speech and
then swung off into the improvised rhythm of Gospel preaching.
Clapping and crying, the crowd yelled "Tell us, tell us" to his "I
have a dream today." "Tell us, tell us," they cried. "I have a dream
today that my four little children will one day live in a nation where
they will not be judged by the color of their skin but by the content
of their character. I have a dream today. . . ." Watching on television, President Kennedy commented, "That guy is really good."

11.   "I DON'T BELIEVE WHAT I JUST READ." Warren G. Harding conducted his 1920 presidential election campaign from his front porch. Sometimes his managers gave him ghost-written speeches to read to the delegations that called on him. On one such occasion Harding stumbled over a passage, paused, and then admitted to his audience, "Well, I never saw this before. I didn't write this speech and don't believe what I just read."

12.   CARRYING ON IN A BLIZZARD A snowstorm raged on Inauguration Day, March 4, 1853, but by eleven-thirty it began to clear. Outgoing President Millard Fillmore picked up President-elect Franklin Pierce at his hotel and they rode together in an open carriage to the Capitol. The weather held while Pierce took the Oath of Office outdoors before a huge crowd. Then he launched into a lengthy inaugural address. A northeast wind began to blow and the snow came down with driving force. The crowd dwindled. Pierce went on and on. The speech was more than three thousand words long and Pierce had memorized every word. It was the first and only time a president gave an inaugural speech without notes. By the time he'd finished, the weather was so grim that the parade back to the White House was called off.

Pardonable Offenses

1.   THEY ALLOWED WOMEN TO VOTE When three Rochester, New York, voting inspectors refused to pay a twenty-five-dollar fine, they were put in jail. Their offense was allowing Susan B. Anthony and fifteen other local women to vote in the November 5, 1872, elections. Anthony had convinced them that the newly adopted Fourteenth Amendment could be interpreted to enfranchise women. In all, the men spent about a week in jail before Anthony's friends were able to obtain pardons from President Ulysses S. Grant. Upon their release, the inspectors found themselves heroes—in the eyes of both men and women. At the next election they were returned to office by the still all-male electorate.

2.   A DOLL'S OFFENSE The Lincoln boys, Willie and Tad, imitated the military life they saw around them at the White House by playing soldiers. One day they burst in on a presidential meeting, breathlessly pleading with "Paw" for a pardon for their doll, Jack. Jack had been court-martialed and was to be shot and then buried

in the Rose Garden but the gardener had objected. They were destroying his roses. Lincoln pulled out a piece of executive stationery and wrote, "The Doll Jack is pardoned by order of the President. A. Lincoln."

3. UNREPENTANT After the fall of the Confederacy, the Southern leaders who had participated in the rebellion had to sign an Oath of Allegiance and request a presidential pardon to have their citizenship rights restored. Jefferson Davis, once the president of the Confederacy, refused to apply. "It has been said that I should apply to the United States for a pardon, but repentance must precede the right of pardon, and I have not repented. . . . I would do it again just as I did in 1861." Wild applause interrupted Jefferson Davis as he spoke these words in 1884.

4. PRAYER, WATERGATE, AND GOLF Sunday morning, September 8, 1974, President Gerald Ford went to St. John's Episcopal Church on Lafayette Square at eight A.M. to "pray for guidance and understanding" before announcing his pardon of Richard Nixon for the Watergate cover-up. He then returned to the Oval Office where his press secretary, Jerald terHorst, resigned in protest. "I cannot in good conscience support your decision to pardon former President Richard Nixon," his typed resignation note read.

Undeterred, Ford went on national television within an hour to tell the American people he had granted "a full, free and absolute pardon unto Richard Nixon for all offenses against the United States." President Ford then went off to play golf. He had been president for a month and wanted to put the Watergate scandals behind the nation. His favorable rating in the Gallup Poll dove from 71 to 49.

5. HIS NAME WAS MUDD In the opinion of Secretary of War Edwin Stanton, anybody connected with the plot to kill Abraham Lincoln ought to receive the death sentence. But the four who were not directly involved—Dr. Samuel Mudd, who had set Booth's leg as he was fleeing south, Michael O'Laughlin, Edward Spangler, and Samuel Arnold—were sentenced to life imprisonment at hard labor. Stanton did not think their punishment was severe enough, so he had the prisoners moved from a New York State prison to Dry Tortugas, a swampy hellhole off Florida called America's Devil's Island.

Nevertheless, the four were model prisoners. When yellow fever broke out in August 1867 and the prison doctor died, Dr. Mudd volunteered his services, saving the lives of both prisoners and soldiers. The officers of the post appealed for a pardon for Dr. Mudd, and President Andrew Johnson granted it in February 1869, just before he left office. Spangler and Arnold, who had worked as Dr. Mudd's assistants, were pardoned at the same time. Michael O'Laughlin had already died at the Dry Tortugas prison.

6.   PIRATES TO THE RESCUE Just before the Battle of New Orleans in the War of 1812, three British officers made a surprise call on the pirate Jean Lafitte at his headquarters in the Louisiana bayous. The pirates were well supplied with cannon, guns, and expert gunners, and the British wanted their help for the coming attack on the Americans at New Orleans. Lafitte would not talk business until after his astounded guests had enjoyed a long and lavish meal served in heavy silver dishes and accompanied by the best French and Spanish wines. Then, over brandy and fine Cuban cigars, Jean Lafitte listened as the British offered him thirty thousand dollars, land, and a captaincy in the British army for his help. He said, "Your plan seems almost perfect," and told them he would let them know. Then he informed the Americans of the British intentions.

Once General Andrew Jackson found he was able to enlist Lafitte's aid against the British, the pirates changed from "hellish banditti" to "privateers" and then to "gentlemen" in Jackson's reports. Lafitte supplied seventy-five hundred flints for Jackson's guns and loaned his expert cannoneers, veterans of the Napoleonic Wars. He helped decimate the British frontal attack. Andrew Jackson became a national hero and, one month after the Battle of New Orleans, Jean Lafitte and his pirates received a full pardon from President James Madison for all past crimes.

Political Mudslinging

1.   THEY CALLED HIM DEBAUCHED As president, George Washington was accused of stealing from the Treasury and of legalized corruption, ostentation, treachery, and being "the dishclout" of "dirty speculation." Benjamin Franklin Bache, Franklin's grandson, wrote: "If ever a nation was debauched by a man, the American nation has been debauched by Washington." The beleaguered Washington complained of attacks in "such exaggerated and indecent terms as could scarcely be applied to a Nero, a notorious defaulter, or even to a common pickpocket." He declined a third term most vehemently.

2.   THERE'S A CERTAIN LOGIC TO IT "I would never call Nixon a son of a bitch because he claims to be a self-made man," said Harry Truman.

3.   JUST A PASTRY PUFF Theodore Roosevelt was clamoring for war with Spain, and when President William McKinley procrastinated, TR declared that the president had no more backbone than "a chocolate eclair."

4.   THE MISSING MISTRESSES Opponents of President John Adams circulated a story that Adams had sent General Pinckney to England in a U.S. frigate to procure four pretty girls as mistresses, two for Pinckney and two for Adams. When the story reached Adams, he wrote: "I do declare upon my honor if this be true General Pinckney has kept them all himself and cheated me out of my two."

5.   DIRTY POOL? In 1824, Andrew Jackson's campaigners tried to smear straitlaced John Quincy Adams by making a great issue out of a billiard table that Adams had purchased with his own money. A Pennsylvania newspaper charged Adams with "royal extravagances" including the "purchase of *Tables and Balls, which Can be used for no purpose but for gambling.*"

The odd tilt of James
Buchanan's neck led to
rumors that he had tried
to hang himself over an
ill-fated romance.
COURTESY OF THE NEW-YORK HIS-
TORICAL SOCIETY, NEW YORK CITY

6.   A SORDID HANG-UP? Newspapers speculated that presidential candidate James Buchanan bore the scar of an unsuccessful hanging. Actually, his neck was twisted due to a birth injury that had caused his head to tilt at an odd angle. The hanging, the rumor mongers suggested, was a result of bachelor Buchanan's undeniable despair over a broken engagement thirty-seven years earlier.

7.   HE MARRIED A MARRIED WOMAN "Ought a convicted adultress and her paramour husband be placed in the highest office

of this free and Christian land?" was the provocative question Andrew Jackson's opponents asked the public. The reference was to the fact that he had inadvertently married Rachel Donelson before her divorce came through and had to go through the ceremony a second time. Jackson was very touchy on the subject, carried a loaded pistol with him, and defied anyone to mention the subject to his face.

On *the* Vice-presidency

1.   Congress originally set the vice-president's salary at five thousand dollars a year, a fifth of the president's. Some thought it too high and proposed payment on the basis of work done.

2.   The country's first vice-president, John Adams, said his country in its wisdom placed him in "the most insignificant office that ever the invention of man contrived or his imagination conceived."

3.   Daniel Webster refused the job by saying, "I do not propose to be buried until I am really dead and in my coffin."

4.   New York political boss Thomas Platt maneuvered Theodore Roosevelt into the vice-presidency to get him out of state politics. Platt claimed that he went to William McKinley's inauguration ceremonies not to see the president sworn in but to "see Theodore Roosevelt take the veil."

5.   Woodrow Wilson's VP, Thomas Marshall, sat idling away the hours in his Capitol office. When visitors peered in at him, he would quip, "If you can't come in, throw me a peanut."

6.   Nelson Rockefeller maintained he never wanted to be vice-president of anything: "I always said I am just not built for standby equipment." But as his presidential dreams faded, he accepted Gerald Ford's offer and was appointed to the number-two spot.

7.   "The Vice-Presidency is filled with trips around the world, chauffeurs, men saluting, people clapping, chairmanship of councils, but in the end it is nothing," said Lyndon Johnson. "I detested every minute of it."

8.   When President Franklin D. Roosevelt told his chief of staff, Admiral Leahy, that he had picked Harry Truman as his running mate, Leahy's response was, "Who the hell is Harry Truman?"

9. John Nance Garner, FDR's first vice-president, said the job was not worth "a pitcher of warm spit."

10. William King was nominated for vice-president in 1852 even though it was known that he was terminally ill with tuberculosis. King went to Cuba to try to regain his health and a special act of Congress allowed him to be sworn in there by the American consul. He was so weak his aides had to prop him up so that he could take the oath. When he realized that the end was near, he insisted on returning home to Alabama and within a week had died. King was the only vice-president never to perform his duties.

11. California Senator Hiram Johnson was proposed as Warren G. Harding's running mate in 1920. He declined, saying, "We're living in a day of strange events, but none so strange as that I should be considered second to Senator Harding." Calvin Coolidge took the job and became president two years later when Harding died.

Democracy in Action

1. HE KNOWS WHERE HE STANDS When asked by a voter why he was for free silver, Nebraska Congressman William Jennings Bryan made this reply: "I don't know anything about free silver. The people of Nebraska are for free silver and I am for free silver. I will look up the arguments later."

2. ILLEGAL LEGAL EXPENSES? Erie Railroad magnate Jay Gould packed $500,000 in a briefcase and went to Albany to get the legislature to legalize the newly printed stock issued to avoid takeover by railroad rival Cornelius Vanderbilt. He said, "In a Republican district, I was Republican; in a Democratic district a Democrat; in a doubtful district I was doubtful; but I was always for Erie." Gould succeeded with the New York legislature by outbidding Vanderbilt in a battle for influence and running up over $1 million in "legal expenses."

3. VOTING FOR A DEAD MAN *New York Tribune* editor Horace Greeley, the man who offered the famous advice "Go west, young man," ran for president in 1872. He received sixty-six electoral votes, but before the electoral college could meet, Greeley died. Most electors switched their allegiance to Thomas A. Hendricks of Illinois,

but three insisted on voting for the late Horace Greeley. Congress refused to count those three votes.

4. INCOMPETENT WITNESSES A Georgia law of the early 1800s said: "No Indian or descendant of any Indians, residing within the Creek or Cherokee Nation of Indians shall be deemed a competent witness in any court in the state to which a white person may be a party."

5. ADDING THREE AND TWO Of the Continental Congress in 1774, John Adams wrote: "Every man in it is a great man, an orator, a critic, a statesman. . . . The consequence of this is that business is drawn and spun out to an immeasurable length. I believe if it was moved and seconded that three and two make five, we would be entertained with logic and rhetoric, law, history, politics, and mathematics, and then—we should pass the resolution unanimously in the affirmative."

6. A TIE WITH HIS OWN VP In the election of 1800, Thomas Jefferson neatly defeated incumbent President John Adams but, because of a constitutional quirk, nearly lost the presidency to his running mate, Aaron Burr.

Originally the Constitution stated that the members of the electoral college each had two votes to cast. The candidate who received the highest total would be president and the runner-up would be vice-president.

What the Founding Fathers had not foreseen was the rise of political parties. Jefferson and Burr ran as a team and each received 73 electoral votes. Since Burr would not withdraw, the tie had to broken by the House of Representatives. There, Alexander Hamilton, leader of the rival Federalists, used his influence. He disagreed violently with Jefferson but respected him. Burr was a man he distrusted outright. On the thirty-sixth ballot, Hamilton's influence prevailed and Jefferson was elected. The Constitution was then amended to prevent a recurrence of these bizarre events.

7. LINCOLN JUMPS OUT THE WINDOW Abraham Lincoln was elected to the state legislature of Illinois in 1834. The capital was then the primitive little town of Vandalia. Lincoln was the leader of a minority group trying to prevent the passage of a bill on state banks.

The strategy Lincoln devised was for his fellow Whigs to stay away so that no quorum—and therefore no vote—would be possible. The sergeant at arms tried to round up the Whigs, but he couldn't find them. The Democrats, however, caught Lincoln by surprise. They had located some members who were ill and brought them in and locked the doors. Frantically, Lincoln and two Whigs who had been stationed at the chamber to keep an eye on things jumped out the window five feet to the ground, but they were too late. A quorum had been reached and the Democrats passed the bill.

8. THE VOTES WASHINGTON DIDN'T GET On April 6, 1789, both houses of Congress met to count the electoral votes in the first-ever election for U.S. president. All 69 electoral votes went to George Washington, making him the unanimous choice. However, he actually only carried ten of the thirteen states. North Carolina and Rhode Island had not yet ratified the Constitution and therefore couldn't vote. New York didn't vote either because its Governor Clinton, who opposed the idea of centralized government, had neglected to appoint any electors.

9. A SEXIST LOOPHOLE By 1807, one by one the states had passed laws denying women the vote, except New Jersey. One enterprising politician there decided to take advantage of this loophole and stuff the ballot box with votes from his female supporters. He won his local election, but women lost the right to vote. The New Jersey legislature quickly passed a law barring them from the polls.

10. JACKSON SCREAMS FOUL PLAY Andrew Jackson has the dubious distinction of being the only presidential candidate to get the most popular votes and the most electoral votes and still lose the election. Unfortunately for Jackson, four candiates ran in 1824. Though he was clearly the front-runner, he did not have a majority of the electoral votes. The election was thrown into the House of Representatives, where Henry Clay, the number-three candidate, threw his support to John Quincy Adams, making him the winner. Adams then made Clay secretary of state and an enraged Jackson called it a "corrupt bargain." Four years later Jackson won easily.

PART X

Joys and Sorrows, Love and Death

War-torn Loyalties

1. THE TALL MAN'S FRIEND Long before the Civil War, Abraham Lincoln knew Confederate General George Pickett, famous for his gallant charge at Gettysburg. Lincoln had helped him get into West Point and become an officer. In 1865, as the Confederacy was collapsing, Lincoln visited Union-occupied Richmond and walked through the still-smoldering ruins looking for Pickett's house. When he found it, he knocked at the door. Pickett's wife opened it fearfully, her baby in her arms. She was alone. The servants had run off and the city was filled with Yankee troops. The tall man standing there said, "I am Abraham Lincoln."

"The President," she gasped.

"No, Abraham Lincoln, George's old friend," he replied.

2. ONE NATION INDIVISIBLE After Union General George Meade turned back General Robert E. Lee's invasion at Gettysburg, he announced that he had defeated "an enemy superior in numbers" and urged his men "to drive from our soil every presence of the invader." When Abraham Lincoln read of this he leaped from his chair and exclaimed, "Drive the invader *from our soil*! My God!" To Lincoln it was all one country, all "our soil." That was "what the war is about and these damn fools cannot grasp it," he said.

Lincoln did not like to think of the Confederates as enemies and Lee shared his feelings. He referred to the North as "those people."

3. A SIDE OF BEEF THROUGH THE LINES General Israel Putnam, hero of the Battle of Bunker Hill, was a close personal friend of General Thomas Gage, commander of British troops in Boston. Putnam had served with Gage in the French and Indian War and Gage had offered Putnam a chance to be a major general in the British army. With Boston surrounded by swarms of American troops, meat became scarce in the city, so Putnam sent a side of beef through the lines to Mrs. Gage.

4. UNGENEROUS TERMS FROM A FRIEND The first important Northern victory of the Civil War was at Fort Donelson in Tennessee. An obscure Union general, Ulysses S. Grant, led the attack, and when the Southern general, Simon Bolivar Buckner, asked for surrender terms, Grant's famous reply was no terms except "an unconditional and immediate surrender." Buckner was not at all happy about a message like that from Grant, who had been his friend at

West Point. The last time they had met in New York, Grant was down on his luck and Buckner had lent him money and paid his hotel bill. Buckner replied that conditions "compel me . . . to accept the ungenerous and unchivalrous terms you propose." Afterward the rival commanders sat down together and reminisced. At Grant's funeral, Buckner was one of the pallbearers.

5. SURRENDERING TO FRIENDS Most of the top Civil War officers knew each other from their days at West Point. In the graduating classes for the tiny pre–Civil War army there were only about thirty cadets, and the army officer corps was a close group until the war divided them about evenly. Major Robert Anderson, Union commander at Fort Sumter, surrendered to his former West Point instructor, Confederate General Beauregard. When Confederate President Jefferson Davis, another West Point graduate, heard of Anderson's surrender, he telegraphed Beauregard to "tender my friendly remembrance to Major Anderson."

6. SPARE THAT MAN! The British attack on Bunker Hill met withering American volleys from close range. As the smoke cleared, the British troops could be seen retreating back down the hill except for a lone British officer who appeared to be dazed. "There's an officer. Let's get him!" Americans shouted. But General Israel Putnam suddenly recognized him as his old friend John Small. Putnam jumped off his horse shouting, "Don't. For God's sake spare that man. I love him like a brother." Major Small made a correct bow of gratitude and turned down the hill. To have ducked or run would have been beneath the dignity of a British officer. Major Small said later of that moment on the hill, "I prepared myself for death."

7. A "SPY" IN THE WHITE HOUSE From the time the Civil War broke out, Kentucky-born Mary Todd Lincoln had to endure rumors questioning her loyalty to the Union. Most of her relatives were Confederates. Her favorite half-brother, Little Aleck, was killed at Baton Rouge. Another half-brother, Sam, died at Shiloh. "Little Emilie," her youngest sister, was married to Confederate General Ben Helm. When he was killed at the Battle of Chickamauga in September 1863, Emilie, pregnant and accompanied by two young children, went to Atlanta to bury him.

On her way back to Kentucky she was stopped in Virginia and held because she refused to take the Oath of Allegiance. When the officers found out she was the president's sister-in-law, a cable was sent to the White House. Lincoln, who was fond of Emilie and had pleaded with her husband to fight for the Union, said immediately, "Send her to me." She stayed for several weeks despite talk that there was a "spy" in the White House.

Guns Against the Helpless

1. BOSTON, MARCH 5, 1770 A fire alarm at night brought out a crowd. It was a false alarm, but a gang of toughs stayed on to harass a British sentry. A crowd gathered, hurling sticks, ice, and threats.

The sentry called for help and Captain Preston arrived with a squad of soldiers. The crowd grew larger and pressed so closely the men could not get back to the guardhouse. Voices in the crowd taunted, "Damn you, you sons of bitches, fire." Preston had given orders not to fire unless he specifically ordered it. Nobody believed it would come to that, but it was dark, things were thrown, the situation was confused. A soldier was knocked down. He rose and fired. A second soldier fired. Before Captain Preston could gain control of his men, four colonists were dead and six wounded, one fatally. Boston termed it a massacre and used the incident to fan anti-British sentiment.

2. SAND CREEK, NOVEMBER 29, 1864 Indian trouble was brewing in the Colorado Territory. Governor John Evans wanted "to prevent friendly Indians from being killed by mistake," so he ordered those who were not at war "to go to places of safety." Thus, Black Kettle and White Antelope led the Cheyennes to Fort Lyon seeking peace. They were told to camp at Sand Creek, thirty miles away.

Colonel John M. Chivington arrived at Fort Lyon from Denver with seven hundred volunteers who were purposefully out to get Indians. Chivington's view was to "kill and scalp all, big and little; nits make lice." He led a dawn attack against the trusting Indians. Black Kettle did not fight but raised the U.S. flag and rallied his people around it as he had been told no soldier would fire at him while under it. It did no good. Chivington's men raced through the camp shooting everyone, even pleading squaws huddled together. A girl carrying a white flag was laughingly used as target practice. White Antelope refused to fight; he stood with arms folded singing his death song as he was shot down. Of the dead, 105 were women and children, most of them horribly mutilated.

3. WOUNDED KNEE, DECEMBER 29, 1890 The army, alarmed by the Indians' wild religious Ghost Dances, issued orders to capture and disarm the "fomenters of disturbances." Big Foot's name was on this list. He was the leader of a ragtag band of about 350; of these, 230 were women and children.

Two thirds of the Indians whose hearts—and souls—were buried at Wounded Knee were women and children.
MONTANA HISTORICAL SOCIETY, HELENA

They were herded into camp along the frozen creek called Wounded Knee and surrounded by 2,500 troops. When the soldiers asked the Indians to turn in their weapons, they did, but when the warriors were ordered to remove their blankets and submit to a search, tempers rose. A shot went off and a fight erupted. The soldiers on the surrounding hills poured rifle and machine-gun fire into the camp. Twenty-five soldiers died and 39 were wounded, some by the indiscriminate firing of their fellow soldiers. About 300 Indians died, two-thirds women and children.

4. MY LAI, MARCH 16, 1968 G.I.'s from Charlie Company swarmed into this Vietnam hamlet expecting to meet the 48th Vietcong Battalion. What they found were mostly women, children, and old men, many cooking breakfast rice over outdoor fires. There was not even sniper fire.

Some Vietnamese were rounded up and killed on the spot. Others were herded into drainage ditches and shot. One G.I., Harry Stanley, told the army's Criminal Investigation Division he saw "some old women and some little children—fifteen or twenty of them—in a group around a temple where some incense was burning. They were kneeling and crying and praying, and various soldiers . . . walked by and executed these women and children by shooting them in the head with their rifles. The soldiers killed all fifteen or twenty of them."

The civilian deaths totaled 347 that morning in My Lai. The incident was covered up for almost a year, and it wasn't until eighteen months later that several of the participants were brought to trial. The only man convicted was Lieutenant Calley, the twenty-four-year-old leader of Charlie Company.

5. KENT STATE, MAY 4, 1970 It was noontime at Ohio's Kent State University and a crowd gathered on the campus commons for a Vietnam War protest rally. Some of the students were shouting, "Pigs go home," others were just passing between classes. The Ohio National Guard had been sent to Kent State because of a student riot in town. General Robert Canterbury, Guard commander, said, "These students are going to have to find out what law and order is all about." He ordered the students to disperse, and when they did not, the Guard, edgy from twelve-hour shifts and lack of sleep, was ordered to clear the commons. A reporter who had heard the order to load guns, fix bayonets, and don gas masks said, "I could not believe it."

Tear gas was fired and the commons was cleared, but about seventy-five of the Guard, under orders, moved up a hill and down near a practice football field. They were faced with rock throwing and verbal abuse, and shouts of "Shoot! Shoot!" A senior, Bill Reymond, said, "All of a sudden everything just blew up." In thirteen seconds twenty-six guardsmen fired fifty-nine shots. Four students were killed, the closest one 265 feet away. General Canterbury said, "I felt that, in view of the extreme danger to the troops, they were justified in firing."

Tearful Times

1. TREACHERY GRIEVES WASHINGTON When George Washington received the stunning news that Benedict Arnold had turned traitor, observers noted how he stayed calm and gave the necessary orders to try to intercept Arnold. Then Washington went into another room with Lafayette and gave way "to an uncontrollable burst of feeling." He threw his arms around Lafayette's neck and wept.

2.   WEDDING WOES Nellie was Ulysses S. Grant's only daughter and he doted on her. She was thirteen when she moved into the White House. At eighteen she met an Englishman, Algernon Sartoris, on board a ship that was returning to America, and they fell in love.

Her White House wedding, which befitted a princess, was the most publicized event of the Grant administration. On May 21, 1874, Nellie, wearing a lace-covered gown with a six-foot train, entered the East Room on her father's arm. During the ceremony, Grant "looked steadfastly at the floor" and wept. Afterward he went off to her room by himself and sobbed like a child. Perhaps it was an omen, for Nellie's marriage was unhappy and ended in divorce.

3.   INDIAN CRIES AT LITTLE BIG HORN Crow Indians often served as scouts with George Armstrong Custer, and when they heard the news that the general and his command had been wiped out at the Little Big Horn, one by one they went off by themselves and sat down, rocking to and fro, weeping, and chanting. Lieutenant Bradley reported that except for relatives and personal friends "there were none in this whole horrified nation of forty millions of people to whom the tidings brought greater grief."

4.   A TEAR-STAINED BATTLE FLAG In his old age, Jefferson Davis, ex-president of the Confederacy, was the living symbol of a lost cause. In 1887, when he visited Macon, Georgia, fifty thousand people came out to greet him. Confederate veterans were so carried away they broke ranks and swarmed around their former chief, endangering his frail body. A faded battle flag was draped over him and the seventy-nine-year-old statesmen buried his face in the folds to conceal his tears.

5.   "MANLY TO WEEP" On the death of George Washington in 1799, the Senate addressed President John Adams: "Permit us, sir, to mingle our tears with yours. On this occasion it is manly to weep. . . . Our country mourns her father."

6.   WAR AGAINST HIS WILL H. H. Kohlsaat, an old friend of President William McKinley's, described a conversation they had had together on the South Porch of the White House. McKinley, a gentle and peace-loving man, had spoken of "being forced" to involve the U.S. in the 1898 war with Spain. "As he said this he broke down and wept as I have never seen anyone weep in my life. . . . He asked me when we got into the light if his eyes were red, and I told him they were, but if he blew his nose very hard just as we

entered where the others were, the redness of his eyes would be attributed to that cause."

7. THE TRAIL OF TEARS When the Creek Indians of Alabama and Georgia were defeated in the Creek War of 1813–14, they were ordered to leave their homes and migrate west to lands designated as Indian Territory. Those who refused were rounded up and held in stockades. The men of the tribe marched west under heavy guard. They were followed by two to three thousand women "shedding tears and making the most bitter wailings." Hardships and disease killed more than one fourth of them on the journey that has been named the Trail of Tears.

8. MARY LINCOLN BECOMES OVERWROUGHT As the Civil War neared an end, the president and Mary Lincoln journeyed to Virginia to review the Army of the James at Ulysses S. Grant's headquarters. During the ceremonies the president rode ahead on horseback. Mrs. Lincoln followed in an open carriage with Mrs. Grant.

A young officer rode up and said, "The President is very gallant, Mrs. Lincoln. He insists on riding by the side of Mrs. Ord" (the wife of General Edward Ord, commander of the troops under review). Mary flew into a jealous rage and became so overwrought she tried to leap from the carriage. When she caught up with General Ord's wife, she let loose such a torrent of verbal abuse, Mrs. Ord dissolved in tears and retired to her quarters.

9. WILSON BREAKS DOWN To rally public support for the League of Nations, President Woodrow Wilson went on a speaking tour even though he was nearing physical collapse. September 25, 1919, found him in Pueblo, Colorado. Arriving at the auditorium, he was unable to negotiate the single entrance step. During his speech, he stumbled over a sentence, stopped and tried again, stopped and stood still. His Secret Service agent tensed himself, expecting the president to fall again.

But Wilson gathered himself together and went on. Near the end, as he began to speak movingly of those who had died in World War I, some in the audience began to reach for handkerchiefs. Then Wilson halted. He looked at the audience and they looked at him. The president was crying. At the end of his speech, his wife, Edith, ran up to him. They were both in tears. That night Woodrow Wilson had a stroke, the speaking tour was canceled, and his special train headed back to Washington.

10. A SON PAYS HIS RESPECTS Lafayette came to America in 1776 as a twenty-year-old volunteer dedicated to fighting for freedom. In 1824 he returned to America an old man with many memories. He made the pilgrimage to Mount Vernon and the tomb of the man who had been almost a father to him. He knelt alone by the marble sarcophagus, came out in tears, and then took his son, George Washington Lafayette, back into the tomb where they both knelt and kissed the sarcophagus. After emerging, he said, "I pay a silent homage to the tomb of the greatest and best of men, my paternal friend."

11. HE KNEW HOW TO CRY Though much of America was in tears during Richard Nixon's televised "Checkers" speech in which he emotionally defended himself against corruption charges, the vice-presidential candidate remained dry-eyed. Afterward he flew to West Virginia to meet with his running mate, Dwight Eisenhower, who told Nixon he was not going to be dropped from the Republican ticket.

Eisenhower met him at the airport and cameras caught an emotional scene that included Nixon weeping on the shoulder of Senator William Knowland. Tears came easily to Nixon. His old high school Drama Club director saw the pictures and recalled that in school plays Nixon "knew how to take direction and could cry real tears at each performance."

12. HARRY'S HOMECOMING Returning from World War I, Captain Harry Truman sailed into New York harbor. The Statue of Liberty came into view and the band on the boat played "Home Sweet Home." As Truman wrote his future wife, Bess, "You know the men have seen so much and been in so many hard places that it takes something to give them a real thrill, but . . . there were not very many dry eyes. The hardest of hard-boiled cookies even had to blow his nose a time or two."

13. WIPING TEARS FROM HER EYES On Wednesday, October 19, 1960, Martin Luther King, Jr., spent the night in jail for the first time. He'd been arrested along with a number of other protesters at a sit-in at a segregated Atlanta snack bar. Four days later, everyone was released except King. He was escorted to nearby De Kalb County, where he'd been fined earlier for driving with an expired Alabama license.

His sentence had included a clause putting him on probation for one year. Since the sit-in arrest was considered a violation of this probation, King was sentenced to four months in jail. In the court-room, Coretta King, six months' pregnant, burst into tears. She was even more frightened when, in the middle of the night, King was taken in handcuffs and leg irons to a more remote state prison. The fate of a black man in a Georgia prison could be precarious.

Concerned, presidential candidate John F. Kennedy made a risky move. He picked up the phone and called Mrs. King to express his sympathy, a call that might well have alienated white voters. King was released shortly thereafter. Martin Luther King, Sr., told re-porters that he'd planned to vote for Richard Nixon but had shifted his support to Kennedy because "this man was willing to wipe the tears from my daughter-in-law's eyes." In the November election, the black vote helped secure a victory for Kennedy.

Celebrations

1. CHEESE TASTING When Andrew Jackson was president, an admirer from Oswego County, New York, sent him a fourteen-hundred-pound Cheddar cheese decorated with Jacksonian slogans and draped in bunting. It was four feet in diameter and arrived in a cart drawn by twenty-four gray horses. Jackson put it in the White House vestibule, where it stayed for two years.

Then, a month before he left office in 1837, Jackson decided to celebrate George Washington's birthday by inviting the public to come and help themselves. Shops and offices closed as citizens de-scended on the White House. It was a mob scene. In two hours the cheese was demolished. The White House carpets were a mess, the wide floorboards were stained, and the odor of Cheddar is said to have lingered for years.

2. A NEW YORK WELCOME After his historic nonstop flight from New York to Paris, Charles A. Lindbergh returned to Washington where President Calvin Coolidge pinned the Distinguished Flying Cross on him. Then, on June 13, 1927, he came back to New York where he was greeted by four million people, the largest crowd in the city's history. He piloted an amphibian plane to the lower har-bor and then boarded Mayor Jimmy Walker's yacht.

Boats of all descriptions surrounded him, all tooting deafeningly, and fireboats sprayed water into the air. He transferred to a big open touring car for the ticker-tape parade up Broadway—a bliz-

zard of eighteen hundred tons of paper. It was an emotional welcome unequaled in the city's history, before or since.

3.   DOING THE CHARLESTON When South Carolina's Ordinance
of Secession was ratified, a joyful celebration broke out in Charleston that lasted for days. Bells rang, cannons boomed, champagne
flowed, bonfires were made by lighting barrels of rosin, and snake-
like parades wound through the streets.

4.   DRINKING ON THE LAWN After Andrew Jackson's inauguration, his enthusiastic admirers were invited back to the White
House. He had been elected as a man of the people and the people
were determined to celebrate. Crystal and china were broken, men
climbed on tables and sofas with muddy boots to get a better view,
fights broke out, ladies fainted. The crush was so suffocating, Jackson left, but the party continued without a policeman to be seen.
Men climbed through windows to get out. Finally punch was set
out on the lawn in washtubs and the crowd began to disperse.

5.   PRAIRIE-DOG SALAMI When Grand Duke Alexis of Russia arrived in the U.S. in 1871, he was headline news for months, especially when he asked to go on a buffalo hunt. Generals Sheridan
and Custer took a break from Indian fighting to preside. Buffalo Bill
Cody, then an army scout, was enlisted to lead the hunt. Cody was
delighted because champagne corks flew every time the Grand Duke
managed to shoot a buffalo. "I was in hopes he would kill five or
six more buffaloes before we reached camp," observed Cody, "especially if a basket of champagne was to be opened every time."

When the grand duke turned twenty-one in the course of the
hunt, all stops were pulled. For dinner, a vast spread of western
specialties was prepared, including buffalo with mushrooms, salami
of prairie dog, roast elk, antelope chops, buffalo calf steaks, black-
tail deer, wild turkey, broiled teal, and mallard. Vegetables were
sweet and white mashed potatoes and green peas. Tapioca pudding
was served as dessert. Of course, champagne, whiskey, brandies,
and ale flowed throughout the meal.

6.   A CAPITOL COOKOUT The proposed Federal City was still
being carved out of the woods when President George Washington
and other notables gathered for the laying of the cornerstone of the
U.S. Capitol on September 18, 1793. They crossed the Potomac and
then formed up in a parade, marching "two abreast in the greatest
solemn dignity with music playing, drums beating, colours flying,
and spectators rejoicing."

They were heading to Jenkins' Heights, now Capitol Hill, which planner Pierre L'Enfant had said "stands as a pedestal waiting for a monument." At its foot was Tiber Creek, which caused them to break ranks and cross it by jumping from stone to stone. When they reached the hilltop, President Washington, wearing a Masonic apron, used a silver towel for laying the stone. There followed speeches, prayers, and the firing of artillery volleys. Then everyone pitched into a barbecue, which featured a roasted five-hundred-pound ox.

7. THE DIET AFTER THE FEAST Though the Pilgrims' harvest in 1621 was small, their first Thanksgiving was heartfelt. Starvation had been a real possibility. Much of their English seed had failed. Their Indian savior, Squanto, had taught them to plant Indian corn by putting the kernels and three herrings in little hillocks. The ninety-six thousand hillocks then had to be guarded from wolves and crows.

When the harvest was finally reaped, Governor William Bradford called for rejoicing and sent four men out fowling. Chief Massasoit was invited—and showed up with ninety braves. They went off into the woods and killed "five fine deer" as their contribution.

It was a three-day celebration. The Pilgrims demonstrated their matchlock muskets and a cannon, the noises both delighting and dismaying the Indians. They also introduced the Indians to wine and its astonishing effects. From the Indians, the Pilgrims learned how to pop corn.

The Pilgrims thought they had enough food to get through the winter, but a few weeks later the *Fortune* arrived with thirty-five new settlers but no food or equipment. Bradford quickly put the colony on half-rations.

Popping the Question

1. ON THE WHITE HOUSE PORCH Less than a year after his wife's death, President Woodrow Wilson unexpectedly met his cousin's friend Edith Galt coming out of the White House elevator. The president was immediately taken by this attractive widow and, after a whirlwind courtship, asked the approval of his daughters and his cousin to remarry. Then, on May 4, 1915, he wondered if they could "try to arrange for me to have a few moments alone with Mrs. Galt this evening. I'm going to pop the question."

After dinner the president and Mrs. Galt found themselves alone on the South Portico as the others walked about the White House lawns. Mrs. Galt responded to Wilson's question by asking for time to consider it. Her moment of acceptance came during an automobile ride in Rock Creek Park with the chauffeur and Secret Service agent in the front seat and Wilson's cousin with them in the backseat. Mrs. Galt put her hand in the president's and whispered that she was "ready to be mustered in as soon as can be."

2.   IN THE KITCHEN While thunder and lightning shook the old Weymouth, Massachusetts, parsonage, John Adams was in the kitchen with the Reverend Smith's daughter, Abigail. He poured out his heart to her and she agreed to marry the man she would always refer to as her "dearest friend."

3.   VIA THE MAIL General Benedict Arnold was the American military commander of Philadelphia when he started to court pretty Peggy Shippen. He was forty-seven years old. She was nineteen and sympathetic to the British side. Arnold reworked two letters of proposal he had made shortly before to another woman and turned them into a single letter to Peggy. He had begged his earlier love to let her "heavenly bosom . . . expand with friendship," while he urged Peggy to let her "heavenly bosom" expand "with a sensation, more soft, more tender" than friendship.

His reworked letters did the trick, and Peggy married him about the time he began to write other letters—to the British, suggesting terms for turning traitor.

4.   ON HORSEBACK Henry Brewster Stanton's invitation to go horseback riding sounded innocent enough to twenty-four-year-old Elizabeth Cady. She thought that the handsome abolitionist was engaged to someone else. However, as their horses passed through a quiet grove, Stanton proposed. Cady accepted. They had known each other one month and ended up eloping, over the objections of wealthy Judge Daniel Cady. Though Elizabeth Cady Stanton became one of the preeminent leaders of the feminist movement and overshadowed her husband, the marriage lasted nearly half a century.

5.   THE PRESIDENT IS SPEECHLESS For Edward Cox, proposing to Tricia Nixon hadn't been a problem. But in 1971, after a two-year secret engagement, the time had come to broach the marriage question with Tricia's father. As Tricia recalled, "Eddie was white as a sheet when he went in to see the President. We had been watching the *Greatest Show on Earth* and we got so nervous that we had to go

out and take a walk around the grounds. Then he talked to my father." Richard Nixon, she said, "was speechless for a moment, but you know how fathers are."

Unlikely Marriages

1. THE GENTLEMAN AND THE SQUAW John Rolfe admitted the strangeness of being "in love with one whose education hath been rude, her manners barbarous, and so discrepant in all nutritive of myself." Nonetheless, he asked seventeen-year-old Pocahontas to marry him. He obtained the permission of the royal Governor Thomas Dale, but when King James heard about the marriage, he was outraged.

Pocahontas, born to one of Powhatan's many wives, was a princess, and the king feared Rolfe's heirs might inherit the royal holdings in Virginia. Rolfe was accused of treason, but after a while the king's temper abated.

Pocahontas renounced paganism, and was baptized into the Church of England and renamed Rebecca. She could not read or write English, but she memorized the Apostle's Creed, the Lord's Prayer, and the Ten Commandments. The devoted couple visited London in 1616 and were waiting to return to America when Pocahontas died of smallpox at age twenty-one.

2. THEY DIDN'T TELL THE FAMILY Abraham Lincoln and Mary Todd seemed to have had an enduring marriage of love and understanding, although the beginning was hardly auspicious. Mary came from a distinguished Kentucky family, knew French, was raised by a black mammy, and loved cotillion parties. Lincoln came from ignorant backwoods stock, was shy and ill at ease at parties, tending to sit around with his hands under his knees. Mary was five feet two and one of the prettiest belles in Springfield, Illinois. Lincoln was six feet four, ungainly, and even thought himself ugly.

By December 1840, the two were engaged. Mary's sister and brother-in-law, with whom she lived in Springfield, argued that she was throwing herself away. Mary defended Lincoln, but her patience was tried when he worked long hours, lapsed into melancholy spells, and didn't attend parties with her. Misunderstandings flared and finally Lincoln asked Mary to be released from the January 1, 1841, wedding date. He went into a severe depression, closing himself up in his boardinghouse room for a week. "I must die or get better," he wrote.

Eventually a matchmaking friend invited the two to a party. They were reconciled and, on the evening of November 4, 1842, were married. Mary didn't tell her sister until the morning of the wedding; Lincoln never told his family until much later. He stood up alone. An Episcopal minister performed the ceremony and Lincoln gave Mary a simple gold ring inscribed "Love Is Eternal."

3. HE DIDN'T WANT TO MARRY HER MOTHER The year Grover Cleveland was twenty-seven, his future wife, Frances Folsom, was born. The daughter of his law partner, he bought her first baby carriage; she called him "Uncle Cleve." When her father died in an accident in 1874, he became the child's guardian.

In 1885, Cleveland entered the White House still a bachelor, but that year Frances graduated from Wells College and he asked her to marry him. She agreed to keep the engagement quiet until she returned form a postgraduation trip to Europe with her mother. However, the press got wind of a romance when Cleveland sent an affectionate bon voyage telegram to the ship. The operator made a copy for himself—and the newspapers. But no one suspected that young Frances was the object of the president's affection; the rumors that flew were about Cleveland and *Mrs.* Folsom. "I don't see why the papers keep marrying me to old ladies all the while," he complained.

On June 2, 1886, he and Frances were married at the White House, the first and only presidential wedding there. The Clevelands had five children and Mrs. Cleveland commented on her marriage: "I can wish the women of our Country no greater blessing than that their homes and lives may be as happy."

4. SHE CHANGED HER MIND In 1843 wealthy David Gardiner took his twenty-three-year-old daughter, Julia, along on a visit to the White House. President John Tyler, who was fifty-three and whose wife had died while he was in office, was immediately taken with Julia's olive-skinned beauty and soon sought her hand. Julia declined but a freak accident changed her mind.

Julia, her father, and Tyler were all attending a February 1844 party on board the warship *Princeton* when a huge cannon exploded during a demonstration firing. Gardiner and others were killed. Julia, who had been in the main cabin, fainted. Tyler took her in his arms, carried her ashore, and comforted her in her grief. Three months later the two were quietly married in a private ceremony in New York.

Julia established an almost regal atmosphere in the White House. She received visitors seated on a low dais with twelve "maids of honor" around her and wearing a flowered headdress resembling a crown. She loved it when Senators Daniel Webster and John C. Calhoun toasted her as "Mrs. Presidentress." Tyler was transformed too. He adored Julia and even learned to approve of the waltz which he had previously condemned as "vulgar." The Tylers had a long and fruitful marriage. At the age of seventy, Tyler, who had been born when George Washington was president, fathered a child who died when Truman was president.

5. TWENTY-SEVEN WIVES The first woman who married Brigham Young, Marion Works, had him all to herself. She died shortly after he converted to Mormonism and Young went on to become the Church leader, leading the Mormons on their famous trek to the valley of the Great Salt Lake.

He accepted the church rule on polygamy reluctantly, saying it would be "great toil and labor for my body." He was tall, broadchested, and had at least twenty-seven wives but possibly seventy. In the evening he put a chalk mark on the door of the wife he would be visiting and then fortified himself by eating eggs to boost his virility. When he died in 1877 he left an estate of over $1 million and was survived by fifty-six children.

6. A TWENTY-FIVE-INCH-TALL GROOM When two of showman P. T. Barnum's midgets, Tom Thumb and Lavinia Bump, became engaged, he offered them fifteen thousand dollars to postpone their wedding a month. The reason was that the Lilliputian couple's appearances at Barnum's American Museum were bringing in thousands of curious visitors and up to three thousand dollars in receipts a day.

Tom Thumb, who had beaten out another midget to win Lavinia's hand, declared that not even "for fifty thousand dollars" would he delay his wedding. It was held on February 10, 1863, and photographed by Mathew Brady, the famous Civil War photographer. President and Mrs. Lincoln sent Chinese fire screens as a wedding present. When the newlyweds visited the White House after their reception, Lincoln told Tom Thumb, "My boy, God likes to do funny things; here you have the long and the short of it." The Thumbs were happily married for twenty years, living in a thirty-thousand-dollar Bridgeport, Connecticut, house with scaled-down furniture.

Man and His Horse

1. HIS HORSE HEARD HIS CUE When Sitting Bull toured with Buffalo Bill's Wild West Show, he had a trick horse, which was given to him as a keepsake. The horse was outside his cabin on the reservation when policemen came to arrest Sitting Bull on the morning of December 18, 1890. The chief was being taken into custody as a precaution because the army was alarmed by the spread of the Indians' Ghost Dances.

In the confused scuffle that followed, shots were fired and Sitting Bull was killed. His horse thought the gunshots were the cue for his act and began doing his tricks. He sat down and raised one hoof, to the terror of the Indians who supposed that the spirit of Sitting Bull had entered his horse.

2. WHITEY AT THE WHITE HOUSE Old Whitey, who served Zachary Taylor through his famous Mexican War battles, had earned the right to graze on the White House lawn. He was ancient and shaggy but a favorite of the tourists. Whitey loved music and when a parade came along Pennsylvania Avenue he would join right in. When Zachary Taylor died after fifteen months in office, Old Whitey marched in the funeral procession with boots reversed in the stirrups—his last parade.

3. SETTING A GOOD EXAMPLE "Here lies the body of my good horse, 'The General,'" reads the marker over the burial plot of President John Tyler's horse. "For twenty years he bore me around the circuit of my practice, and in all that time he never made a blunder. Would that his master could say the same!"

4. A PONY IN THE WHITE HOUSE Theodore Roosevelt's son Archie was bedridden with the measles. His brother, Quentin, thought it would cheer him up if he could see his calico pony, Algonquin. With the help of the White House coachman, Quentin snuck Algonquin through the basement and up the elevator to Archie's room. Archie's spirits were indeed lifted and Algonquin was well behaved.

5. THE BURDENS OF STATE Secretary of War Elihu Root heard reports that William Howard Taft, governor of the newly acquired Philippine Islands, was ill and cabled him to ask about his health. The three-hundred-pound Taft replied that he was feeling fine and had just returned from a twenty-five-mile horseback ride. Root cabled back, "How is the horse?"

6. LUCKY BONES Two years after Robert E. Lee's death, his horse, Traveller, who had been a familiar sight during the Civil War, stepped on a nail and died of tetanus. Traveller was buried on the grounds of Washington and Lee University, where Lee had been president. Thirty-five years later his bones were exhumed and put on display in the cellar of the chapel, where he was a tourist attraction for sixty years. Students began to sign their names on the skeleton and the legend grew that initialing Traveller was the secret to a passing grade. Finally, in 1971, the horse's bones were reburied on the university grounds.

7. A BLIND MAN'S SOLACE Gentle old Ruff shared mountain man Jim Bridger's final explorations. In 1875, Bridger, who had discovered the Great Salt Lake, was aging, ailing, and almost totally blind. Confined to his Missouri farm, he would roam about his property on old Ruff. But, as his daughter Virginia wrote, "at times father would draw the lines wrong and the horse would go wrong and then they would get lost in the woods. The strange part of it was the old faithful dog, Sultan, would come home and let us know that father was lost. The dog would bark and whine until I would go out and look for him, and lead him and the old horse home on the main road."

8. HORSE OVERBOARD When Buffalo Bill Cody's Wild West troupe was sailing back from their London tour, a tragedy occurred that was reported on both sides of the Atlantic. Charlie, Cody's horse, had caught a chill and died. "I should have preferred to carry him home and bury him on the prairie, but this was impossible," wrote Cody. His funeral was set for 8:00 P.M. on May 17, 1888. "During the day he lay in state on the deck, decently wrapped in a canvas shroud and covered with the Stars and Stripes. At the appointed hour, the entire ship's company assembled. The band played 'Auld Lang Syne,' lights were burned and as the faithful creature glided gently into the water the ship's cannon boomed a last farewell to my consistent friend and companion of the last fifteen years."

9.   TWICE MOURNED When the Lincolns moved into the White House someone gave Willie a pony. He loved it so much that he rode it in all kinds of weather. One day he was out riding in the rain and caught a chill. It turned into a serious cold and soon a fever. The president kept a vigil at his bedside night after night, and when Willie died, both he and Mary were overwhelmed with grief. Mary Lincoln could not bear to look at her son's picture. She gave away all his toys, but the pony stayed on in the White House stables. Then, on February 10, 1864, at 9 P.M., Lincoln looked out the window and saw flames shooting out from the stables. He raced to the scene of the fire, only to learn that Willie's pony, like the rest of the horses, had refused to come out of the burning stables. Lincoln, who still mourned for his son, went into a deep depression that lasted for days.

PART XI

Adventure and Intrigue

Jailbreaks, Escapes, and Quick Getaways

1. TO THE OUTHOUSE—AND OUT OF TOWN Billy the Kid, captured and jailed at Lincoln, New Mexico, needed to go to the privy. He chose a moment when the deputy marshal and other prisoners were across the street having dinner at the hotel. His only guard, Deputy Sheriff Bell, undid the Kid's chains, which were fastened to the floor, and escorted him to the outhouse.

On the way back, the Kid slipped out of his handcuffs and produced a gun, which was either hidden in the privy or wrested from the jail's armory. He shot Bell and gunned down the only other lawman, the deputy marshal, who was running across the street from dinner. He then asked a townsperson for a prospecting pick, which he leisurely used to break out of one of his leg shackles. He demanded a horse and rode out of town.

Sheriff Garrett was away at the time, but he recalled, "The inhabitants of the whole town of Lincoln appeared to be terror-stricken. The kid, it is my firm belief, could have ridden up and down the plaza until dark without a shot having been fired at him, nor an attempt made to arrest him."

2. THE WARDEN LOSES HIS PRISONER In 1875 William Marcey "Boss" Tweed of New York City's infamous Tweed Ring was finally arrested for embezzling $6 million. Unable to post bail, which was set at $3 million, he was confined to Ludlow Street Jail. Every afternoon Tweed was allowed to leave in a closed carriage accompanied by two jailers who took him to an uptown rural section for a walk. On the way back they often stopped off at Tweed's luxurious home for dinner.

On December 4, 1875, Warden Dunham and Keeper Hagan sat in a downstairs drawing room with their prisoner. Tweed asked to go upstairs for a minute to talk to his wife. Five minutes later they reportedly went to find him but he was not there.

Warden Dunham said he immediately rushed out the front door and looked up and down the block, but his prisoner had made a sensational escape. No one knew exactly how he had managed to disappear, but high-ranking police officers didn't accept the warden's story; they believed that Tweed had been gone for hours at that point.

Tweed later turned up in Spain, a getaway that reportedly cost

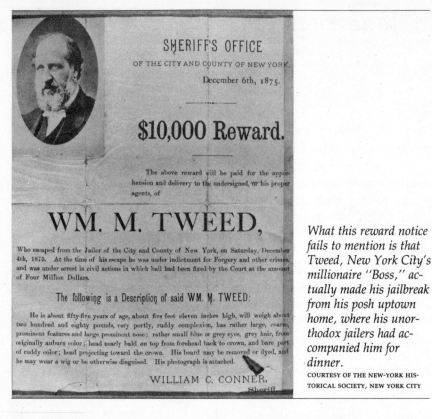

SHERIFF'S OFFICE

OF THE CITY AND COUNTY OF NEW YORK,

December 6th, 1875.

$10,000 Reward.

The above reward will be paid for the apprehension and delivery to the undersigned, or his proper agents, of

WM. M. TWEED,

Who escaped from the Jailor of the City and County of New York, on Saturday, December 4th, 1875. At the time of his escape he was under indictment for Forgery and other crimes, and was under arrest in civil actions in which bail had been fixed by the Court at the amount of Four Million Dollars.

The following is a Description of said WM. M. TWEED:

He is about fifty-five years of age, about five feet eleven inches high, will weigh about two hundred and eighty pounds, very portly, ruddy complexion, has rather large, coarse, prominent features and large prominent nose; rather small blue or grey eyes, grey hair, from originally auburn color; head nearly bald on top from forehead back to crown, and bare part of ruddy color; head projecting toward the crown. His beard may be removed or dyed, and he may wear a wig or be otherwise disguised. His photograph is attached.

WILLIAM C. CONNER,
Sheriff

What this reward notice fails to mention is that Tweed, New York City's millionaire "Boss," actually made his jailbreak from his posh uptown home, where his unorthodox jailers had accompanied him for dinner.
COURTESY OF THE NEW-YORK HISTORICAL SOCIETY, NEW YORK CITY

him sixty thousand dollars. However, his freedom was short-lived. He was apprehended by Spanish authorities and returned to the U.S.

3.   ELUDING THE SHAWNEES It was snowing when Daniel Boone left Boonesboro, the town he had founded on the Kentucky frontier, to go out hunting alone. He was jumped by a war party of Shawnees and he tried to escape on foot but soon realized it was a lost cause. He placed his rifle in front of a tree as a sign of surrender and hid behind the tree.

The Shawnees were delighted to capture the famed frontiersman. They shook hands with him cordially and took him back to Ohio. Chief Blackfish treated him as a son. Boone hunted with the Indians and played in their games, although he was always careful to stay on their good side by letting them win.

All the while he secretly stored food and powder. When he realized the Shawnees were planning an attack on the fort at Boonesboro, he knew he needed to warn his family and friends. Finally, on June 16, 1778, his famous escape began. He chose a moment when the men were out hunting. Friendly squaws were aghast at what he was attempting and warned him he would die in the woods. But Daniel Boone made it to Boonesboro—160 miles in four days, an amazing feat of endurance and woodsmanship.

4. JEFFERSON TAKES TO THE WOODS During the Revolutionary War, Banastre Tarleton, the feared British leader of dragoons, set out to capture Thomas Jefferson, then governor of Virginia. The British intended to send him to England in chains to be tried for treason.

The raiding party, en route to Monticello, Jefferson's mountaintop home, stopped at Cuckoo Tavern. There young Jack Jouett overheard their plans and rode off to warn Jefferson. He arrived at daybreak, his face covered with cuts from his wild all-night ride through the bush. Jefferson immediately sent his wife and children away to safety but lingered to tidy up his affairs. Periodically he would use his telescope to look for signs of the dragoons. He was just finishing a leisurely breakfast when a slave rushed in with the news that the British were coming up the drive to Monticello. Surprised by the speed of their arrival, Jefferson quickly went to the woods where he had hidden a horse and made a narrow escape.

5. BONNIE SPRINGS CLYDE—FOR A WHILE Bonnie Parker taped a .38 pistol to her thigh and went to visit her lover, Clyde Barrrow, in prison. The pistol had a Bisley handle narrow enough to slip through the bars. That night, Clyde made his escape. He got as far as Ohio before he was caught in a bungled burglary. He went back to jail but was only separated from Bonnie for twenty months because his mother pleaded with the governor for a pardon. The two lovers then went on to rob, shoot, and kill like the best of the 1930s gangsters—until they were shot dead in an ambush.

6. ESCAPE FROM THE WHITE HOUSE When Andrew Jackson, elected as a "man of the people," opened the doors of the White House for his first inaugural reception, his admirers responded in droves. Crowds kept pushing in, china broke, the punch spilled, and fights broke out. The wooden floors trembled beneath so many feet. There were no security guards.

As the crush became greater, Jackson had to keep backing up until he was pressed against a wall office, gasping for air and nearing collapse. Finally, friends had to link arms creating a human fence to give the president room. They helped him escape out a back window to the South Portico and then down the stairs. The exhausted president was taken to Gadsby's Hotel and put to bed.

7.   MILLIONAIRES GO WEST Entrepreneurs Jim Fisk and Jay Gould pulled out all the stops to thwart Cornelius Vanderbilt's takeover of their Erie Railroad. The faster Vanderbilt bought up their stock, the faster they printed new stock, flooding the market. When Vanderbilt discovered he had been duped, he became furious. He had a friendly New York City judge order the Erie's records seized. Warned while eating dinner at Delmonico's, Fisk and Gould took off and crammed the Erie's stocks and bonds, plus six million dollars in cash, into suitcases. Then they jumped in a hack and raced at top speed for the Hudson River docks. In hot pursuit were carriages of the deputy sheriffs, who lost their quarry as Fisk and Gould boarded a ferry that was headed west to New Jersey.

When interviewed in Jersey City, safely out of the reach of New York law, Fisk recalled New York newspaperman Horace Greeley's famous words about heading west for success. He said, "Tell Mr. Greeley from us that we're sorry now that we didn't take his advice sooner—about going West."

8.   DON'T LEAVE HOME WITHOUT GEORGE The British were coming and everyone seemed to be leaving Washington on August 24, 1813. Everyone except Dolley Madison. She hoped the president and his cabinet would be home for dinner. Servants were ordered to roast the meat and decant the wine. Finally, a message from Madison bade her leave and she packed the last wagon with crimson draperies from the Oval Room, books, and silverware. Then Dolley remembered George Washington. His portrait was in a frame that was screwed to the State Dining Room wall. She refused to leave him behind. Three men tried to undo the frame and finally Dolley agreed to have them break it. The canvas was rolled up and escorted to a safe haven, as was Dolley's pet parrot. Then, with little time to spare, she locked the front doors, scooped up a framed copy of the Declaration of Independence, and left. Soon thereafter, the British burned the White House.

9.   DILLINGER WIELDS A WASHBOARD "I don't want to kill anyone," said bank robber John Dillinger to the attendant at the supposedly escape-proof Crown Point, Indiana, prison. It was March 3, 1934. Dillinger pointed what looked like a gun. Actually it was the top of a washboard he'd carved with a razor and coated with bootblack. Since none of the prison guards were in a mood to buck

Dillinger's command of "Do as I tell you," the outlaw was able to make his escape. He took Sheriff Lillian Holley's car and two hostages, one of whom was another sheriff. Across the state line in rural Illinois, he let his captives out, giving them four dollars for food and transportation home. "I'd give you guys more but that's all I can spare," said Dillinger, who waved as he drove off.

Running Up the White Flag

1.   A REVOLUTIONARY MOMENT On the morning of October 17, 1781, more than one hundred American guns were pounding the besieged British lines at Yorktown with almost no answering fire. As the morning haze lifted, the Americans were able to make out a small, spindly legged drummer, clad in scarlet and wearing a bearskin cap. He was beating a call for a parley. Then a British officer appeared on the parapet "holding up a white handkerchief." The firing ceased. Americans approached, tied the handkerchief over the British officer's eyes, and led him into American lines where he gave a note to General Washington. It agreed to discuss surrender terms and closed, "I have the honor to be Sir Your most obedient and most humble Servant, Cornwallis." The last battle in the American Revolution was over.

2.   THE CASE OF DR. BEANES Francis Scott Key received President James Madison's permission to go to the British fleet in a "flag-of-truce packett" and ask Admiral Cochrane to release a Dr. William Beanes. The Americans charged that Beanes was a noncombatant "taken from his bed, in the midst of his family and hurried off almost without clothes" in "departure from the known usages of civilized warfare." Key's mission was successful, but he and the doctor were forced to stay with the British fleet as the attack on Baltimore and Fort McHenry was about to occur.

It was from a small boat on the British side of the fight that Key saw the "bombs bursting in air," and later, when the early-morning fog lifted, the star-spangled banner. He was so moved that he began to write a poem on an envelope. It was set to the tune of "To Anacreon in Heaven," a popular drinking song, and became an immediate favorite.

3.   A LINEN TOWEL ENDS IT "Tell General Lee I have fought my corps to a frazzle," said Confederate General Gordon. As Lee said,

there was nothing left but surrender, though he "would rather die a thousand deaths." Union troops saw a small white object appear and thought it was a signal for the rebel infantry to begin firing. Instead, three men approached carrying a white flag—actually a fringed linen towel, which was all that could be found in a hurry. Soon white flags were flying up and down the line. Lee and Grant arranged to meet in the little town of Appomattox Court House and the war was over. After the surrender, the fringed linen towel was given to a rising military star, George Armstrong Custer, who at twenty-one had been the Union's youngest general. Custer gave it to his wife as a keepsake.

4. AN OUTLAW GETS A SQUARE MEAL Billy the Kid and four outlaws were surrounded at a deserted cabin near Stinking Springs, New Mexico. In the moonlight of December 22, 1880, they'd been tracked through the snow by Sheriff Pat Garrett and his posse. The next morning, Garrett, as he told it, suggested the Kid come out and get some breakfast. "Can't do it Pat," Billy replied. "Business is too confining. No time to run around." Garrett, hungry himself, got provisions at a nearby ranch. Later, he said, "we built a rousing fire and went to cooking. The odor of roasting meat was too much for the famished lads." Out the window came "a handkerchief that had once been white, at the end of a stick." An imprisoned Billy the Kid told the Las Vegas *Gazette*, "I thought it was better to come out and get a square meal—don't you?"

5. HONOR REQUIRED A BATTLE When American Commodore Dewey was getting ready for an attack on Manila during the Spanish-American War, victory was relatively certain. The Spanish fleet had already been crushed and General Juadenes was willing to turn over the Philippine capital, but his honor demanded a battle. Dewey was forced to make a show of attacking the Spanish. "I had to fire, to kill a few people," he explained.

Juadenes agreed not to use the fort's big guns if the U.S. fleet did not bombard Manila. At 8:45 A.M. on August 13, 1898, Dewey deployed his ships for an attack. At 9:35 A.M., they opened fire on an old fort on the outskirts of Manila. At 11:20 A.M., Spain flew a white flag, the prearranged signal, and the "battle" was over. Only five Americans had been killed.

6. COLONIAL WIGFALL TO THE RESCUE The firing was fierce at Fort Sumter during the Civil War's opening battle. Union Private Thompson was about to reload his cannon when, to his astonish-

ment, he saw a strange figure with a red sash outside the gun opening. The man carried a sword with a white flag on it and announced
he was Colonel Louis Wigfall of the Confederate army.

He had been rowed over to the fort amid the crashing cannonballs by two very reluctant Negroes. This was his own quixotic
peace mission; he had come without any authority from anyone.
Unable to enter through the main gate because it had gone up in
flames, he had walked to the gun embrasure. Wigfall convinced the
startled Private Thompson to allow him to climb in and went to talk
to the fort's commander, Major Anderson. He told him, "You have
defended your flag nobly, sir. It's madness to persevere in useless
resistance."

Anderson knew he was defending an ultimately hopeless position on an island in the Charleston harbor and agreed to surrender.
It was 1:30 P.M. on Saturday, April 13, 1861, when the Stars and
Stripes came down and a hospital sheet was raised, ending the first
battle of the Civil War.

Dueling: An American Pastime

1. HIS SON DIED ON THE SAME SPOT Aaron Burr was vice-
president of the United States when he challenged former Treasury
Secretary Alexander Hamilton to a duel for defaming him with such
words as "despicable." Hamilton accepted the challenge although
he was opposed to dueling. He had held his only son, Philip, in his
arms as the young man died from a duel at the very spot set for
the fight with Burr.

At dawn Hamilton and Burr crossed the Hudson from New York
City to New Jersey. At ten paces both fired. Burr was not hit; Hamilton was shot in the groin and died an agonizing death. The vice-
president went into hiding. After four months he reemerged. Though
still wanted for murder in New Jersey, he was never prosecuted.

2. A NAVY HERO KILLED Stephen Decatur had a history of heroics, both in the War of 1812 and in fights with the Barbary pirates.
It was he who toasted "our country, right or wrong."

Decatur also had a history as a duelist. In 1799 he wounded one
opponent in the hip in a duel. He served as a second for Midship-
man Joseph Bainbridge and helped him win against an expert
marksman by insisting they fire from only four paces.

His last and fatal duel came when he was challenged by Captain James Barron. In 1808 Barron had been suspended by a military court headed by Decatur. This led to a heated correspondence and finally Barron's challenge. Decatur selected the close range of eight paces in deference to Barron's faulty eyesight and said he would aim low to avoid mortal injury.

They fired at the same time. Barron was wounded in the thigh, but the forty-one-year-old Decatur was shot through the body and killed. President James Monroe and all high-ranking Washington officials turned out for Decatur's funeral.

3.   BITING THE BULLET Sam Houston's problem began when he referred to John P. Erwin, the postmaster of Nashville, as a "scoundrel." Erwin challenged Houston to a duel and, as etiquette required, had his second deliver the message to Houston's second. But Houston's friend refused to accept it on the grounds that the messenger was a nonresident of Tennessee.

The postmaster then found a new second, General William A. White, who delivered the challenge directly to Houston. He refused to accept on the grounds that a second can only deliver a challenge to a second. However, Houston did offer to fight General White, even though he only knew him slightly.

After much complicated maneuvering and exchanging of notes, White decided to challenge Houston on the grounds that his friend, the postmaster, had been offended. Houston disavowed any personal animosity toward White but consented to the duel anyway.

Houston then sought out his friend and veteran dueler Andrew Jackson for advice. Jackson told him that biting on a bullet as he drew his gun would help to steady his aim.

Houston and White crossed the border into Kentucky at dawn and used pistols at only fifteen feet. Both fired at once. Houston was unharmed; White received a bullet in the groin but later recovered. Houston told him he was sorry but "you know it was forced upon me." "I know it," White replied, "and forgive you." Houston refused any glory from the encounter. He was opposed to dueling, he said, and gratified that "my adversary was injured no worse."

4.   LINCOLN CHOOSES CAVALRY SWORDS When Abraham Lincoln was courting Mary Todd, Mary and her girlfriend wrote anonymous letters to Springfield's *Sagamore Journal* ridiculing Illinois state auditor James Shields. The two laughed and thought Shields a pompous little man. However, Shields didn't see anything funny in their satire and demanded to know who wrote the letters.

Lincoln, who had written one of the letters, decided to assume responsibility and tried to mollify Shields. The letters, he said, were "wholly for political effect" and were not intended as a personal affront. Shields would not be placated and insisted his honor must be served in a duel.

Lincoln, as the party who was challenged, had the choice of weapons. He specified a face-to-face fight using cavalry broadswords within an eight-foot circle. Shields was short; Lincoln stood six feet four in his "sock feet" and had exceptionally long arms that were well-muscled from splitting rails. The situation was ludicrous and serious at the same time. On September 22, 1842, they crossed to Missouri where dueling was not illegal. At the last moment friends were able to persuade Shields to accept Lincoln's explanation and the fight was avoided. Lincoln was mortified that the situation had nearly come to a duel and would never even talk about it again.

5.   "A HIGH-TONED DUEL" It was April 8, 1826, when Speaker of the House Henry Clay politely greeted U.S. Senator John Randolph on the Virginia side of the Potomac River where the two were meeting for a duel. Randolph had referred to Clay as a "blackleg," meaning a dishonest gambler.

The two men faced each other at ten paces and fired their pistols. Both missed their marks. Another senator, Thomas Hart Benton, tried to persuade them to call it off, but neither would agree. Clay's second shot pierced Randolph's coat but didn't wound him. Randolph intentionally shot into the air. He then went to Clay, offering his hand, and Clay met him halfway. They shook. Clay said, "I trust in God, my dear sir, you are untouched; after what has occurred I would not have harmed you for a thousand worlds." Senator Benton's comment was that it was "about the last high-toned duel" he ever witnessed.

6.   A TWIST IN TIME For Andrew Jackson, being called a "worthless scoundrel; A poltroon, and a coward!" was enough to get his dander up. But Charles Dickinson, a Tennessee lawyer, had also made insulting remarks about Mrs. Jackson, who had inadvertently married Jackson before she was properly divorced from her first husband. The result was that, in 1806, Jackson found himself twenty-four paces from Dickinson, his pistol loaded.

Dickinson, reputed to be the best shot in Tennessee, fired first and cried, "My God! Have I missed him?" The bullet tore into Jackson's chest where his heart should have been. But Jackson had worn a bulky overcoat and twisted his lean body inside it to throw off his opponent's aim. The rules required that Dickinson stand still while Jackson took his turn. Jackson then took careful aim and proceeded to shoot his opponent dead. As he walked away with his second and the surgeon, blood began to drip from his shoe. "I believe he pinked me," Jackson admitted. Dickinson's bullet stayed near his heart for the rest of his days.

Close Calls

1.   A TRUE CLIFF-HANGER Enamored of the American West, Theodore Roosevelt would go to any lengths to get a good angle for a picture. Once when he was out in the Dakota Territory he concluded that the best photo opportunity was halfway down a cliff. He had himself lowered two hundred feet by a rope.

When the men in his party found they couldn't pull Roosevelt back up, TR's solution was simple—cut the rope and let him drop sixty feet into an ice-filled river below. This sounded suicidal to his companions, so they raced back to camp for more rope. They could only find an additional twenty-five feet. After two hours of suspense and suspension, they lowered him as far down as the rope would permit and then cut him loose.

When Roosevelt was pulled out of the icy stream onto a raft, he was only half conscious. One of his companions reported, "He was stiff and sore for several days, from all the bruises across his chest and under his arms, but he did no moaning about it."

2.   A PROFILE IN COURAGE John F. Kennedy's most famous brush with death came one night in 1943 when a Japanese destroyer loomed up in the darkness and crashed into PT-109 at high speed. But his closest call came in 1954.

Then a popular U.S. senator, he underwent a complicated operation to alleviate spinal pain from his war injury. The operation was extremely risky because Kennedy also had Addison's disease, the result of his exposure to the ocean and malaria. A Boston clinic refused to operate. Kennedy, unable to endure back pain that had become almost crippling, found new doctors in New York.

After the operation, an infection set in. Kennedy lapsed into a coma. His family rushed to his side and the Last Rites of the Church were administered. Despite the odds, the steel-willed JFK managed to recover slowly.

3.   ALMOST CAUGHT IN THE WHITE HOUSE CLOSET She called him "Wurren." He called her "Duchess." To the American public the Hardings seemed like a nice White House family, but the president was having an affair with young Nan Britton. Harding had the Secret Service slip Nan into the White House, but he had a difficult time finding a secluded place where, in Nan's words, "we might share kisses in safety." She added that his solution was "a small closet in the anteroom. . . . There the President and his adoring sweetheart made love."

The closet had two doors, one from the presidential office and one from an outside corridor. Harding prudently stationed a Secret Service agent at the door in the corridor. The Duchess had her own spy system and somehow got suspicious. She came rushing down the stairs but was stopped by the guard. Then she hurried down the corridor to the Rose Garden to get into the Oval Office from the other side. Meantime, the agent rapped on the door warning Harding. When the First Lady stormed into the Oval Office, Wurren, adjusting his tie, asked, "What's the matter, Duchess?"

4.   ALMOST PLASTERED TO DEATH Thomas Jefferson was eighty-two years old and in poor health when an itinerant sculptor, John Browere, almost killed him. Browere made life masks, actual casts of a man's head, which were the only accurate representations possible in the days before photography. He had covered Jefferson's head and neck with plaster, leaving the necessary holes for breathing, but let it sit too long. Jefferson began groaning and the family feared he would suffocate. The "vile plasterer," as Jefferson's granddaughter called Browere, had to use a chisel and mallet to get the mask off. Jefferson survived, apparently no worse for his close call. A bronze bust made from Browere's mask is on display in Cooperstown, New York.

5.   A SNEEZE WOULD HAVE BEEN FATAL Martin Luther King, Jr., was autographing books in a Harlem department store in September 1958 when a middle-aged black woman pushed through the crowd and asked, "Are you Mr. King?" When King nodded, she stabbed him with a seven-inch steel letter opener, then started beating him with her fists.

King was rushed to Harlem Hospital. The letter opener lodged so close to the main heart artery that if he had sneezed or coughed he would have died. It took a three-hour operation to remove the weapon. His assailant, Mrs. Izola Ware Curry, also had a loaded pistol in her purse.

6.   SHOCKING A TURKEY Two days before Christmas, 1750, Benjamin Franklin decided to try a new electricity experiment to see if he could "kill a turkey by the shock from two large glass jars" that served as batteries and contained "as much electrical fire as forty common phials."

Franklin inadvertently touched both wires, and he served as the conductor, instead of the turkey. Witnesses told him there was a flash and a crack "as loud as a pistol," but Franklin's hearing and sight had vanished as "a universal blow" went through his body from head to foot. He suffered a violent shaking. His senses began to return but his hands felt "like dead flesh" for another eight or ten minutes. After recovering and realizing what had happened, Franklin commented, "Well, I meant to kill a turkey and instead I nearly killed a goose."

7.   A LOYAL BROTHER Fifteen-year-old Dwight Eisenhower fell in the stable yard and skinned his knee. Blood poisoning developed and soon his entire leg began to throb and bloat up. The doctor insisted an amputation was the "only chance of saving your life." Ike refused, saying, "I'd rather die," and got his older brother Edgar to stand by his bed. "You got to promise me you won't let 'em do it," he sobbed. Edgar stood watch for two days and nights, eating in the room and sleeping up against the door, before the infection subsided. Eisenhower said it showed him that sheer will was a powerful weapon.

Ransoms and Other Payoffs

1.   TRADED FOR A RACEHORSE George Washington Carver's mother, Mary, was a slave belonging to Missouri farmer Moses Carver. One night during the Civil War, raiders carried off Mary and her infant son, George. Moses Carver enlisted the aid of a neighbor, John Bentley, who was a Union scout, to search for the mother and son, offering a racehorse for ransom.

Six days later, Bentley rode up and handed Moses a small wet bundle—the baby George, barely alive. Mary was never seen again, but Bentley was rewarded with the racehorse. Carver's wife stripped the baby naked, held him by the fire to warm him, and fed him droplets of milk sweetened with sugar. The infant survived and grew up to become an internationally acclaimed agricultural scientist. But the continuous coughing Carver suffered as a frail child left its mark. His vocal cords had been torn and even as an adult he had a high squeaky voice.

2.   LINDBERGH'S LOSS In 1932 nineteen-month-old Charles Augustus Lindbergh was sleeping in his crib when a kidnapper climbed through a second-story window of the Lindbergh home in Hopewell, New Jersey, and abducted him. A note left in the baby's bedroom was "signed" with two red interlocking circles. Blue filled in the overlapping area and a square hole was punched in each of the three areas.

A key piece of evidence against Lindbergh baby kidnapper, Bruno Hauptmann, was the ladder he used to climb into the second-story window. At his 1935 trial souvenir vendors in the courthouse lobby made a profit selling miniature ladders.
UPI/BETTMAN NEWSPHOTOS

When the ransom note arrived, it had the identifying signature and the words "70,000$ make one packet." It also said to put an ad in the New York *American* saying "MONEY IS READY." Dr. Condon, who acted as an intermediary, drove with Lindbergh to a dirt road alongside a cemetery at night. Dr. Condon paid the ransom and brought back a note saying the child could be found on a boat— "a small Boad 28 feet long." Lindbergh was elated but soon found that there was no boat. His son had been killed.

3.   HELP NOT WANTED When a strong British force approached Alexandria, Virginia, in the War of 1812, the town fathers did not want their city to be burned the way Washington, D.C., had been. The British agreed to hold their fire in return for a price—permission to help themselves to American naval stores and also to flour, wheat, and tobacco. When the U.S. Army sent a relief force toward the city, Alexandria officials headed them off by saying it would be "injurious to the interests of the town for any troops to enter at this time."

4. PACIFYING THE PIRATES The Barbary pirates had a lucrative habit of seizing ships passing through the Mediterranean and holding prisoners for ransom. On July 13, 1796, the U.S. was forced to pay the dey of Algiers, leader of one of the Barbary states, $200,000 for 122 Americans taken prisoner, even though 37 of them were already dead and buried. Of the 85 who survived, many did not live long because of cruel treatment in the Algerian prisons. Large-scale payoffs ceased in 1815, but only after the young and weak U.S. Navy grew strong enough to send the marines to Tripoli and Algeria to defeat the Barbary pirates.

5. CASTRO'S RANSOM In April 1961, a band of Cuban exiles invaded their homeland intending to overthrow Fidel Castro. Orchestrated by the CIA, the attack at the Bay of Pigs quickly proved a disaster. More than one thousand Americans were held prisoner and Castro demanded $62 million for their release. He eventually settled for $53 million in food and drugs. On Sunday, December 23, 1962, the first returning prisoners reached Florida. The following Saturday, lined up in the Orange Bowl, they were given a hero's welcome. President John F. Kennedy flew down and greeted them before a crowd of forty thousand. He was given the brigade flag that the invaders had used and in an emotional speech said, "I can assure you that this flag will be returned to this Brigade in a free Havana." Castro boasted that he had been able to hold the U.S. up for ransom.

6. PROFITS OF WAR In 1864 Frederick, Maryland, found itself surrounded by the army of Confederate General Jubal Early, who threatened to sack the town if he didn't receive $200,000. Since Union supplies worth over $1 million were stored in the town, everyone scurried to meet Early's demand. The ransom was raised by borrowing from several banks. The town of Frederick had to repay the loan, though they hoped the federal government would eventually pick up the tab. It never has, although the matter was still under consideration as recently as 1986.

Sunken Ships

1. A SIGN FROM GOD It was just after midnight on Christmas, 1492, when Christopher Columbus's *Santa Maria* hit a coral reef off what is now Haiti. It seemed that the helmsman had given the tiller

to a small boy and gone to sleep. The hull filled with water and Columbus ordered the ship abandoned. Indians helped to salvage equipment and build a fort from the ship's timbers. Columbus believed that the lost ship meant that God intended him to found a colony. He named it Christmas Town—Villa de la Navidad—and some of the *Santa Maria*'s crew volunteered to stay there since there wasn't room enough on the *Pinta* and *Niña* to take them all back to Spain.

2.   A CAUSE OF WAR The U.S.S. *Maine* was riding at anchor outside Havana, Cuba, on the calm tropical night of February 15, 1898. It as 9:40 P.M. and Captain Charles Sigsbee was writing a letter to his wife when his cabin was rocked by a thunderous explosion. Shock waves shattered glass across the water in Havana and the city's lights went out. The *Maine* sank in forty feet of water. Out of a crew of 350, 260 were lost.

A navy court of inquiry sent divers down to the muddy bottom to examine the twisted steel and came to the conclusion that a submarine mine had caused the explosion of the ship's forward ammunition magazine. This conclusion was disputed in later years, but in 1898 it was enough to push the U.S. into a war with Spain. In 1911 the *Maine* was raised and the wreckage examined to see if the explosion had been from an external mine or internal causes. When no decisive answers were found, it was towed to sea and sunk with military honors in water deep enough to make further examination impossible.

3.   THE WILD WEST GOES UNDER "Outfit at bottom of the river, what do you advise?" Buffalo Bill Cody cabled his partner in Denver. The Wild West Show, packed on a boat heading down the Mississippi, had hit another boat and sunk. Cody wrote, "We lost all our personal effects, including wagons, camp equipage, arms, ammunition, donkeys, buffaloes and one elk. We managed, however, to save our horses, Deadwood coach, band wagon and—ourselves. The loss thus entailed about $20,000." In eight days, however, he had rounded up another herd of elk and buffalo plus wagons, et cetera, and opened the show in New Orleans.

4.   A ONE-BATTLE HERO On its first day of duty, the Union ship *Monitor* fought its famous Civil War battle with the *Merrimac* and saved the North's fleet of wooden ships from destruction. That two-hour fight turned out to be the *Monitor*'s only battle. Eleven months later it was lost off Hatteras.

The specially designed iron-sided *Monitor* was unable to travel on its own in ocean waters, so it was being towed to North Carolina for new duty. A storm came up; huge waves rolled across the deck and even over the turret. The seam between the hull and the deck split. Commander John Bankhead knew he could not save the ship.

A red lantern—a prearranged distress signal—was hoisted and the sidewheeler *Rhode Island*, which was towing the *Monitor*, pulled alongside. Bankhead shouted into a trumpet, "We are sinking. Send boats." In cutting the *Monitor* loose from the *Rhode Island*, one volunteer was swept overboard. A second was also lost to the waves. Some of the crew of the *Monitor* refused to go into the wildly bobbing relief boats, and they were among the sixteen who were lost. Twenty of the survivors would "humbly beg" the navy to be "discharged from further service."

Souvenir Hunters

1. A ROCK REDUCED BY THE AGES When the Pilgrims first sighted Plymouth Rock in 1620, it was probably 80 percent larger than it is today. In the intervening centuries, souvenir hunters chiseled off pieces of it for their mantels. This was relatively easy in the years when it was situated in places such as the town square. But since 1920, the rock has been enshrined in a Greek temple and is protected by an iron grill.

2. A HORSE'S TAIL Old Whitey served in Zachary Taylor's famous Mexican War campaigns and accompanied him to the White House. Knock-knee and uncurried, Old Whitey peacefully cropped the grass on the White House lawns and was unconcerned when visitors pulled hairs from his tail as souvenirs. By the time of Taylor's funeral, sixteen months after he took office, Old Whitey had hardly a hair left on his tail.

3. THRICE EMBATTLED Wilmer McLean was a pacifist who found himself unexpectedly involved in the first battle of the Civil War. It was fought across his farm. He lived on fourteen hundred acres near a creek called Bull Run. His house became a hospital and a morgue. A later year, the scene was repeated with the second Battle of Bull Run. McLean vowed to move "where the sound of no battle would ever reach." He chose the tiny Virginia village of Appomattox Court House and the Civil War ended in his parlor—literally.

Unaware of McLean's past, staff officers picked his house, the best in the tiny town, for Generals Grant and Lee to meet to sign the surrender terms. Afterward, his parlor furniture was chopped up and taken for souvenirs. Despite his protests, cavalry officers took off with his chairs on horseback and his upholstery was cut into ribbons and handed out.

4. "HOW COULD THEY?" That's what President Abraham Lincoln asked sadly after the reception for his second inauguration. The White House, from the time of John Adams, was considered to belong to the people. When Lincoln was sworn in, visitors made themselves very much at home. They cut souvenirs from the brocaded window treatments and snipped floral designs from the lace curtains. Charles Crook, a bodyguard, said the parlors "looked as if a regiment of rebel troops had been quartered there—with permission to forage."

5. GRIM REAPINGS Confederate Captain Henry Wirz presided over the ghastliest of prison camps—Andersonville, where one in three Union soldiers died. The North made him a scapegoat and he was hanged as a war criminal in 1865. Spectators cut up the noose and the scaffold to take home as mementos.

6. A REAL SHOCKER In 1885 ex-President Ulyssess S. Grant, dying of cancer, retreated to a cottage in New York State where he was racing the clock to finish his memoirs. Veterans in uniform guarded the house, but still souvenir hunters managed to climb onto the roof and make off with the lightning rod. Before it could be replaced, a storm came. Lightning struck, collapsing part of the ceiling and narrowly missing Ulyssess III in his nursery. Three soldiers suffered shocks and burns.

7. A DUPLICATE TOMB Visitors today at Monticello stop to see the famous obelisk tombstone designed by Thomas Jefferson himself, but it is only a copy. The original was so badly chipped by souvenir hunters that Congress commissioned a reproduction in 1883 and ordered it surrounded by a heavy iron fence.

8. A SNIP IN TIME At President Abraham Lincoln's funeral, his riderless horse, Old Buck, was led behind the hearse. Old Buck was covered in a red, white, and blue blanket, which had literally gone to pieces by the time he got back to the stable. Spectators along the way had helped themselves to bits of the blanket until nothing was left.

9. LINDBERGH MANIA "When I arrived at the police-guarded hangar, it was a shock to see my plane," wrote Charles Lindbergh of *The Spirit of St. Louis* in Paris. Souvenir hunters had cut holes in the plane's fabric and "some collector, apparently stronger than the rest, had pulled a grease cup off my engine. When I looked over the equipment in my cockpit, I discovered only one loss, but it was a great one—the log of my flight had been stolen."

Hoaxes, Deceptions, and Put-ons

1. A FALSE THREAT TO A LOVER In March 1915, Edith Bolling Galt entered into Woodrow Wilson's life like a spring breeze. The president was deeply depressed over the loss of his wife, Ellen, who had died some months earlier. Friends feared he had lost his will to live, but the widowed Mrs. Galt changed all that. Wilson launched a whirlwind courtship, sending her flowers every day. When he suddenly proposed marriage, his advisers were shocked. Wilson's 1916 reelection campaign was under way and they feared a swift remarriage would alienate voters.

Close aides decided to take action. Secretary of the Treasury William Gibbs McAdoo, Wilson's son-in-law, went to the president with a fabricated story that if the wedding were pursued, Mary Hulbert Peck would publish effusive letters Wilson had written her during his first marriage. Wilson was devastated but he told Mrs. Galt the whole story of his friendship with Mrs. Peck. She responded with a passionate pledge of her love and loyalty: "I will stand by you— not for duty, not for pity, not for honor—but for love." Wilson went ahead and was married in Mrs. Galt's Washington home on December 18, 1915. He won a second term with her at his side.

Years later, after Wilson had died, another aide, Colonel House, admitted to Mrs. Wilson that the story was a hoax—he and McAdoo had dreamed it up to prevent what they considered to be a politically damaging marriage.

2. FRANKLIN ATTACKS THE HESSIANS During the American Revolution, a provocative letter appeared in a Parisian newspaper. It was supposedly written by a German count who had hired his troops to England's King George. The count expressed his happiness that 1,605 of his soldiers had been killed. After all, King George

paid him extra if his men died. He also begged the baron, who was commanding his troops in America, not to take too much trouble to keep the wounded alive. He recalled the Spartan army's fight to the death at Thermopylae and said, "How happy should I be could I say the same of my brave Hessians." The letter was actually penned by Benjamin Franklin, the American minister in Paris who was exercising his talent for satire.

3. A USEFUL PHONY When the Revolution broke out, George Washington was faced with raw militia ignorant of the most basic military commands. The man who drilled them during the winter at Valley Forge was Baron Friederich von Steuben. The baron, who came over from Germany barely knowing a word of English, had been recommended to the Continental Congress by Benjamin Franklin. He presented himself as a lieutenant general who had served under Frederick the Great, though actually he had been only a half-pay captain. Von Steuben's claim to his title was tenuous, but Franklin was willing to go along with the embroidery because he knew that Congress needed to be impressed. Franklin even arranged for his passage to America since the baron was virtually penniless. Quite simply, von Steuben's services were vital, a fact that George Washington knew well. At the end of the Revolution, he deliberately made his last official act a letter of commendation to von Steuben.

4. "A MOST CRUEL HOAX" Vice-President Thomas Marshall was speaking at Atlanta's civic auditorium on November 23, 1919, when suddenly he was interrupted. He was told a call had been received saying that President Wilson had died. The vice-president was overwhelmed. He explained to the audience, "I cannot continue my speech. I must leave at once to take up my duties as Chief Executive of this great nation." Wilson's health was fragile as he was recovering from a stroke, but the president was very much alive. Afterward, Marshall referred to the episode, perpetrated by an unknown crackpot, as "a most cruel hoax."

5. HE KNEW A TRICK In the 1930s, Ronald Reagan was starting out as a sports announcer on radio. He loved horses and as a sideline wanted to join the cavalry reserves. The cavalry, however, presented an obstacle: the eye exam. Reagan was nearsighted, but, as he said, "I did know a trick." Instead of holding a black card over one eye while he read with the other, he held his hand over his eye

and squeezed his fingers to make a narrow slit which acted as a lens and enabled him to read the chart. This got him through the exam and he became a lieutenant in the U.S. cavalry.

Lost, Misplaced, or Led Astray

1.   LOST IN THE WOODS Abigail Adams, the first First Lady to live in the White House, got lost trying to find it. She was traveling from Baltimore to the new capital in Washington and was "obliged" to go eight miles through the woods, "where we wandered two hours without finding a guide, or the path."

2.   THE SECRET'S IN THE WRAPPER A Confederate officer chose an unlikely wrapper for a bundle of cigars: a copy of General Robert E. Lee's secret special order #191. Somehow he lost the parcel in the evacuation of Frederick, Maryland. It was found by two Union soldiers who turned the secret order over to the occupying Union general, George B. McClellan. Lee's special order #191 revealed that Confederate forces were scattered and convinced McClellan to attack the Confederates at Antietam. It was one of the bloodiest battles of the war. Lee was forced to retreat into Virginia and Lincoln had the victory he needed to issue the Emancipation Proclamation from a posture of strength.

3.   A MYSTERY OF HISTORY The first band of 108 settlers that Sir Walter Raleigh sent to the New World came back. They landed briefly at Roanoke Island but were deterred by unfriendly Indians and a lack of food. In 1587, Raleigh recruited another 150 settlers who were instructed to land on the shores of the Chesapeake Bay, but they only got as far as Roanoke Island. Twenty-seven days later, Virginia Dare was born, the first English child born in America. Supplies ran dangerously short and the colony's leader, John White, returned to England for more.

When he was finally able to return to America in 1590, he found everyone had disappeared. The fort stood but the houses had been dismantled. Carved in a palisade of the fort was the word *Croatoan*, the name of an Indian tribe, but no inscribed cross, the agreed-to sign that they had left due to danger. A trumpeter marched around the island playing English tunes in case the colonists were in hiding. Roanoke, the lost colony, remains a historical enigma.

4.   PAINE'S REMAINS Thomas Paine, the great writer of the Revolutionary cause, was buried on his farm in New Rochelle, New York. Ten years later his remains were dug up and taken to England, where he had been born. An English admirer, William Cobbett, intended to raise a monument to the author of *Common Sense*. However, Cobbett died and Paine became a part of Cobbett's estate. A probate court refused to recognize Paine's body as an asset. In 1844 the body and the coffin were acquired by a furniture dealer—their last known address.

5.   THE EIGHTEEN MISSING PAGES When the conspirators in Lincoln's assassination plot were tried, Colonel Conger, under oath, described all the items he had removed from Booth's body but failed to mention Booth's diary. The diary lay hidden away in the War Department archives. After two years its existence was revealed when Lieutenant Baker of the Secret Service wrote a book. The House Judiciary Committee then got hold of it but found there were eighteen pages missing—carefully cut out with a razor. Nobody could explain the missing pages.

The diary did reveal that Booth's plans had changed from kidnapping to murder only the day before Lincoln's assassination—a fact that surely would have benefited those defendants who were charged and convicted with conspiring to murder the president. The diary, open to where the eighteen pages were cut out, is on display today in Ford's Theatre in Washington.

6.   WHICH WAY IS IRELAND? Charles A. Lindbergh had only crude instruments to help him navigate on his nonstop flight from New York to Paris. At night he had to use a flashlight to get readings. When dawn came, he thought he might be lost. He spotted a fishing boat on the ocean below, so he glided down to within fifty feet, throttled back the engine, and yelled, "Which way is Ireland?" Nobody answered but soon he picked up the Irish coast and was amazed to find he was right on course.

7.   SHERMAN LOST IN A HOLE? On November 15, 1864, General William T. Sherman took sixty thousand men and left Atlanta. He began his famous march to the sea, destroying and burning everything in a sixty-mile-wide strip before emerging on the Georgia coast. The Union command lost contact with Sherman and his army for over a month and anxious Northerners wanted to know where he was. President Lincoln told them, "I know the hole he went in at, but I can't tell you what hole he will come out of."

8. LOOKING FOR THE RED RIVER "What! Is this not the Red River?" an astonished Zebulon Pike asked a Spanish officer who informed him that he had gone beyond the bounds of the Louisiana Territory and was trespassing in Spanish lands. The American explorer lowered the U.S. flag and his men were taken to Santa Fe by the officer "and 50 dragoons."

Being captured by the Spanish was something Pike may have anticipated. One goal of his 1807 expedition was to learn about Spanish doings on the other side of the Red River, the border of the new Louisiana Purchase. He had written General James Wilkinson, the commander who had sent him on the expedition, that if captured by the Spanish he felt he could still gain information and escape without harm by claiming to be "uncertain aboute the head waters of the rivers." He had even seemingly alerted the Spanish to his presence by allowing a member of his expedition to go into Santa Fa and take care of some personal "pecuniary demands."

Pike and his men were held for several months and then escorted back to U.S. territory. After his return, Pike was able to make valuable maps from notes hidden in the empty gun barrels.

9. LEE'S CITIZENSHIP IS LOST FOR A CENTURY After the Civil War, Southerners who had headed the rebellion had to apply for a presidential pardon to have their citizenship restored. Many refused, but Robert E. Lee led the way toward healing the nation's wounds. In 1865 he signed an Oath of Allegiance, the first step in receiving a pardon. Mysteriously, it was lost until 1970. The paper had been sent to Secretary of State William Seward, who somehow assumed it was simply for his information and gave it to a friend. It was discovered in a Washington office in a dusty bundle of State Department papers more than one hundred years later. On August 5, 1975, President Gerald Ford signed a law restoring the citizenship of the South's greatest hero.

10. THE MISSING PILGRIM The first summer in Plymouth, young John Billington "lost himself in the woods," as Pilgrim leader William Bradford put it. The problem with rescuing him was that he was last seen near the domain of the unfriendly Narraganset Indians. There were only thirty-two adult male Pilgrims who had survived the winter. Sending an armed rescue party could leave the colony vulnerable to attack. Ten men were sent to search the coast in a shallop. After two menacing encounters with Indians, they came upon the chief of the Nausets, followed by one hundred braves. On the shoulder of one of them was John Billington, who, it turned out, had been kidnapped and passed from tribe to tribe. The chief was rewarded with a knife and the Pilgrims headed back to their fledgling colony.

11.   A BEWILDERING QUESTION Aging Daniel Boone was asked if he'd ever been lost in the woods. "Well," he replied, "once I was *bewildered* for three days."

Fake Burials and Other Grave Situations

1.   A HERO COMES HOME—AFTER ONE HUNDRED YEARS Revolutionary War sea captain John Paul Jones, the man who had "not yet begun to fight," went off to Europe after his American exploits and was feted from Paris to Moscow. When he died in Paris in 1792, the French National Assembly sent a deputation to his funeral. He was buried in the Protestant cemetery in a coffin made of lead, a substance that would help protect his remains in case the U.S. decided to reclaim its famous veteran.

However, no one was very interested in Jones's body until one hundred years after his death. By then the exact whereabouts of his grave had been forgotten. A six-year search ensued, and in 1905 his body was located and escorted to Annapolis, Maryland, by a U.S. naval squadron. In 1913, Jones's coffin was placed in a crypt of the chapel of the U.S. Naval Academy in an elaborate and ornamental tomb that cost Congress seventy-five thousand dollars.

2.   SMITHSON GOES TO THE SMITHSONIAN James Smithson, an English scientist, had never even set foot in America when he bequeathed his entire estate of over $500,000 to the United States. It was used to found the Smithsonian Institution, which Smithson finally visited eighty years after his death. When he died in 1820, he was in Genoa, Italy, and was buried in the English cemetery on a hill overlooking the harbor. As the years went on, the Italians began quarrying the hill to fill in the harbor. The cemetery was in danger of caving in, but the English couldn't do anything about it because, as it turned out, they owned the surface of the hill but not the ground underneath. Finally, on December 31, 1903, Smithson's grave was opened and his skeleton, "in perfect condition," was transferred to a metal casket and shipped to Washington. In 1904 a

troop of cavalry and a marine band escorted the body to a new sarcophagus behind an iron railing in the institution he founded.

3. THEIR CASKETS WERE FILLED WITH SAND Joseph Smith founded the Mormon Church in 1830 but was unable to find a peaceful home for his followers. Public hostility kept him on the move until 1844, when he and his brother Hyrum were murdered by an Illinois mob. The bodies of the slain brothers were viewed by twenty thousand Mormons. Crowds filed into the cemetery to watch their coffins lowered into the ground, but the burial was actually a charade. The pine boxes contained bags of sand. The Mormons feared the graves would be desecrated, so the Smiths were buried during the night in the basement of Nauvoo House, a Mormon hotel. Broken stone and rubbish were piled over the spot. Joseph Smith's wife, Emma, later had the bodies exhumed and buried at their summer cottage.

4. WITH HIS BOOTS OFF When Robert E. Lee died, the local undertaker was in a quandary. His stock of coffins had drifted off in a flood. Two volunteers had braved the current in a small boat and managed to retrieve one, but it turned out to be too short for Lee. His body could just barely be stuffed in and his boots had to be removed. So Robert E. Lee, the great Civil War hero, was buried in his socks—a fact that was kept quiet until two generations after his death in 1870.

5. HE SAW LINCOLN IN THE TWENTIETH CENTURY When Abraham Lincoln died in 1865, more than one million people viewed his body as his funeral train stopped in major cities on its twenty-day trip to Springfield, Illinois. He was buried in Oak Ridge Cemetery, but in 1876 robbers broke into his tomb, so the Lincoln Monument Association decided to hide his body. For two years, unbeknownst to the public, his tomb was devoid of a coffin, which was kept under loose boards in a dark passageway behind the catacombs. In the next twenty-three years, his body was moved seventeen times until a decision was made to build a new, larger tomb where, on September 26, 1901, Lincoln's coffin was embedded in steel and concrete six feet beneath the floor, so that it could not be disturbed again. But first the casket was opened for the last time. Those who viewed the body included a young boy who could grow up saying he saw Lincoln in the twentieth century.

6. EXHUMING A PATRIOT The British were astounded to find the body of Dr. Joseph Warren among the dead at Bunker Hill.

Warren was the president of the Provincial Congress and a leading spokesman for the colonial cause. A British officer in charge of burying the dead after the battle reported that he "stuffed the scoundrel in a hole with one of his fellows and there may he and his seditious principles remain." There they did not rest, however. When the British left Boston, Warren's body was exhumed and reburied with masonic funeral rites.

7.   A SECRET BURIAL PLOT After killing Abraham Lincoln, John Wilkes Booth fled south and was shot at night in a Virginia tobacco shed. His body was brought back to Washington, but Secretary of War Edwin Stanton, aware of all the emotion of the time, wanted to prevent Booth from becoming a Civil War symbol. So he ordered a fake burial at sea. While crowds watched, a shroud weighted down by cannonballs was rowed out to sea and lowered overboard.

Meanwhile, the actual body was secretly buried under the warehouse floor of a Washington arsenal where felons often found their final resting spot. Three and a half years later, the body was quietly dug up at night, transferred to an unmarked pine box, and taken to a funeral home behind Ford's Theatre. There it was turned over to Booth's brother Edwin, a famous actor, who had it reinterred in the family plot in a Baltimore cemetery.

Royal Encounters

1.   KING KALAKAUA IS CAREFUL On December 18, 1874, President Ulysses S. Grant received the first reigning king to visit the U.S.—King Kalakaua of Hawaii, dubbed the "Merry Monarch" because he had brought back the hula and other native customs suppressed by the missionaries. King Kalakaua wanted to negotiate a trade treaty to allow Hawaiian sugar to enter the U.S. on favorable terms, so he decided on an American tour. When Grant gave a state dinner for him, the Hawaiian had three of his royal retinue stand behind him. One carefully examined each dish before passing it to the king.

2.   THE TSAR'S SON ON A BUFFALO HUNT Grand Duke Alexis, the son of Tsar Alexander I of Russia, sailed for America in September 1871 escorted by a Russian battle fleet. He was feted in New York and Washington, but what the young grand duke really wanted to do was to go west and hunt buffalo. General Philip Sheridan,

General George Armstrong Custer, top army brass, and Buffalo Bill Cody were recruited to help set up a royal hunt.

The grand duke arrived on a special train and was given Cody's celebrated buffalo-hunting horse, Buckskin Joe, to ride. When the first herd was sighted, the duke emptied his pistol at twenty feet and missed. Buffalo Bill gave him a second pistol but the result was the same. Finally, Buffalo Bill lent him "my old reliable 'Lucretia' " and maneuvered the duke's horse to within ten feet of the herd. "Now is your time," he told the duke, who fired, felled a buffalo, "dropped his gun on the ground, and commenced waving his hat." He then cut off the tail as a souvenir, and sat on the carcass waving the dripping tail and cheering. The feat was celebrated with champagne all around.

3.   OUT OF THE MOUTHS OF BABES "How is everything," the Prince of Wales asked seven-year-old Henry Ford II on a 1924 visit to the Michigan home of the Edsel Fords. "Well," said young Henry, pointing to his brother Benson, "he just threw up, and Grandmother is hiding behind the screen." The Ford household was in a tizzy because the prince had arrived an hour and a half late. Grandmother Clay had run off to the nursery, never guessing that would be the prince's first stop.

4.   A KISS FROM KING GEORGE III John Adams had the touchy assignment of representing the new United States of America as its first minister to Great Britain. King George had been surly about the loss of his colonies, saying that he was better off rid of them. When it came time for Adams's wife, Abigail, to be presented to the king, she was understandably nervous. She removed her white gloves expecting a cold formal handshake, but found that the gracious King George "saluted my left cheek."

5.   THE INDIAN PRINCESS AND QUEEN ANNE Pocahontas arrived in England on June 12, 1616, with her husband, John Rolfe, her infant son, and an Indian retinue of ten that was intended to show her status as an Indian princess. One brave had instructions from her father, Chief Powhatan, to count the number of Englishmen he saw; he started making notches in a stick but soon gave up. Pocahontas was presented to Queen Anne as the savior of Jamestown and daughter of Powhatan. When Sir Walter Raleigh met her, he knelt and kissed her hand, commenting on his joy in meeting so beautiful a princess.

6. A NAVAL HERO MAKES GOOD In 1780 Revolutionary War hero John Paul Jones found himself wooed by royalty all across Europe. The French, his natural fans since they were at odds with the British, had helped outfit his famous ship, the *Bonhomme Richard,* and had cheered when it was victorious at sea. When Jones arrived in Paris, Marie Antoinette presented him with a fob chain and seal and King Louis XVI gave him a gold-hilted sword. On a visit to Denmark, King Christian awarded him an annual pension of fifteen hundred crowns but never actually paid it. Catherine the Great gave Jones his best offer—a rear admiral's commission in the Russian navy, a post he held from 1788–89.

7. A ROYAL FLUSH Buffalo Bill Cody led his Wild West Show to England in 1887, complete with cowboys, Indians, horses, and buffalo. Queen Victoria, who hadn't attended any public entertainment in twenty-five years, traveled to view a special performance on May 11. She liked it so much she requested another on June 20. The highlight, as always, was the Indians' attack on the Deadwood stage and the cavalry's last-minute rescue. To ride in the stage was the ultimate privilege. On this occasion, seating went to four kings—of Denmark, Greece, Belgium, and Saxony—and a future king—the Prince of Wales. They were driven by Buffalo Bill himself.

Afterward, the prince, who had learned about poker, told Cody, "Colonel, you never held four kings like these before." Cody replied, "I've held four kings but four kings and the Prince of Wales makes a royal flush, such as no man ever held before."

8. THE WRATH OF THE ROYAL POODLE Twenty-five-inch-tall General Tom Thumb took London by storm in 1844 with a stage show that included impersonations of Napoleon, Goliath, and Cupid. Queen Victoria invited him to Buckingham Palace and all went splendidly—until it came time to depart. Etiquette required that a visitor never show his back to the Queen. So little Tom Thumb, along with his sponsor, showman Phineas T. Barnum, began to back out of the room. Tom, with his miniature legs, was loosing ground, so he took to running a short distance and then turning around and walking backward again. According to Barnum, this excited "the Queen's favorite poodle-dog, and he vented his displeasure by barking so sharply as to startle the General from his propriety." Set upon by the poodle, Tom Thumb, "with his little cane commenced an attack on the poodle, and a funny fight ensued, which renewed and increased the merriment of the royal party." The queen sent her apologies for her poodle's manners.

9.   OUR FAVORITE MARQUIS The Marquis de Lafayette returned to America in 1824 at the invitation of Congress and President Monroe. Lafayette had been twenty when he first arrived to fight with George Washington. Nearly fifty years later, he was the country's guest and the country could not do enough for him. His visit began with a flower-strewn parade up Broadway in New York and ended more than a year later after a tour to all twenty-four states.

Lafayette's secretary collapsed under the strain of countless banquets, speeches, official functions, and toasts, but the aging hero seemed to thrive on everything, even an unexpected shipwreck on the Ohio River. Congress voted him $200,000 as recompense for expenses he incurred as a volunteer in the Revolution. He was also awarded a township of twenty-four thousand acres in Florida. After a mammoth farewell reception, Lafayette finally headed back to France in September 1825. The U.S. put a forty-four-gun frigate at his disposal for the trip home so that Lafayette could travel in style and have room to load all his gifts, including a live alligator which he had stored in the East Room of the White House.

PART XII

How It Happened

Playing Cards

1. J. P. MORGAN PLAYS SOLITAIRE In 1895 a financial crisis loomed. The gold standard, which President Grover Cleveland firmly backed, required the government to redeem U.S. securities in gold, but a run on gold was threatening the government's dwindling supply. Cleveland sought help from Congress. Meanwhile, the Treasury Department contacted America's most powerful banker, J. Pierpont Morgan, in New York.

Arriving in Washington, Morgan was told that the president wouldn't see him. Cleveland, a Democrat, didn't want to be associated with eastern Republican bankers. "I have come to Washington to see the President," Morgan stated in his deliberate way, "and I am going to stay here until I see him."

He went to a hotel and settled down to his favorite pastime—solitaire. He liked to arrange his cards methodically. Meanwhile, the government supply of gold coin got down to $9 million and a $10-million note was about to be presented for redemption. Congress refused to act. The government was about to run out of gold.

The president's call interrupted Morgan's solitaire and the financier, whose credit was better than that of the U.S. government, put together a syndicate that raised $450 million.

2. VANDERBILT PLAYS WHIST Cornelius Vanderbilt was questioned by a committee of the New York legislature about his railroad manipulations. The commodore claimed he knew nothing of what happened. "I was not there, gentlemen," Vanderbilt, with the utmost aplomb, told the astonished legislators, "I was home playing a rubber of whist, and I never allow anything to interfere with me when I am playing that game. It requires as you know undivided attention."

3. FRANKLIN SHUFFLES THE DECK Benjamin Franklin loved to play cards but felt guilty about wasting his time. He managed to rationalize his habit by telling himself that his soul was immortal and, since he had all eternity, he wasn't really squandering his earthly hours. "Being, like other reasonable creatures, satisfied with a small reason, when it is in favor of doing what I have a mind to do, I shuffle the cards again and begin another game," he explained.

4. DEAD IN DEADWOOD Most people rushed to Deadwood in the Dakota Territory for gold. But in the summer of 1876, Wild Bill Hickok ignored mining and settled down to gambling.

On August 2 he arose at his usual hour of noon, attended to some routine chores, and by three P.M. was at his regular place of business, the No. 10 Saloon. He had his first drink of the day. It was also his last.

He went to join three friends in a poker game. It was Hickok's firm policy always to sit with back against the wall, but Captain Frank Massey, a Missouri River boat pilot, insisted on Hickok's customary seat, saying, "Nobody is going to shoot you in the back."

The play began. Hickok was soon cleaned out and had to borrow fifty dollars in chips from the bartender to stay in the game. It was at this point that Jack McCall, a twenty-five-year-old drifter and aspiring gunfighter, entered the saloon, downed a drink at the bar, and then walked up behind Hickok, who had just been dealt a pair of aces, a pair of eights, and a queen.

McCall fired once with his .45 Colt, shooting Hickok through the head, the bullet embedding itself in Captain Massey's arm. "Take that," said McCall, who had no particular grudge against his victim. The thirty-nine-year-old Hickok slumped to the floor clutching his cards. Two pair, aces and eights, are still known among poker players as a dead man's hand.

5.   A BRIDGE FANATIC By the time World War II came around, General Dwight D. Eisenhower had played poker on army bases around the world for thirty years. He was a serious player and a regular winner but finally gave the game up because he sensed resentment among his fellow officers. He then took up bridge and became a fanatic. When the D-Day invasion of Normandy approached, Eisenhower found his best escape from the strain was a game of bridge.

Naked

1.   GLOVES BUT NO FIG LEAVES President Theodore Roosevelt invited French Ambassador Jules Jusserand along on one of his "point-to-point" walks. What made these walks legendary was that TR insisted no obstacle be circumvented. Walkers had to go through or over everything. Thus, when they came to the Potomac River, they stripped and were about to plunge in when the president, noticing that Jusserand still had on his white gloves, said, "Mr. Ambassador, have you forgotten your gloves?" "We might meet some ladies," was the French ambassador's reply.

2. NO COMMON MODESTY George Washington was upset by the conduct of the untrained militia and issued orders that he did not "mean to discourage the practice of Bathing" but many men had lost "all sense of decency & common Modesty" and are "running about Naked upon ye Bridge." Not only that, there were "ladies of the first fashion" passing over the bridge and the men acted as if "they meant to glory in their shame."

3. NATIVE ATTIRE Christopher Columbus liked the Caribbean natives he found. He called them Indians and thought "they would make good servants" and "could be turned into Christians without difficulty." He also noted that "men and women went quite naked."

4. THE JOY OF NAKEDNESS In London, Benjamin Franklin liked to get up early and sit in his bedroom "without any clothes whatever, half an hour or an hour according to the season, either reading or writing."

5. RUNNING FOR HIS LIFE John Colter went to the Pacific with Lewis and Clark, trapped furs in the Rockies, and discovered the famous Yellowstone geysers and hot springs. While out trapping he was captured by the notoriously cruel Blackfeet Indians. He expected torture and a slow death, but instead the Blackfeet surprised Colter by stripping him naked and pointing to the prairie. He started to walk. An old Indian impatiently signaled him to speed up. Then he saw the braves discarding leggings and excess clothing and realized that he was about to race for his life. With war whoops and spears a large group of Blackfeet came after him.

THE TRAPPER AND THE INDIANS

Trapper John Colter, captured by the fierce Blackfeet Indians, was stripped and given a chance to run for his life. Here he turns and surprises one of his pursuers, whereupon he wrestles away the Indians' spear.
DENVER PUBLIC LIBRARY, WESTERN HISTORY DEPARTMENT

Colter grew weak after a couple of miles and blood gushed from his nose. One Indian finally got close and attacked him with a spear. Colter grabbed at the spear and broke off the iron head as the Indian lunged. He killed the Indian, grabbed his blanket, and ran on as he could hear the shouts behind him. When he reached the Madison River, he hid in a beaver hut. He could hear the frustrated Indians above him.

At night he swam the river and then, still naked except for the blanket which he used at night, walked three hundred miles to Manuel's Fort. It took him eleven days to reach safety and by then he was so emaciated that nobody recognized him.

6. THE PRESIDENT IN THE BUFF In the summer months President John Quincy Adams liked to swim in the Potomac for exercise. On one occasion in June 1825, Adams intended to swim across the Potomac and back. Antoine, his servant, was rowing behind him in a boat when a breeze came up. Antoine lost control of the boat and jumped out. Adams made it to the shore opposite the White House and was left "sitting naked basking on the bank" while Antoine went for a carriage. Adams arrived back at the White House six hours later and found that no one had missed him.

7. MARY LINCOLN'S TROUBLES After her husband was assassinated, Mary Lincoln became increasingly unstable. Her son Tad lovingly took care of her, but when Tad died in 1871 she was bereft. Her persecution complex became so extreme she could not enter a public room without trembling in fear. In March 1875, she went to Chicago to visit her eldest son, Robert, but refused to stay at his home. Distressed, he took a hotel room next to hers and employed a woman to stay with her as much as possible. At night she'd tap on his door, afraid people were trying to rob and poison her. Once, he found her wandering nude in the hall. When he tried to help her back into her room, she screamed, "You are going to murder me."

Uplifting Moments: People Who Were Carried

1. PROSTRATE IN PARIS When Charles A. Lindbergh landed in Paris after his historic nonstop flight from New York, *The Spirit of*

St. Louis was surrounded by thousands of wildly excited Frenchmen who had broken through police barricades. Lindbergh tried to step out but "dozens of hands took hold of me . . . I found myself lying in a prostrate position, up on top of the crowd, in the center of an ocean of heads that extended as far out into the darkness as I could see." A reporter grabbed Lindbergh's helmet and donned it. Someone shouted, "There is Lindbergh," and the crowd mistakenly started carrying the reporter off to the official reception committee, enabling some French pilots to come to Lindbergh's rescue.

2.   OVER THE THRESHOLD When Thomas Jefferson returned to America after several years in Europe, he rode to Monticello in a carriage with his daughters. As he neared his house, all his slaves rushed down the hill, unhitched his carriage, and pulled it up by hand.

Patsy, one of Jefferson's daughters, described what happened: "Such a scene I never witnessed in my life. . . . When the door of the carriage was opened they received him in their arms and bore him to the house, crowding around and kissing his hands and feet— some blubbering and crying—others laughing."

3.   ALOFT IN CONGRESS Seventy-three-year-old Thaddeus Stevens was determined to see his bitter foe Andrew Johnson impeached—even if it took his dying breath. Stevens was fatally ill and so feeble he had to be carried to his seat in the House of Representatives by two boys. Nonetheless, he spearheaded the impeachment vote through the House on May 16, 1868, but then it was up to the Senate to convict Johnson on the impeachment charges.

When the final vote came, the House of Representatives adjourned and marched in a long procession, two by two, to the Senate chamber to witness the event. Old Thaddeus Stevens was a conspicuous figure as he was carried in his chair high above the others in the procession. The Senate failed to uphold the charges by one vote.

4.   THROUGH THE STREETS OF PHILADELPHIA Benjamin Franklin, ailing and in his eighties, attended the Constitutional Convention infrequently. But when he did, he traveled through the streets of Philadelphia in a sedan chair which he had brought from France. It was carried by four prisoners borrowed from jail.

5.   DYING AT THE ALAMO Inside the Alamo, Colonel William Barrett Travis drew a line in the dirt with his sword and asked that all those "determined to stay here and die with me" cross the line.

Jim Bowie, dying of tuberculosis, asked to be carried across in his cot as he was unable to move himself.

6. CARRIED OUT OF THE PRESIDENT'S OFFICE One day when Mary Lincoln was upset, she rushed into her husband's office at the White House and interrupted an important meeting with a torrent of words. Calmly, the six-feet-four-inch president arose, picked up his five-feet-two-inch wife, and carried her out of the office. He then returned, locking the door behind him, and continued the conversation as if nothing had happened.

7. CATCHING THE SUNSET WITH CHURCHILL When President Franklin D. Roosevelt and Prime Minister Winston Churchill finished their wartime conference at Casablanca, Churchill insisted they go to Marrakesh, which was famous, he said, for fortune-tellers, snake charmers, and brothels. It was a 150-mile drive across the desert with U.S. troops guarding the road and fighters overhead. When they reached the villa where they were staying in Marrakesh, Churchill climbed six stories to the roof to see the sun setting on the snow-capped peaks and urged FDR to join him. Since the crippled Roosevelt couldn't navigate the steps, his masseur and Secret Service chief made a human chair and carried him up the winding staircase to the roof, his limp legs dangling uselessly.

On Foot

1. WALKING TO THE HOLY LAND It was fourteen hundred miles from Iowa City to the Mormon settlement in the valley of the Great Salt Lake, and in June 1856, four hundred Mormons set out to walk the whole way pulling their belongings on handcarts. The brethren were told it would not be "an easy task," but "to start with faith, trusting in Israel's God." One seventy-three-year-old woman walked every step of the way. On September 26 the foot-weary Mormons emerged from Emigration Canyon and saw the great Utah valley and the holy city before them. The entire population was lined up to welcome them, offering cool fruit and crying hosannas. The handcart pioneers were the first of thousands to walk the Mormon Trail.

2. JEFFERSON SETS A DEMOCRATIC PACE Newly elected president, Thomas Jefferson, a believer in the "leveling principles of

democracy," was staying at Conrad and McMunn's boardinghouse on New Jersey Avenue in Washington, D.C. He disdained the fancy carriages and horses that outgoing President John Adams had left for him at the White House stables and decided to walk from his lodgings to the Capitol for the inaugural ceremony.

Afterward he walked back to Conrad and McMunn's escorted by many members of Congress. That evening he dined there as usual, but his fellow boarders felt the new president was carrying his leveling principles too far when he insisted on taking his old seat at the foot of the dining-room table.

3.   THE LONGEST YARDS Though FDR's polio-stricken legs were totally useless, he felt it politically important to stand and appear to walk. Working with his son Elliott and a therapist, he developed a technique of leaning on his son's arm and balancing with a cane. Thus supported, he would swing one braced leg into place and shift his weight forward to take a "step." In 1924 he had to use crutches to propel himself fifteen feet to the podium of the Democratic Convention to nominate Al Smith for president. But in 1928, when he again nominated Smith, he managed to "walk," seemingly normally, gripping Elliott's arm and throwing his head back with a huge smile. It was his first attempt to walk in public. Eleanor knitted nervously in the balcony throughout his speech.

4.   A BOY SCOUT HIKE In 1913 Buffalo Bill's Wild West Show was seized by creditors and all the props were auctioned off. A troop of Chicago Boy Scouts who had been part of the show was stranded in Denver. From August until October they marched home, giving exhibition drills along the way to raise money for food.

5.   A STAIRCASE OF SNOW One of the obstacles Alaskan gold prospectors faced on the way to the gold fields was the steep Chilkoot Pass. In summer they could zigzag up its slopes, but in winter they had to line up single file to climb twelve hundred steps cut out of the frozen snow. The slowest prospector set the pace. If anyone dropped out to rest, often he had to wait hours to find a gap in the line so that he could resume his climb. Carrying up a season's supplies might necessitate a dozen trips up the icy staircase.

6.   THE SECRET SERVICE HAD TO SCURRY Harry Truman was seldom tired even after a sixteen- to seventeen-hour day. As president he arose at five-thirty, shaved, dressed, and then tiptoed downstairs. He scanned the newspapers, then at seven set off for a brisk two-mile walk. He carried the gold-headed cane given to him

by his World War I buddies from Battery D and tipped his hat to early risers along F Street. His normal pace was 120 steps to the minute, which made his Secret Service detail scurry to keep up.

Out in the Cold

1. WASHINGTON'S ICY DIP When he was in his early twenties, George Washington was returning from a military mission to the Ohio Valley and he got caught in a blizzard. He and his guide, wary of unfriendly Indians, could not afford to be deterred by the weather and they traveled all night. By the time they reached the Allegheny River, they were exhausted but determined to cross. However, the water near the shore was frozen. Blocks of ice floated in the middle of the river.

George Washington's most treacherous crossing may have been on a makeshift raft across the ice-clogged Allegheny. This illustration depicts the young military man in remarkably dry clothing just before he was thrown into the icy river.
BOSTON PUBLIC LIBRARY PRINT COLLECTION

The two men built a raft and began navigating through the icy river. Washington was steering when his pole got caught and he was thrown headfirst into the water. He was able to grab on to the raft as it went by. Fortunately, there was an island in the middle of the river, and the two men waded ashore. Washington spent the night beating his arms and pounding his feet to keep from freezing to death. In the morning the Allegheny was frozen solid and they were able to walk to the other shore.

2.   THE COLDEST INAUGURATION DAY On March 4, 1873, the day President-elect Ulysses S. Grant was to be sworn in, the temperature hovered around zero; sleet and snow were driven by a bitter wind.

Grant rode to the Capitol in his own open four-in-hand carriage, muffled to the ears in a beaver overcoat. He wore a high silk hat, but every head was uncovered for the oath, which was administered outside on the Capitol steps. Afterward, Grant went through the ritual of reading his speech in the numbing cold. The parade back to the White House passed gaily decorated stands, all deserted. The valves of the musical instruments stuck, and several cadets in the line of march fainted.

3.   A CHILLY WEDDING NIGHT After saying "I do" on New Year's Day, 1772, Thomas Jefferson took his new bride, Martha, to Monticello. It was a long drive from her father's house. Snow was twenty-four inches deep in some parts. Traveling was so slow that by the time the newlyweds arrived, the servants were asleep and the fires out.

Undaunted but chilly, Jefferson and Martha decided not to wake anyone up. They found a bottle of wine to warm their limbs. In high spirits they went to one of the finished rooms of the still uncompleted house.

4.   A COLD AUTUMN IN NEW YORK In 1944 Franklin Roosevelt was campaigning for reelection and the country was concerned that the aging, ailing president would be unable to live out a fourth term. To defy the rumors, which were not far from the truth, FDR broke his wartime security policy and announced he'd ride in an open car through all five boroughs of New York City, a fifty-mile trip, rain or shine.

The president was greeted by millions—and by a driving rain. Roosevelt got so cold that he was secretly taken to heated garages along the parade route. There the crippled president was lifted from the car, laid on blankets, stripped, toweled dry, and redressed. After drinking a shot of brandy, he was lifted back into the car.

5.   A BULLY TIME Theodore Roosevelt's good humor survived even the most chilling circumstances. Once, on an excursion from his ranch in the Dakota Territory, he encountered a thermometer that "was twenty-six degrees below zero . . . we had no food for twelve hours. I became numbed, and before I was aware of it had frozen my face, one foot, both knees, and one hand." TR was undaunted.

To him it was all an adventure. "Luckily," he concluded, "I reached the ranch before serious damage was done."

Up in Smoke

1. FIRE AT THE ALAMO When the Mexicans stormed the Alamo during Texas's struggle for independence, they took no prisoners. The few defenders who survived were rounded up and shot. General Santa Anna ordered his five-thousand-man Mexican army to build a huge funeral pyre of wood and dried branches. The bodies of the Texans—including Colonel Travis, Davy Crockett, and Jim Bowie—were put between the layers of wood. Just before dusk, General Santa Anna ordered the torch applied to the pyre.

2. FOR WHOM THE BELLS TOLLED As British General Howe readied his troops to attack the Americans on Bunker Hill, he ordered Charlestown, across the Charles River from Boston, to be set on fire. He wanted to prevent snipers from shooting out of the windows into the flank of his army. The British navy started the fire by shooting hollowed-out cannonballs filled with hot pitch. Soon wharves and houses were ablaze. Priceless treasures such as the Mather library were destroyed. As the flames reached the church steeple, the weakened timbers set the bells tolling until they fell clanging into the deserted streets.

3. "INSTANTANEOUS CONFLAGRATION" Dolley Madison had fled only hours before an unwelcome guest appeared at the White House. It was British Admiral Cockburn, who was leading the force that was invading Washington during the War of 1812. He broke the lock on the front door and entered the house, which Dolley had spent twelve thousand dollars on to decorate. After taking a yellow cushion from the Ladies' Drawing Room as a souvenir, he ordered his troops to pile the president's furniture in the East Room. Windows were knocked out. Fifty of his men took positions outside the perimeter of the White House. Each was carrying a long pole with a ball of oil-soaked rags on the end. Ceremoniously, a torch was passed from man to man until every pole had burst into flames at the end. Then the command was given. The poles were thrown through the broken windows like spears. "Instantaneous conflagration" was how one spectator described the result.

4. THE FIRE MARSHAL TAKES CHARGE Vice-President Calvin Coolidge was living in the Willard Hotel when a fire drove the guests out. Thinking that the fire was over, Coolidge tried to go back up the stairs, but a fire marshal stopped him and asked, "Who are you?" "I'm the Vice-President," Coolidge replied. This seemed to satisfy the marshal and he let Coolidge proceed up the staircase, but then he had second thoughts.

"What are you Vice-President of?" he demanded.

"I am the Vice-President of the United States," was the response.

"Come right down," the marshal said, "I thought you were Vice-President of the hotel."

It Happened While the Band Played

1. THE BAND SAID IT ALL The British surrender at Yorktown ended the American Revolution. The unthinkable had happened to the mighty British Empire. As their soldiers dejectedly came out of their fortifications to stack their weapons, their band played "The World Turned Upside Down."

2. "GRAND MUSICK" After the battle at Lexington, eight hundred British Redcoats continued on to Concord. Warned of the British advance, about one hundred Concord minutemen marched out of town to meet them, but when they saw such a large force approaching, they realized they'd made a mistake and did an abrupt about-face. That left the two forces marching in the same direction at the same time, both with "Droms and fifes agoing." Together they "had grand musick," as one minuteman put it. Except for a skirmish at Concord Bridge, the minutemen avoided a confrontation at Concord. Instead, they waited until the British marched back to Boston and peppered them from behind walls and trees.

3. A HYMN OF FIRE AND DEATH At dawn on March 6, 1836, the bands of General Santa Anna's Mexican army assembled outside the Alamo and began playing the *Degüello*—a stirring hymn of fire and death. The final assault on the Alamo was about to begin and the *Degüello* symbolized total destruction of the enemy.

4. THEIR FIGHT SONG When Commodore Oliver Hazard Perry attacked the British on Lake Erie in the War of 1812, he sought to inspire his men by raising a blue flag that said DON'T GIVE UP THE SHIP, a famous cry from an earlier battle. Not to be outdone, the British rallied their men to the tune of "Rule Britannia," struck up by a British brass band on the *Detroit*. Perry won the battle and reported his victory with the famous words, "We have met the enemy and they are ours."

5. "AUTUMN" ON THE *TITANIC* While the lifeboats were loading women and children from the stricken *Titanic*, the ship's band played ragtime. The rescued passengers could hear the music floating toward them in the darkness. They watched as people lined the decks and the porthole lights blazed. When the water came over the deck, bandmaster Hartley tapped his violin. The ragtime ceased. As the ship tilted and went under, the band played the Episcopal hymn "Autumn."

6. MAKING SURE THE CHIEF IS HAILED Physically unimpressive, President James K. Polk sometimes went unnoticed when he entered a reception. His wife, Sarah, decided to arrange for the marine band to play "Hail to the Chief," an old Scottish anthem, to announce the president's arrival. The tradition has lasted to this day.

7. MUSIC TO HIS EARS Besieged in Vermont during the Revolution, British General Simon Fraser thought defeat was certain until suddenly he heard loud drums, oboes, brasses, and roaring voices singing German hymns. Help, in the form of German mercenary reinforcements, was audibly on the way.

8. AN IRISH QUICKSTEP When George Armstrong Custer's men marched off to the fight at Little Big Horn, a band, posted on a knoll, struck up "Garry Owen," the old Irish quickstep that the 7th Cavalry had adopted as its regimental marching tune. Private Goldin remembered a hearty cheer as they marched off, the band's notes "still ringing in our ears as we left the river bottom and the band was lost to sight." It was the last music most of the men of the 7th Cavalry would ever hear.

9. CAPTURING DIXIE On the morning after Robert E. Lee's surrender at Appomattox Court House, President Lincoln celebrated by throwing open the White House gates, which had been kept tightly shut during the war. Crowds swarmed on the grounds, to

the dismay of the Metropolitan Police, and a band played on the portico.

From the window above, Lincoln gave a brief speech and then requested a song. "I have always thought 'Dixie' one of the best tunes I have ever heard. . . . I insisted yesterday that we fairly captured it. I presented that question to the Attorney-General, and he gave his legal opinion that it is our lawful prize. I now request the band to favor me with its performance."

10. A SURPRISE WEDDING MARCH In 1886, after President Grover Cleveland announced his engagement to pretty Frances Folsom, who was thirty years his junior, he came to visit her in New York and to review a Memorial Day parade. Cleveland was stationed at the reviewing stand on Fifth Avenue. Miss Folsom, who was staying two blocks away, stepped out onto a balcony and waved her handkerchief. When her fiancé saw her, he tipped his hat. The crowds went wild with enthusiasm.

The Twenty-second Regimental Band passed Cleveland's stand and suddenly changed its tune to play the wedding march. The next band responded to the resultant cheers with another marital song. Another played a new song from Gilbert and Sullivan's *The Mikado*, then playing in town, whose words went, "I think you had better succumb—For he's going to marry Yum-Yum!"

11. BY THE ROCKETS' RED GLARE At 8:00 A.M. on Sunday, December 7, 1941, the navy band at Pearl Harbor started playing the national anthem while the color guard stood at attention for the morning flag raising. Planes were seen diving in the distance but they were thought to be part of a drill. Then a Japanese plane dropped a torpedo at the battleship *Arizona* and flew low over the navy group. Bandleader Oden McMillan kept conducting. Bullets fired by the Japanese rear gunner splattered around them and the flag that had just been raised was torn. Not until "The Star-Spangled Banner" was finished did they all run for cover. Miraculously, no one was hurt.

Occasions for a Song

1. TRYING TO OVERCOME In 1963 Birmingham, Alabama, was a tough steel town, the South's strongest bastion of segregation.

Martin Luther King, Jr., decided to use it to dramatize the civil rights situation. When protest marches only resulted in filled jails, he decided to launch a controversial attack.

On May 2, one thousand black schoolchildren took to the streets singing the Gospel song "We Shall Overcome."

Police chief Eugene "Bull" Conner lost his patience. The children were attacked by police dogs and blasts from fire hoses. Still singing, they were taken off to jail.

The next day the children marched again while the TV cameras ran, and Birmingham became a national spectacle. A week later a negotiated settlement was reached and Birmingham was desegregated.

2. SHE WAS "A SOLDIER OF THE CROSS" Only a few determined drinkers were at the bar on the morning of December 27, 1900, when temperance leader Carry Nation invaded Wichita's finest saloon, the Annex at the Hotel Carey, so called because saloons were illegal in Kansas.

Mrs. Nation wore a bonnet and carried a club. Concealed in her voluminous black alpaca dress were her "smashers," some of the "nicest rocks, round with sharp edges," which she let go as customers dived behind the fifty-foot curved and polished bar. Glasses and bottles shattered. A fifteen-hundred-dollar mirror, a crystal chandelier, and the glass covering a huge nude painting of Cleopatra were all ruined by her smashers and her club. "Peace on earth, good will to men," she shouted.

When arrested, she began to sing. All the way to the police station she went through choruses of "Am I a Soldier of the Cross?"

3. OF LIBERTY SHE SANG Escaped slave Harriet Tubman earned her nickname "Moses" by helping blacks flee to freedom on the underground railroad. During the Civil War she spied for the Union army, scouting Confederate positions disguised as a hobbling old woman. In South Carolina, her information led to a surprise Union attack on two camps—and the freeing of eight hundred slaves. Glad to be freed, the blacks were nonetheless wary of the Union soldiers and flatly refused to board "Lincoln's gunboats," which were supposed to transport them to safety at a Union camp. Colonel Montgomery turned to Tubman and said, "Moses, you'll have to give 'em a song." Improvising quickly, Tubman sang:

> *Come along! Come along! Don't be alarm.*
> *Uncle Sam's rich enough to give us all a farm!*

Come along! Come along! Don't be a fool!
Uncle Sam's rich enough to send us all to school!

The blacks heard her musical message and soon headed for the boats. "I never seen such a sight," Tubman recalled. ". . . Bags on their shoulders, baskets on their heads. . . . Pigs squealing, chickens screaming, young ones squallin'."

4. A DEATHLY ROCK AND ROLL When Buffalo Bill's Wild West Show first sailed to England in 1887, the Indian death song was frequently heard on the boat. The Indians, who numbered ninety-seven in a troupe of about two hundred, had a superstition that those of their race who crossed the ocean would waste away and die. Stormy seas hit and everyone except Annie Oakley became "as sick as a cow with a hollow horn," as Buffalo Bill phrased it. Convinced that their superstition was right, the Indians sang their death song. All, however, survived the passage and even made the trip home safely.

5. "WHOO-PEE" After the battle of San Juan Hill, the members of Colonel Theodore Roosevelt's volunteer regiment sang:

Rough, rough, we're the stuff,
We want to fight and we can't get enough,
Whoo-pee.

Their wish didn't come true. With the end of the San Juan Hill battle, the only real fighting in the war was over.

PART XIII

Crime, Punishment, and the Law

Assassinations That Failed

If you are elected president, the odds are about one in four that somebody will take a shot at you.

1. TWO SHOTS MISFIRE AT CLOSE RANGE Andrew Jackson was crossing the Capitol rotunda leaning on the arm of his Treasury secretary when he heard a gun behind him snap and misfire. As he turned, his would-be assassin pulled out another loaded gun, but its charge also failed to go off. The president set on the man with his cane.

His attacker was Richard Lawrence, an out-of-work housepainter who believed Jackson was a king who had usurped the throne from the rightful ruler, Lawrence's father. Judged insane, he was sentenced to an asylum for life. His prosecutor was Francis Scott Key, who had composed the national anthem. Later, Lawrence's guns were tested and, incredibly, both were shown to be in good working order. Apparently the powder and balls had fallen out in his pocket.

2. "IT TAKES MORE THAN ONE BULLET TO KILL A BULL MOOSE." That was Theodore Roosevelt, the Bull Moose candidate, running for a third term in 1912. Roosevelt had been heading over to a Milwaukee auditorium to make a speech when short, pleasant-looking John Schrank fired a .38 Colt pistol at close range.

The bullet had bored through TR's folded fifty-page speech, punctured his metal eyeglass case, and lodged in his chest. His shirt was soaked with blood, a red puddle formed in his left shoe, but he insisted on giving his fifty-minute speech before leaving for the hospital. When a heckler doubted Roosevelt had been shot, he unbuttoned his vest to show his blood-stained shirt, saying it was "no occasion for any sympathy whatever."

Roosevelt's assailant believed he had acted on instructions from a dream in which the slain President McKinley pointed out TR as his murderer. Schrank aspired to fame and was irate when the doctors decided not to remove the bullet from Roosevelt's rib cage. "That is my bullet . . . and I want it to go to the New-York Historical Society," Schrank said. Judged insane, he was sentenced to an asylum and outlived Roosevelt by twenty-four years. When told of the former president's death, he remarked, "Sorry to learn of it."

Teddy Roosevelt's poor eyesight may have saved his life. His metal eyeglass case, as well as a folded fifty-page speech, helped slow the course of a would-be assassin's bullet.

THEODORE ROOSEVELT COLLECTION, HARVARD COLLEGE LIBRARY

3. "I NO CARE." President-elect Franklin D. Roosevelt had been fishing on Vincent Astor's yacht off Miami. When he came ashore, he decided to schedule an informal speech at a bandstand. It was February 15, 1933.

Two days earlier, immigrant Joseph Zangara, an unemployed bricklayer, had purchased a .32 caliber pistol at a pawn shop. He had thought about taking the bus to Washington to kill Hoover, the cause of the Depression, but decided to shoot FDR since he was in town. "Hoover and Roosevelt—everybody the same," he said.

The crippled Roosevelt spoke from his blue Buick, the top down. Five-feet-tall, 105-pound Zanagara tried to find a way to shoot over the tall crowd, but suddenly Roosevelt's 132-word speech was over. Mayor Anton J. Cermak of Chicago and other dignitaries moved in to greet the president-elect.

Zangara seized a wobbly folding chair and stood on it. He fired five shots. Five bystanders were hit, including Mayor Cermak who fell against FDR's car, fatally shot through the lung. Roosevelt was unscathed. Sentenced to death, Zangara told the judge, "You is crook man, too! Put me in electric chair. I no care." His unclaimed remains are buried in an unmarked prison grave.

4. AN INTERRUPTED NAP Girsel Torresola and Oscar Collazo decided to shoot President Harry S Truman, an act that would probably cost them their lives but which they hoped would dramatize the cause of Puerto Rican nationalism. They bought dress suits and took a train from New York to Washington, D.C. Since they were unfamiliar with the city, they took a cab tour and learned that President Truman was staying in Blair House because the White House was being renovated. They asked the driver to point out Blair House.

Even though it was the first day of November in 1950, the weather in Washington was 84 degrees and humid. At Blair House, Truman went upstairs for his usual after-lunch nap, took off his suit, and stretched out on the bedcover in his underwear. His rest was interrupted at 2:20 when firing erupted as the Puerto Ricans tried to shoot their way in. Truman jumped up and rushed to the bedroom window, which was directly over the front door. A guard yelled, "Dammit! Get back! Get back!"

The raid was over in three minutes—thirty-one shots fired, Collazo wounded, Torresola and one guard dead. Later, Truman told Admiral Leahy, "The only thing you have to worry about is luck. I never had bad luck."

5. AT THE WRONG END OF A GUN—TWICE IN SEVENTEEN DAYS President Gerald Ford was walking toward the office of California Governor Jerry Brown and, as he said, "I was in a good mood, so I started shaking hands. That's when I spotted a woman wearing a bright red dress. . . . I noticed immediately that she had thrust her hand under the arms of the other spectators. I reached down to shake it—and looked into the barrel of a .45 caliber pistol pointed directly at me. I ducked." It was Lynette "Squeaky" Fromme, a twenty-six-year-old disciple of mass killer Charles Manson. Secret Service agent Larry Buendorf grabbed her and wrestled her to the ground.

Seventeen days later Ford was walking from the St. Francis Hotel in San Francisco past a small crowd of spectators. "Bang! I recognized the sound of a shot, and I froze," he said. Agents pushed the president into his waiting car and jumped on top of him. The shot came from a .38 revolver fired by Sara Jane Moore, a middle-aged suburban divorcée who had become involved with political radicals and then turned on them by becoming an FBI informant. She was acting out of desperation and guilt rather than any antagonism to

Ford. In fact, if he had taken any longer in emerging from the hotel, she might not have fired her shot. It was nearly time to pick up her son from school.

Both women are serving life sentences.

6. "JERRY, GET OFF ME. YOU'RE HURTING MY RIBS." So said Ronald Reagan to the Secret Service agent who lay on top of him, sandwiching the president on the transmission hump of his limousine. In two seconds, six shots had been fired by John Hinckley, who had thought that by killing the president he could win the love of young actress Jodie Foster.

Reagan knew that some men in his party were hit but believed himself unscathed. The pain in his ribs, he assumed, was a result of his encounter with the car floor. Then, on the way back to the White House, Reagan coughed up blood. The black limo took off at high speed for the hospital. A bullet had pierced his lung and lodged three inches from his heart. "Honey, I forgot to duck," the president told his wife Nancy before going into a two-hour operation. Hinckley was judged insane and sentenced to a mental hospital.

Assassinations That Succeeded

If you become president, the odds are about one in ten that you will be murdered.

1. MURDER IN THE THEATER Acting was in John Wilkes Booth's blood. His brother and father were famous performers and Booth, though lesser known, had starred in productions at Ford's Theatre. It was like a second home—he even picked up his mail there. A Southern sympathizer who spent the Civil War in the North, Booth wanted to kidnap President Lincoln and take him south as a hostage. For months he plotted but nothing worked.

Then, on the morning of April 14, 1865, he learned that his quarry was coming to Ford's Theatre. His plan changed to murder. He scheduled his attack for 10:15 P.M. At that time he knew there would be only one actor onstage who would give a line that always received a burst of laughter. It would deaden the sound of the shot.

Booth entered a balcony called the Dress Circle. The back hallway to the president's box was temporarily unguarded. He wedged the door to the hallway closed with a board which he had evidently hidden there during the day. Then he looked into Lincoln's box through a little gimlet hole which he had bored in the door. Once he sighted the president sitting in his rocker, he entered, fired a single shot directly into Lincoln's head, and vaulted over the low box railing, landing on the stage twelve feet below.

The one factor Booth hadn't counted on was that Lincoln's box was draped with flags. His spur caught in one of them, disrupting his jump. He tensed and broke a bone in his leg when he landed. Nonetheless, he walked across the stage unmolested and went through a rear door where a stagehand was holding his horse. Mrs. Lincoln's piercing screams brought the doctors in the audience to the president's aid, but they immediately realized there was no hope. Lincoln died the following morning. Booth became the target of an all-out manhunt. He was caught hiding in a Virginia tobacco barn and shot.

2. SHOT IN THE BACK AT A WASHINGTON, D.C., RAILROAD STATION James A. Garfield walked into the Baltimore and Potomac railroad station at nine-thirty on the morning of July 2, 1881. He was catching a train to attend commencement exercises at his alma mater, Williams College. Secretary of State James G. Blaine was at his side when a disgruntled office-seeker, Charles Guiteau, fired at the president from behind. The first shot only grazed his coat, but the second bullet fractured two ribs and lodged somewhere in his lower right side. "My God, what is this?" Garfield cried as he fell to his knees.

Eighty grueling days later he died. Doctors, the best of the day, were unable to locate the bullet and searched for it by poking their unsterilized fingers in the wound. To ease Garfield's suffering when the Washington summer proved sweltering, he was taken in a specially designed railroad car to his house at Elberon on the New Jersey shore. The railroad tracks were extended right up to the front porch so that he wouldn't have to endure a bouncy carriage ride. Garfield died there on September 19. Only with an autopsy were the doctors able to locate the bullet, which had lodged below the pancreas.

3 HE REACHED TO SHAKE THE HAND OF AN ANARCHIST Leon Czolgoz had a handkerchief concealing a pistol in his right hand as he shuffled forward in line to shake hands with President William McKinley. It was September 6, 1901, at the Pan American Exposition in Buffalo, New York. McKinley, thinking Czolgoz's right hand was bandaged, reached to take his good one. Czolgoz then fired two shots from a .32 caliber pistol. "I done my duty," he cried

as he was subdued and beaten. The gentle McKinley implored the crowd not to hurt him.

Czolgoz, a twenty-eight-year-old unemployed laborer, thought himself an anarchist. When a worker from New Jersey killed the king of Italy, Czolgoz had cut out the newspaper account and taken it to bed with him. "I thought it would be a good thing for the country to kill the President," said Czolgoz. McKinley, who died eight days later, had just been reelected with the largest plurality of popular votes up to that time. He was one of the best loved of U.S. presidents.

4. "DALLAS IS A VERY DANGEROUS PLACE." That's what Senator William Fulbright told President John F. Kennedy, adding, "I wouldn't go there. Don't you go." Texas wasn't Kennedy country. It was right wing, conservative. But it was Democratic and the president needed to hold the party together for his 1964 reelection.

November 22, 1963, was warm and sunny. The huge crowds lined the Dallas streets waiting for the president's motorcade. Also anticipating Kennedy's arrival was Lee Harvey Oswald, stationed on the sixth floor of the Texas School Book Depository, where he worked. He earned $1.25 an hour as a clerk, the latest in a series of meaningless jobs.

Meaning was something that had managed to elude Oswald. In search of a way to fit in, he'd joined the marines and quit. He'd denounced the U.S. and gone to live in Russia but found it sterile. He came home and got involved with Castro's Cuban revolution. But his real problem was a loveless childhood and a rocky marriage.

The night before the assassination, he had attempted to make amends with his Russian wife, Marina, but she turned a cold shoulder. He slept little and in the morning kissed his two children and left his wedding ring in a demitasse cup. He went to work with a $19.95 mail-order rifle, a World War II surplus Italian carbine, wrapped in brown paper. When Kennedy's open car came past the Texas School Book Depository, Oswald aimed the power sight on his rifle and fired. Within two hours, Kennedy was dead. Within forty-eight hours, so was Oswald.

He'd escaped from the scene of the crime by bus and taxi, but was arrested shortly thereafter in a movie theater. Then, for no apparent reason, Dallas nightclub owner Jack Ruby walked into the basement of the Dallas police station and shot Oswald, prompting theories of a murder conspiracy which have never been proven.

Arresting Predicaments

1. A PURPOSEFUL TAX EVADER Henry Thoreau was arrested in 1846 for refusing to pay a one-dollar poll tax which he felt would be used to support slavery. The next day Ralph Waldo Emerson came to the Concord jail and paid Thoreau's tax. Passive resistance, felt Thoreau, was a tool for a man of conscience to use to protest government wrongs. His arrest led to his famous 1849 essay "On the Duty of Civil Disobedience."

2. AN UNWITTING KIDNAPPER William Marcy "Boss" Tweed, one of the leaders behind New York City's crooked Tammany Hall, was certainly not a model citizen. He'd been convicted of embezzling six million dollars from the city Treasury and then skipped out of jail. But in Spain, where he ended up, his record was clean. Nonetheless, the Spanish authorities quickly had him arrested for "kidnapping two American children." They had seen a *Harper's Weekly* cartoon by Thomas Nast that showed Tweed in prison stripes. In his right hand was a threatening club and in his left, two small boys who were being lifted off their feet.

   The cartoon was meant to poke fun at Tweed's idea of justice, but the Spanish authorities assumed that it meant Tweed had made off with two children. He was deported. On November 23, 1876, he arrived in New York, where he spent the rest of his life in jail.

3. PRESIDENTIAL GRAVE ROBBERS On November 7, 1876, an Illinois outlaw gang tried to steal the body of Abraham Lincoln from Oak Ridge Cemetery in Springfield, Illinois. They sawed the padlock off an iron door of the tomb, pried the marble lid off the sarcophagus, and got the coffin partway out when they were raided by the police, who had been tipped off. How to arrest them was a problem. There was no law against stealing a body in Illinois and the gang hadn't actually been able to make off with the coffin. They were charged with conspiring to steal a seventy-five-dollar coffin, convicted, and sentenced to a year in prison.

4. AN ILLEGAL VOTER "You may handcuff me as soon as I get my hat and coat on," said Susan B. Anthony to the U.S. marshal who rang her doorbell with a warrant for her arrest. Miss Anthony

When Susan B. Anthony refused to post her five-hundred-dollar bail, her lawyer paid it, saying, "I could not see a lady I respected put in jail." Anthony used the time until her trial to lecture on whether it was a crime for a citizen of the United States to vote.

THE NEW-YORK HISTORICAL SOCIETY

had voted in the 1872 election believing that the new amendment enfranchising freed slaves also gave women the right to vote. The embarrassed marshal charged her with knowingly voting without a lawful right to do so but refused to handcuff her. He escorted her to the streetcar. When the conductor asked for Susan B. Anthony's fare, she loudly announced, "This gentleman is escorting me to jail. Ask him for my fare."

5.   A LADY PORNOGRAPHER In 1872 Victoria Woodhull, an unorthodox feminist and publisher of *Woodhull and Claflin's Weekly*, was arrested, evicted from her home, imprisoned for six months, and forced to suspend publication of her paper. The charge was passing obscene materials through the mail. In one of her articles she had defended her unusual living arrangement, which included both her current and former husbands, and the courts ruled that it constituted obscenity.

6.   DANCING WAS THEIR CRIME Kicking Bear, Short Bull, Mash the Kettle, and sixteen other Indian leaders were arrested in 1895 for participating in the impassioned Ghost Dances, which the Indians believed would end the white man's rule. Their punishment was unorthodox. They were sent abroad with Buffalo Bill's Wild West Show.

7.   SHE WRECKED SALOONS "Madam, I must place you under arrest," said the Wichita, Kansas, detective to temperance leader Carry Nation after she had destroyed the city's finest saloon. "Arrest *me!*" she cried. "Why don't you arrest the man who runs this hellhole?" The crusader had a point. Saloons were illegal in Kansas. The charges were subsequently dropped.

8. A NOISY DRUMMER On September 20, 1810, Blount County Court in Tennessee ordered that Samuel Houston be fined five dollars for "disorderly riotously, wantonly with an Assembly of Militia annoying the Court with the noise of a Drum." Seventeen-year-old Sam didn't pay—he left town and went to live with Indians.

Hanged Men (and a Woman)

1. A THINLY DISGUISED HERO "I only regret that I have but one life to lose for my country," said young Nathan Hale in 1776. But the one life he did give need not have been so short. Hale had volunteered to spy against the British and his mission was ill-fated from the start.

First of all, it was far from a secret. Every officer in his regiment had seen twenty-one-year-old Hale step forward and accept the assignment no one else would take. He was sent behind British lines on Long Island without a secret code or contacts, pretending to be a wandering schoolteacher. He had a facial scar, which made him readily identifiable, and a Tory cousin who may have betrayed him. Hale was easily caught and hanged in Manhattan in September 1776 near what is now Grand Central Terminal.

2. A SPY EVERYBODY LIKED British Major John André was handsome, charming, and considered a "man of the first abilities" by George Washington. He was also technically a spy. The job of negotiating Benedict Arnold's treason had fallen to André, who had rashly let Arnold lead him inside the American lines. He was caught on his way back to British-held New York with a cloak thrown over his uniform and the plans to Arnold's fort at West Point in his boot.

Washington called together a board of officers to decide André's fate. If they found that he was a British officer captured in the line of duty, then André was a prisoner of war and could be exchanged. It was found, however, that he was guilty of spying. The normal sentence for that was hanging. André argued with Washington for his right to be shot, not strung up like a common criminal. Alexander Hamilton and other American officers vehemently pleaded his case. Reluctantly, Washington concluded that André had to die a spy's death but did not tell him.

On the day of the execution, André ate a breakfast Washington had sent from his own table. Then he shaved, donned his scarlet

uniform, and said, "I am ready, gentlemen." When he saw the gallows, he realized his fate. Biting his underlip and shaking his head,
he said, "I've borne everything but this is too degrading." The ex-
ecutioner had a disguise of tarred grease over his face and hands.
André said, "Take your black hands off me," and put the rope around
his neck himself, making the knot snug under one ear. He climbed
onto a wagon under the gallows; the hangman led the horse away.
American officers cried openly as the body dropped.

Mrs. Surratt went to
the scaffold with three
other Lincoln conspira-
tors on a day so scorch-
ing that spectators took
refuge under umbrellas.
BOSTON PUBLIC LIBRARY PRINT
COLLECTION

3.   DID SHE KNOW OR DIDN'T SHE? On the day of Mary Surratt's hanging, horsemen were posted along the route to the White
House in anticipation of a pardon from President Andrew Johnson.
Mrs. Surratt ran the boardinghouse where John Wilkes Booth and
friends had met to plot Lincoln's assassination. Evidence as to
whether she knew of their plans was slim, but times were emotional. A closed military—rather than a civil—court found her guilty.
The day of her hanging was hot and she fainted on the way to the
scaffold. A priest held an umbrella over her. Afterward, Andrew
Johnson said he would have signed a pardon but through mysterious political circumstances never saw any request. Mrs. Surratt was
the first woman hanged in the U.S.

4.   TWO LESS MEN AT THE BATTLE OF BUNKER HILL British
General Howe was getting ready to lead the attack up the Ameri-
can-fortified Bunker Hill when General Robert Pigot of the Royal
Marines approached. Pointing to five men surrounded by an armed
guard, he said, "They tried to desert, sir. Ran for the American
lines." Howe was aghast. Discipline was sacred to the British. He
reminded the deserters that the morning orders had clearly stated
that any man who "quit his rank on any pretense" would be executed without mercy. "I would like to hang the five of you," he

said, "but I need men." Then, pointing to two in the middle, he commanded, "Hang those two." Howe turned and left the men on their knees begging for mercy. As the British soldiers formed lines to go up Bunker Hill, they could see the bodies of two of their comrades slowly twisting on the ropes.

5. A MAN WHO DIDN'T "AVOID LEWD WOMEN" Almost twenty thousand spectators turned out to watch the hanging of Thomas Hickey in New York City on June 28, 1776. A sergeant under George Washington, he had been caught plotting to help the British invade New York and even to poison Washington. On the day of his hanging. Hickey broke down and alternately sobbed and shouted defiance. Washington made a lesson of the situation in his orders by stating that the "most certain method" to avoid this type of treachery was "to avoid lewd women, who, by the dying confession of this poor criminal, first led him into practices which ended in an untimely and ignominious death."

6. THE "ANDERSONVILLE SAVAGE" Even a bloody battle like Gettysburg left a Civil War soldier with a better chance of survival than a stint in a prison camp. Both Confederate and Union camps were grim, but one of the most certain death traps was Andersonville, Georgia. The man who ran it was Confederate Captain Henry Wirz. His manner was abrupt and irritable due to a painful arm wound he'd received in the war. Prisoners at his camp were dying at the rate of one hundred a day; those who survived looked like human skeletons. Wirz could not get the tools or even the manpower to bury the dead properly. He was a doctor himself, yet his hospital was a horror. Supplies were scarce. New shipments were nearly an impossibility because at this point in the war most of the railroads had been torn up and food was hard to find even for Confederate troops.

When the fighting ended, the Northern press sought a scapegoat and Wirz was it. They called him the "Andersonville savage." He was charged with murder "in violation of the laws and customs of war." The court refused to hear any evidence comparing the Andersonville camp to those in the North.

Sentenced to hang on November 10, 1865, Wirz climbed the thirteen steps of the scaffold and told the major in charge, "I know what your orders are, Major. I am being hanged for obeying them." They shook hands and soon Captain Henry Wirz, CSA, a black mask over his contorted face, swung from a greased noose. All the men accused with him were released without trial.

7. A MOLDERING IN HIS GRAVE It was the moonlit Sunday morning of October 16, 1859, when a handful of shots rang out at the U.S. arsenal at Harpers Ferry, Virginia. Fiery old John Brown, a religious fanatic who had sworn to destroy slavery because the Bible told him it was wrong, had captured the arsenal with the intent to distribute its arms to lead a slave uprising.

Once the news of his daring act was out, he was certain that blacks would flock to his stronghold. The only men who arrived, however, were those in the U.S. Army led by a colonel named Robert E. Lee. Quickly, Brown was captured and brought to trial for treason. His lawyers attempted to save his life by introducing an insanity plea. Brown would have none of it. Eyes flashing, the bearded old man leaped off his courtroom cot, where he had been resting from his wounds, and hotly defended the rationality of his acts. When he was convicted of treason, he rejoiced, saying, "I am worth inconceivably more to *hang* than for any other purpose." He rode to the scaffold sitting on his coffin. The North made him a martyr and kept his memory alive in a song.

8. AN ASPIRING AMBASSADOR TURNED KILLER Charles J. Guiteau bought a pistol with a fancy handle because he thought it would look better in a museum. He had just been rejected in a far-fetched quest for an appointment as ambassador to Paris. The man who turned him down: President James Garfield. "Like a flash" it came to Guiteau, unemployed and a wife-beater with a history of mental illness, that the new president should die. God commanded him. With his last twenty cents in his pocket and a new pistol, he walked up behind Garfield in a Washington, D.C., train station and fired a shot which eleven agonizing weeks later proved fatal. Lawyers tried to prove insanity, but Guiteau, the second man to kill a president, was hanged.

9. HUNG UP OVER AN EIGHT-HOUR WORK DAY When the verdict of guilty came in the wake of Chicago's Haymarket Square bombing, defendant Albert Parsons waved the anarchists' red handkerchief and tied the cords of the window shade into a noose. Outside, the hostile mob cheered at the prospect of his death.

Parsons's primary crime had been to be present at a May 4, 1886, labor demonstration in favor of an eight-hour workday. A bomb from an unknown source had been thrown into the police ranks, unleashing five minutes of firing. Six policemen died, sixty were wounded, and countless workers were maimed.

The labor leaders were quickly rounded up and, in an emotional trial, convicted of murder. Of the seven condemned men, one committed suicide in his prison cell by setting off a dynamite cap in his mouth. Two were pardoned by the governor. The remaining four went to the scaffold unrepentant. "Hurrah for Anarchy!" cried one in German, another in English. A third shouted through his hood, "The day will come when our silence will be more powerful than the voices you strangle today!" Before Parsons could speak, the trap was sprung. Within eight minutes all were dead.

10. VALUED AT $375 AND THEN HANGED Nat Turner was thirty-one years old and considered by his master to be a smart, hard-working, well-behaved slave. But inside Turner was seething. He was deeply religious and believed it was his mission to lead the slaves to freedom.

On Sundays he was allowed to preach to other slaves. After church on August 21, 1831, he began the South's bloodiest slave rebellion. It started when he and six other blacks took axes and attacked the Travis farm, hacking to pieces seven whites, including an infant. Then the uprising spread across Virginia's Southampton County, gathering force from other slaves as it went.

Panic and fear swept the white community, but within forty-eight hours the revolt was halted by the white militia. Turner's men suffered from disorganization and drunkenness. Some slaves joined his rebellion but others warned their masters and even fought for them, out of loyalty, decency, or fear. Nat Turner was caught on Sunday, October 30. Since legally he belonged to Putnam Moore, a young child killed in the uprising, the court described him as "Nat alias Nat Turner a negro man slave the property of Putnam Moore an infant."

The verdict was never in doubt. First the court set his value at $375 so that the state could repay the estate of Putnam Moore. Then the sheriff took Turner out to the gnarled hanging tree. A large crowd gathered; the noose was affixed and the rope thrown over a limb. Nat Turner was pulled up with a jerk. His wife and daughter were sold off to slave traders.

Prison Stories

1. THE ULTIMATE INSULT Jefferson Davis was arrested at the end of the Civil War and held without bail in Fort Monroe for two

years. A moat surrounded the fort, which had walls ninety-five feet thick. Davis was put in a dark, dank cell behind heavy doors and bars. A squad of seventy soldiers was placed on duty. Guards with clumping feet paced outside and inside his cell, preventing sleep. A lamp burned day and night.

Yet the ultimate insult to the former Confederate president came when he was put in heavy leg irons like a criminal. A burly smith with a sledgehammer had riveted the chain around his ankle. Davis wept, unable to find words to express his humiliation.

2.   STANTON'S TORTURE While awaiting trial before a military court, four of the men accused of complicity in the plot to assassinate Abraham Lincoln were held in separate cells.

On April 23, 1865, Secretary of War Edwin Stanton ordered that "for better security against conversation" each prisoner "shall have a canvas bag put over the head . . . and tied about the neck, with a hole for proper breathing and eating, but not seeing." There were small openings for the nose and mouth. Cotton pads were placed over the ears and eyes, resulting in the eyeballs being pushed far back into their sockets. Each prisoner's hands were cuffed to the end of a fourteen-inch-long bar of iron so that his arms were kept stiffly apart and no object could be grasped with two hands. On his feet were chains tied to a seventy-five-pound cannonballs.

The men were not allowed visitors, not even a lawyer. The prison surgeon, Dr. George Porter, told Stanton that the hot summer days and the constant pressure on the head might bring on insanity, but Stanton was not moved and the hoods were kept on.

3.   HIS KIND OF JAIL When New York law finally caught up with William Marcy "Boss" Tweed, head of the ring that swindled millions of dollars from the city, he was confined to Ludlow Street Jail. There the warden obligingly rented his quarters for seventy-five dollars to Tweed and allowed him the services of a servant named Luke. Tweed had a flowered courtyard to walk in and a grand piano. He liked to sit by the window and call to those who passed. Many of them he knew well, but after his fall from power few would call him their friend. He died at the Ludlow Street Jail.

4.   THE "HOTEL WITH THE GRATED DOOR" Wealthy Robert Morris, signer of the Declaration of Independence and "Financier of the Revolution," lost his fortune in land speculation after the war. His debts amounted to almost three million dollars on February 15, 1798, when he was sent to debtor's prison.

He had a spacious room with a writing desk, bedstead, settee, chairs, and mirrors. Although he was penniless, the prison charged him rent. He had many visitors, including Alexander Hamilton and George Washington. Morris spent three and a half years in what he called his "hotel with the grated door" before a settlement was reached with his creditors. Five years later he died in poverty and obscurity.

PART XIV

History in Perspective

Shortsighted Reactions to Great Leaps Forward

1. "WHAT USE COULD THIS COMPANY MAKE OF A TOY?" This was the reaction of William Orton, president of Western Union Telegraph Company, when offered Alexander Graham Bell's patents for the telephone for $100,000. The Bell Telephone Company became the industrial giant American Telephone and Telegraph Company and Bell's patent is now considered the single-most valuable one ever issued by the Patent Office. Orton has gone down in history for making one of the worst decisions in American business history.

2. "I CONSIDER IT AN IMPOSSIBILITY." Lee DeForest, radio pioneer and inventor with more than three hundred patents including the Audion tube, was talking about television broadcasting.

3. "CUT OUT THE WILD-CAT STUFF." This was a Cleveland newspaper editor's response to a stringer in Kitty Hawk, North Carolina, who had reported that on December 17, 1903, two brothers named Wright had traveled almost one thousand feet at a height of sixty feet in a flying machine.

4. FULTON'S FOLLY Robert Fulton sometimes "loitered unknown" on his way to his shipyard and "heard the loud laugh at my expense" and "the dull and endless repetition of the *Fulton Folly*." On August 9, 1807, Fulton took his new paddle-wheel steamboat, the *Clermont*, out for a trial run. It still was not completely framed in and to spectators on shore it looked like "a backwoods sawmill mounted on a scow and set on fire."

Ten days later Fulton heard "many sarcastic remarks" as his ship pushed off into the Hudson River with forty passengers, mostly friends and relatives. The 150-mile trip to Albany went without incident at the remarkable upstream speed of about five miles an hour. He easily passed sloops and schooners that challenged him. Barges with double-manned oars tried in vain to keep pace. The New York papers ignored the event, but the steamboat era had begun.

5. TAMPERING WITH DIVINE WILL When Benjamin Franklin proved that lightning was electricity by flying his famous kite, he was careful to give credit to "God in his Goodness." Lightning was considered to be an expression of divine wrath and was to be warded

off by prayer or the ringing of church bells, which were sometimes inscribed *"Fulgura frango"*—"I break up the lightning." During storms the lives of countless bell ringers were lost because of this belief.

When Franklin invented a rod that could render lightning harmless by conducting it from steeple to ground, Boston clergymen opposed the idea, maintaining that lightning was God's punishment. Others feared the lightning rod because they believed that if lightning was led down into the bowels of the earth, earthquakes would result. When Boston was struck by an earthquake in 1775, one minister preached that it was a warning from on high. He claimed that too many were defying divine will by using lightning rods, which were the work of the devil. Long after Franklin's day, opposition to the lightning rod continued.

6. NOTHING LIKE IT ON EARTH When shipbuilder and inventor John Ericsson's model of the warship *Monitor* was shown to the navy board, it was rejected. The design was too revolutionary—it was made entirely of iron, its deck was only one foot above the water, and it had two cannons in an iron turret that revolved.

Captain Davis told Ericsson to take the model home and "worship it. It will not be idolatry. It is in the image of nothing in the heavens above, or in the earth beneath." Officers brought up on wooden decks and sails didn't understand the new age of iron and steam. But President Lincoln liked the idea and Ericsson had a second hearing. The navy board changed its mind and awarded him a contract. The *Monitor* was finished just in time to fight the Civil War's most famous naval battle with the Confederate's ironclad *Merrimac.* The battle was a draw, but the *Monitor* prevented the destruction of the Northern navy's wooden ships.

The Clouded Crystal Ball

1. OUR OWN SAHARA? Explorer Zebulon Pike, who lent his name to a famous Colorado peak, saw the great plains as uninhabitable and predicted they would become "as celebrated as the sandy deserts of Africa."

2. HELL TO RENT "The reign of tears is over. The slums will soon be a memory. We will turn our prisons into factories. . . . Hell will be forever for rent." So said preacher Billy Sunday when the Prohibition act was passed.

3.   AN ATOMIC EXPERT WHO BOMBED "This is the biggest fool thing we have ever done. The bomb will never go off and I speak as an expert on explosives." Vannevar Bush, head of the Office of Scientific Research and Development, was explaining the atomic bomb to President Harry Truman.

4.   NO CLUE ABOUT THE CRASH "We in America today are nearer to the final triumph over poverty than ever before in the history of any land. The poorhouse is vanishing among us." Herbert Hoover was speaking on August 11, 1928, just before the 1929 stock-market crash and the worst Depression in history.

5.   WHO NEEDS DUST AND CACTUS? "What do we want with this vast, worthless area?" asked Daniel Webster as the United States and Great Britain wrestled over claims to the Oregon Territory. To Webster, Oregon was a "region of savages and wild beasts, of deserts, of shifting sands and whirlpools of dust, of cactus and prairie dogs" and he had little interest in acquiring it.

6.   THE POLL THAT TOOK A TOLL On August 22, 1936, one of America's leading magazines, the *Literary Digest,* announced the start of its annual presidential poll. Its "smooth-running machine" was "swinging into action" with "the swift precision of thirty years' experience" to reduce guesswork to hard fact and would soon let the country know the results of the upcoming election to "within a fraction of 1 per cent." The *Digest*'s sure winner was Alf Landon, with 370 electoral votes. When Election Day arrived, Landon was swamped by Franklin D. Roosevelt, who won every state except Maine and Vermont. The *Literary Digest* was on its way to oblivion.

7.   SO LONG, DICK Richard Nixon was so upset by losing the race for governor of California in 1962 that he asked Herb Klein to go down to the hotel lobby and read the concession speech for him. Nixon watched on television as the reporters upbraided Klein—they wanted Nixon personally. At first Nixon said, "Screw them. I'm not doing it," but then he changed his mind. In an emotionally charged speech he said, "You won't have Nixon to kick around anymore, because, gentlemen, this is my last press conference." Six years later he ran for president and was elected twice, enduring many more press conferences.

Had They Only Known

1. AN UNHEEDED WARNING While George Washington was preparing to cross the ice-clogged Delaware on Christmas night, 1776, Colonel Rall, the Hessian commander at Trenton, was drinking applejack and playing cards. He received a note from a British loyalist warning him of the imminent attack, but it was late, Rall was groggy, and the note was in English, which he couldn't read. He put it in his pocket. Washington attacked at dawn and took one thousand prisoners in a much-needed victory. Rall was wounded in the battle. As he lay dying, the note was found and translated into German. Had he read it earlier, he admitted, "I would not be here."

2. FOUGHT FOR NAUGHT When Major General Andrew Jackson arrived in New Orleans on December 1, 1814, he found it alarmingly unprepared for an expected British attack. Jackson was ill with dysentery, but he furiously set about gearing up the city's defenses, even accepting aid from the pirate Jean Laffite. When the British army of more than eight thousand men did move in on New Orleans, they suffered a smashing defeat. The Americans, firing from behind earthworks, lost only seven men.

What no one knew was that the War of 1812 had ended two weeks earlier when a peace treaty was signed in Ghent, Belgium. Jackson's stunning victory was unnecessary, but it did make him a national hero and help propel him to the presidency.

3. NO RUSH ABOUT GOLD At the close of the Mexican War in 1848, a treaty was drawn up ceding California and lands north of the Rio Grande to the United States for fifteen million dollars. What neither the Mexicans nor the Americans knew was that gold had already been discovered at Sutter's mill in California two weeks earlier. News still hadn't reached the East a month later when the Senate debated the treaty for eleven days. It underwent thirty-eight roll-call votes before it passed. The Whigs tried to tack on amendments excluding California and New Mexico from the treaty. A full four months after the discovery of gold, Mexico formally signed away half of its lands. With California alone, it ceded territory that yielded an average of twenty-six million dollars a year in minerals right through 1900.

4.   THE RESULT OF A CUT CABLE In the Spanish-American War, Admiral Dewey crushed the Spanish fleet in the Philippines and then cut the islands' only communication link to the outside world—an underwater cable from Manila to Hong Kong. He controlled the harbor, but the Spanish, who still held the city of Manila, refused to share the cable with the Americans. Ultimately, that decision cost Spain the Philippines. On August 13, 1898, the U.S. finally invaded Manila. The armistice had been signed the day before, but without a cable the news came too late. When apprised of Dewey's victory, President McKinley wasn't sure what to do with the islands but eventually decided to demand that Spain cede them to the U.S.

5.   DON'T WORRY ABOUT IT Early Sunday morning on December 7, 1941, Privates Joseph Lockard and George Elliott were operating a radar station at Opana on Oahu. Their tour of duty ended at 7:00 A.M., but the truck had not arrived to pick them up. Elliot, who was in training, was fiddling with the controls at 7:02 when he picked up the biggest blip either of them had ever seen. Lockard pushed him away. At first he thought the set was broken; then he realized it was a huge flight of planes—the very ones heading to attack Pearl Harbor.

At 7:06 the two tried using the headphones to contact the control room, where all flights were plotted on a huge map. The line was dead—the men in the control room had gone to breakfast.

Elliott tried the regular phone circuit and got through to Lieutenant Kermit Tyler, a pilot who was the only person on duty. "There's a large number of planes coming in from the north, three degrees east." Lieutenant Tyler was unimpressed. Lockard got on the line and tried to convince the lieutenant that it was important—he had never seen so many planes on the screen. "Well, don't worry about it," Tyler finally said.

At 7:45 A.M. the truck came and the two privates shut down the station and left. At 7:55 A.M. the first bombs fell on Pearl Harbor.

What They Were Doing When

1.   EATING LUNCH ON A ROCK When it was clear that President William McKinley was dying of an assassin's bullet, it suddenly became a top priority to find Vice-President Theodore Roosevelt, who was hiking in the Adirondacks. He'd undertaken

the trip with the blessing of McKinley's overly optimistic doctors. TR was eating his lunch on a rock when a woodsman came out of a thicket with a note from Secretary of State Elihu Root. Upon reading the grim news, he immediately, hurried down the mountain. He was met by relays of drivers and horses who took him on a wild ride in total darkness over washed-out roads. At the nearest town a special train was waiting to take Roosevelt to Buffalo, New York. By the time he arrived the next day, McKinley was dead. The new president borrowed formal attire and was immediately sworn in.

2. SITTING FOR HIS PORTRAIT When news of the critical American victory at Saratoga reached General George Washington, he was having his portrait painted by Charles Wilson Peale. The battle, which had taken place two weeks earlier, was a turning point in the Revolution. Washington commented, "Ah, Burgoyne is defeated," and continued to sit for what was to become a classic image.

3. JUST A FACE IN THE CROWD After the Confederacy crumbled, the Union army issued an all-out alert to "capture or kill Jefferson Davis, the rebel ex-president." He was quickly arrested in Georgia. On his way to federal prison, he was taken through Augusta, Georgia. Among the onlookers was eight-year-old Woodrow Wilson, son of the town's Presbyterian minister.

4. OUT AT THE OLD BALL GAME On April 17, 1964, the Washington Senators were battling against the California Angels. President Lyndon Johnson had thrown out the first ball and seventeen senators—including Hubert Humphrey—were watching the game. At the end of the third inning a call came over the public-address system: "Attention please! All senators must report back to the Senate for a quorum call." The attendance call had been forced by the conservative Southerners as a means of delaying a key civil rights bill, which was already besieged by a filibuster. Senator Humphrey and his liberal colleagues quickly jumped into waiting limousines and made the one-mile trip back to the Senate in time for the quorum call.

5. "THE BEST THING IS TO PRAY." When John F. Kennedy was shot in 1963, Lyndon Johnson's daughter Luci was sitting in Spanish class at the National Cathedral School for Girls in Washington, D.C. A friend told her the news. "I thought she was kidding," Luci recalled. "Then the class began buzzing. The bells started ringing continuously. My teacher never said a word. The class stood up

and walked to the chapel . . . everyone was so thunderstruck. My principal, Katherine Lee . . . said the best thing is to pray. My first reaction was I was the only one who knew President Kennedy. It never entered my mind that I was the President's daughter."

One of the two tiny heads in the second-story window of this New York City house belongs to young Theodore Roosevelt, as Lincoln's funeral procession marched by.
THEODORE ROOSEVELT COLLECTION, HARVARD COLLEGE LIBRARY

6. WATCHING OUT THE WINDOW When Abraham Lincoln's funeral procession wound up Broadway in New York City, it·passed by Union Square, where six-year-old Theodore Roosevelt and his brother Elliott were peering out the window.

7. IN HIS BAN-LON SHIRT While the House Judiciary Committee was voting articles of impeachment against him, Richard Nixon was swimming at Red Beach near his San Clemente, California, home.

"I was getting dressed in the beach trailer when the phone rang and Ziegler gave me the news," he recalled. "That was how I learned that I was the first President in 106 years to be recommended for impeachment: standing in the beach trailer, barefoot, wearing old trousers, a Ban-Lon shirt, and a blue windbreaker emblazoned with the Presidential Seal."

Historic Moments on the Night Shift

1.   FOLLY AT FOUR A.M. Secretary of State William Seward was in his Washington, D.C., home playing whist one night in March 1867 when the Russian minister, Baron Edouard de Stoeckl, dropped in. His government had just cabled him permission to sell Alaska to the U.S. Seward was one of the few who saw any value in Alaska and he wanted to push the treaty through the Senate, which was going to adjourn the next day. He offered to close the deal at once, but the Russian protested that it was night and the State Department offices were not open.

"Never mind that," Seward said. "Before midnight you will find me at the Department, which will be open and ready for business." Clerks were rounded up, the State Department lights were turned on, and by four A.M. the treaty selling Alaska to the U.S. for $7.2 million—about two cents an acre—was signed and sealed.

Seward sent it off to the Senate, where it eventually passed by one vote.

2.   PROMOTED IN HIS SLEEP Vice-President Calvin Coolidge was visiting his family at Plymouth Notch, Vermont. After a day spent haying a field with a neighbor, he had gone to bed as usual at nine P.M. Sometimes after midnight on August 3, 1923, he was awakened by his father coming up the stairs calling, "Calvin, wake up. You're President of the United States." Warren G. Harding had died of a cerebral hemorrhage in San Francisco. This news had been telegraphed to nearby Bridgewater, Vermont, where the local telegraph operator, Winfred A. Perkins, had rushed up the mountain in a car with the message. He had awakened Coolidge's father who slept downstairs and announced the news before anyone had a chance to open the envelope with the telegram.

The new president came downstairs and walked over to Miss

Florence Cilley's general store, which had the only telephone in the valley, and contacted Attorney General Daugherty. On his advice, Coolidge had his father, a notary public, administer the Oath of Office. The thirtieth president was sworn in at 2:47 in the morning in the sitting room of a simple Vermont farmhouse, the kerosene lamp casting a pale light on the faded wallpaper—the homeliest of inaugurations.

3.   WITH GOD'S HELP "I walked the floor of the White House night after night," President William McKinley said, explaining how he reached his decision on what to do with the Philippine Islands, which had been captured in the 1898 Spanish-American War. "I went down on my knees and prayed to Almighty God for light and guidance. . . . And then one night it came to me this way . . . there was nothing left for us to do but to take them all, and to educate the Filipinos, and uplift and civilize and Christianize, and by God's grace do the very best we could by them, as our fellow men for whom Christ also died. And then I went to bed and went to sleep and slept soundly."

4.   A DARK HORSE IN A SMOKE-FILLED ROOM Senator Warren G. Harding did so poorly in the presidential primaries, he didn't feel he had any chance to get the Republican nomination in 1920. But his campaign manager, Harry Daugherty, made an uncannily accurate prediction to reporters that the convention would be dead-locked and that the worn-out leaders would "get together in some hotel about 2:11 in the morning" and choose Senator Harding as the compromise candidate. Sure enough, Harding was called to the proverbial smoke-filled room of the Blackstone Hotel at 2:00 A.M. Reporters asked Harding to comment. The awed candidate used the poker-playing terms he was most familiar with: "We drew to a pair of deuces and filled."

5.   A SHOT IN THE DARK STARTS THE CIVIL WAR On April 11, 1865, Edmund Ruffin, an ardent Southern firebrand, went to bed with his uniform on. He wanted to be ready at a moment's notice because Captain George Cuthbert of the Palmetto Guards told him he was to have the honor of firing the first shot if the Confederates decided to attack Fort Sumter. Since Ruffin was aging and partly deaf, news of this honor had to be shouted in his ear.

While he slept, the Confederate command reached the momentous decision to fire on the federal fort. Drums called the men to their stations just before 4:00 A.M., and at 4:30 A.M. Edmund Ruffin, his wispy white hair down to his shoulders, pulled the lanyard on the cannon that sent a cannonball toward Fort Sumter in the Charleston, South Carolina, harbor. The North and South were at war.

What Else Happened on the Fourth of July?

1. JULY 4, 1776 Amid the Continental Congress's debates on whether to accept the Declaration of Independence, Thomas Jefferson, the document's author, found time to run errands. He made the rounds of a number of Philadelphia shops and bought a thermometer and seven pairs of women's gloves.

2. JULY 4, 1804 Explorer William Clark, heading up the Missouri River to the Pacific with Meriwether Lewis, wrote that his crew "ussered in the day by a discharge of one shot from our Bow piece." He also noted that "Jos. Fields got bit by a Snake."

3. JULY 4, 1826 On the fiftieth anniversary of the adoption of the Declaration of Independence, two signers and former presidents died. John Adams and Thomas Jefferson had been friends and co-workers for independence, but later they were political enemies. In old age they reached a rapprochement, resuming their correspondence and friendship.

John Adams passed away quietly in Quincy, Massachusetts. His last words were, "Thomas Jefferson still survives." But his compatriot had already died earlier in the day in Virginia.

4. JULY 4, 1831 President James Monroe, impoverished due to the burdens of public service, died in New York at his daughter's house. His funeral procession was the grandest the city had ever seen. Bells tolled across the country as the nation mourned one of its last Revolutionary War heroes.

5. JULY 4, 1850 President Zachary Taylor participated in the Fourth of July ceremonies at the Washington Monument, which was just being built—his last official act. The speeches were long and the day was hot. Taylor remarked that the sun was stronger than it was in Mexico, where he'd become a hero in the 1848 war. At the ceremonies, he quenched his thirst with ice water. On returning to the White House, he drank ice milk and ate ripe cherries. That evening he was beset with stomach cramps and taken upstairs to bed. He died five days later.

6. JULY 4, 1863 When the Confederates surrendered Vicksburg, Mississippi, on July 4, President Lincoln said, "the Father of Waters again goes unvexed to the sea." The South had lost its last major post on the Mississippi River. The people of Vicksburg would not celebrate the Fourth of July again until 1945, when World War II patriotism finally healed Civil War wounds.

7. JULY 4, 1872 In rural Plymouth Notch, Vermont, Calvin Coolidge was born in the downstairs bedroom of a house that also served as a store and post office. No newspaper reported the event. He was originally named John Calvin after his father, proprietor of the village store, but the John was dropped.

8. JULY 4, 1894 The Republic of Hawaii was proclaimed. Sanford B. Dole, representing American business interests, became its first and only president. It was annexed to the United States four years later.

9. JULY 4, 1898 Independence Day fell in the middle of the Spanish-American War. From Cuba, Admiral Sampson cabled: "The fleet under my command offers the nation as a Fourth of July present the whole of Cervera's fleet." His men had destroyed the Spanish squadron without the loss of a single ship.

Buffalo Facts

What this pioneer woman holds in her wheelbarrow was a key factor in the taming of the West—buffalo droppings, also called buffalo chips, which provided fuel on the treeless prairie.
COURTESY OF AMON CARTER MUSEUM, FORT WORTH, TEXAS

1. A bull buffalo stands six feet tall and weighs a ton—the largest animal in North America. Running singly he can reach speeds of thirty to thirty-five miles an hour and tire out a horse.

2. In the mid-nineteenth century there were more buffalo than people in the United States. Buffalo were the most numerous land mammals on earth.

3. The Sioux and other nomadic tribes who followed the buffalo herds and lived off them only did so after the white settlement of North America. Before the Spanish brought the horse to America, the Indians had no means of chasing buffalo.

4. Even in storms, cowbirds rode on the backs of the buffalo, foraging for insects in their fur.

5. The Indians admired the stubborn courage of the bull buffalo. Names such as Tall Bull and Sitting Bull were given to braves who had demonstrated their courage.

6. Buffalo were a major cause of breakdowns in telegraphic communication across the plains. They liked to scratch their backs by rubbing against the poles and often knocked them over in an effort to relieve an itch.

7. Migrating herds stretched as far as the eye could see. They delayed transcontinental trains and could take five days to pass one point.

8. The Sharps rifle, a breach loader that allowed rapid firing, enabled hunters to kill herds en masse. Buffalo were dull-witted with few natural enemies. When shot at from a distance, they didn't understand the source of their danger and tended just to stare stupidly at their dying mates rather than move off. Once the herd did get going in one direction, they tended to keep in a straight line for miles. Thousands drowned in rivers, and herds could be led over cliffs.

9. William F. Cody won the nickname "Buffalo Bill" by killing large numbers of buffalo for food for the railroad construction workers. The secret to his success, as he tells it, was "to get them circling by riding my horse at the head of the herd, shooting the leaders, thus crowding the followers to the left till they would finally circle round and round. On this morning the buffaloes were very accommodating, and I soon had them running in a beautiful circle, when I dropped them thick and fast, until I had thirty-eight."

10. From 1868 to 1881, $2.5 million was paid for buffalo bones. The older cracked, weather-beaten ones were ground up for fertilizer. The fresher ones were used for bone china. Settlers were paid about 10 cents a skeleton or about $10 a ton. It took one hundred buffalo to make a ton of bones.

11. In the ten years from 1872 to 1882, more than one million buffalo were killed each year.

12. Buffalo existed in the East as well as the West. The last buffalo was chased out of the city of Buffalo, New York, in 1803.

The Rise and Fall of the Horse in America

1. A SPLASH ENTRANCE AFTER EIGHTY-FIVE HUNDRED YEARS The horse was extinct in the New World for eighty-five hundred years, until Columbus set sail on his second voyage. Before he left Spain, he had a supply of horses hoisted aboard by means of leather bellybands attached to ropes and pulleys. The horses spent the one-hundred-day voyage penned in on the open deck with no room to move. Miles from the island of Hispaniola, now Haiti and the Dominican Republic, they smelled land and excitedly began pawing and neighing. About a half mile from shore, they were pushed overboard. As there were no docking facilities in the New World, the horses had no choice but to make a splash entrance.

2. THE POOP ON URBAN LIFE New York City in the early 1900s had some 150,000 horses, resulting in an accumulation of manure at the rate of more than three million pounds a day.

3. WAR HORSES During the Civil War, Confederate cavalrymen supplied their own horses. They were allowed forty cents a day for the animal's care. If the horse was killed or disabled in battle, then the owner was paid the appraised value and given thirty days leave to find a replacement.

4. THE HORSE SURPRISES THE INDIANS Until the Spanish arrived, the North American Indians had never seen a horse. When confronted with the strange animals mounted by Europeans with

sickly white skin, they were not sure if they were faced with one animal or two.

5. MUSIC TO GO WEST BY The tractor-trailer truck of early America was the Conestoga wagon, which carried three to four tons of cargo. The standard hitch was a six-horse team—the front "leads" were the lightest and liveliest, the middle pair were the "swings," and the "wheelhorses" were the largest and strongest. An arch of four bells hung over each horse's mane—small soprano bells on the leads, medium tenor bells on the swings, and large basso bells on the wheelhorses. They averaged fifteen to twenty miles a day.

6. THE PONY EXPLOSION Between 1900 and 1910 the growth in the horse population far outpaced that of the human population. With the flood tide of immigrants, the number of people in the United States increased by 21 percent, jumping from 76 to 92 million. In the same period the horse population grew a dramatic 70 percent— from 13 to 23 million.

7. NOMADIC POSSIBILITIES As the horse flourished, the life-style of the plains Indians was totally altered. The horse enabled them to follow and hunt the huge roaming herds of buffalo, which became the center of their culture.

8. THE TRACTOR FACTOR In the 1920s, the greatest increase in farm productivity was brought about by the decline of the horse. When the gasoline-powered tractor came into use, the teams of up to fifty horses that had pulled combine harvesters were no longer necessary. Millions of acres that had been used to raise feed for horses were freed up to raise food for people. Throughout the 1920s the horse population decreased by almost half a million a year and would continue to decrease as America shifted to different kinds of horsepower.

Notes

PART I: All in the First Family

PRESIDENTS ON THE PRESIDENCY

1. Marcus Cunliffe, *George Washington: Man and Monument* (New York: New American Library, 1982), p. 116.
2. Sid Frank and Arden Davis Melick, *The Presidents: Tidbits and Trivia* (New York: Greenwich House, 1984), p. 49.
3. John B. Moses, *Presidential Courage* (New York: Norton, 1980), p. 69.
5. Paul F. Boller, *Presidential Anecdotes* (New York: Oxford University Press, 1981), p. 127.
7. Boller, *Presidential Anecdotes*, p. 166.
8. Ibid., p. 170.
9. Ted Morgan, *FDR: A Biography* (New York: Simon & Schuster, 1985), p. 43.
10. Boller, *Presidential Anecdotes*, p. 199.
11. Arthur Bernon Tourtellot, *The Presidents on the Presidency* (New York: Doubleday, 1964), p. 363.
12. Ibid.
13. Donald McCoy,*Calvin Collidge* (New York: Macmillan, 1967), p. 148.
14. Tourtellot, *The Presidents on the Presidency*, p. 370.
15. Helen Thomas, *Dateline: White House* (New York: Macmillan, 1975), p. 22.

PRESIDENTIAL IMBIBERS AND ABSTAINERS

1. Boller, *Presidential Anecdotes*, p. 286
2. Philip Klein, *President James Buchanan, A Biography* (University Park: Pennsylvania State University Press, 1962), pp. 210–211.
3. Francis Russell, *The Shadow of Blooming Grove: Warren G. Harding in His Times* (New York: McGraw-Hill, 1968), pp. 446–448; Marianne Means, *The Woman in the White House* (New York: Random House, 1963), p. 168.
4. Boller, *Presidential Anecdotes*, p. 165.
5. Edward Wagenknecht, *The Seven Worlds of Theodore Roosevelt* (New York: Longmans, Green, 1958), pp. 92–93.
6. Rexford Guy Tugwell, *Grover Cleveland* (New York: Macmillan, 1968), pp. 39–42.
7. Lately Thomas, *The First President Johnson* (New York: William Morrow, 1968), pp. 295–297.
9. Richard Goldhurst, *Many Are the Hearts: The Agony and the Triumph of Ulysses S. Grant* (New York: Reader's Digest Press, 1975), p. 58; W. E. Woodward, *Meet General Grant* (New York: Horace Liveright, 1928), p. 121.
10. Alden Hatch, *Woodrow Wilson* (New York: Henry Holt, 1947), pp. 132–133.

TRYING OUT FOR COMMANDER IN CHIEF

1. Marcus Cunliffe and the editors of *American Heritage, The American Heritage History of the Presidency* (New York: American Heritage Publishing Co., 1968), p. 971; Ronnie Dugger, *The Politician: The Life and Times of Lyndon Johnson* (New York: Norton, 1982), pp. 238–250.

2. Carl Sandburg, *Abraham Lincoln: The Prairie Years and the War Years* (New York: Harcourt Brace Jovanovich, 1954), pp. 62–66.
3. Bailey, *Presidential Greatness*, pp. 84–85; Joan and Clay Blair, *The Search for JFK* (New York: Berkley, 1976), pp. 236–269.
4. Bruce Mazlish and Edwin Diamond, *Jimmy Carter: A Character Portrait* (New York: Simon & Schuster, 1978), p. 112.
5. Burke Davis, *Old Hickory* (New York: Holt, 1960), pp. 5–6.
6. John William Tebbel, *George Washington's America* (New York: Dutton, 1954), pp. 38–40.

PRESIDENTS ON THE RIGHT AND WRONG SIDES OF THE LAW

1. Edmund Morris, *The Rise of Theodore Roosevelt* (New York: Coward, McCann & Geoghegan, 1979), pp. 322–323.
2. Lou Cannon, *Reagan* (New York: Putnam, 1982), p. 31.
3. Roger Butterfield, *American Past: A History of the United States from Concord to Hiroshima* (New York: Simon & Schuster, 1947), p. 196; Joseph Kane, *Facts About the Presidents* (New York: H. W. Wilson, 1959), p. 420.
4. Hope Miller, *Scandals in the Highest Office* (New York: Random House, 1975), p. 157.
5. Charles and Barbara Whalen, *The Longest Debate: A Legislative History of the 1964 Civil Rights Act* (New York: New American Library, 1985), p. 74.
6. Kane, *Facts About the Presidents*, pp. 419–420.
7. Claude G. Bowers, *The Young Thomas Jefferson, 1743–1789* (Boston: Houghton Mifflin, 1945), p. 215.
8. Edwin A. Wein, *Woodrow Wilson: A Medical and Pyschological Biography* (Princeton, N.J.: Princeton University Press, 1981), p. 372.

LIFE IN THE WHITE HOUSE

1. William Seale, *The President's House* (Washington, D.C.: White House Historical Association, 1986), pp. 93–94.
3. Ibid., p. 129.
4. Butterfield, *American Past*, p. 106; Michael DiSalle, *Second Choice* (New York: Hawthorn Books, 1966), p. 41.
5. Arthur Hadley, *Power's Human Face* (New York: William Morrow, 1965), p. 197.
6. Margaret Truman, *Women of Courage: From Revolutionary Times to the Present* (New York: William Morrow, 1976), p. 49.
7. Dixon Wecter, *The Saga of American Society* (New York; Scribner, 1937), p. 86.
8. Thomas, *Dateline: White House*, p. 4.
9. Glenn Kittler, *Hail to the Chief* (Philadelphia: Chilton Books, 1965), p. 73; Editors of *American Heritage*, *The American Heritage Pictorial History of the Presidents of the United States* (New York: American Heritage Publishing, 1968), p. 347; Lonnelle Aikman, *The Living White House* (Washington, D.C.: White House Historical Association, 1966), p. 24.
10. Amy Jensen, *The White House and Its Thirty-four Families* (New York: McGraw-Hill, 1965), pp. 201–202.
11. Means, *The Woman in the White House*, p. 167.

12. Jensen, *The White House and its Thirty-four Families*, pp. 63–64.
13. Seale, *The President's House*, p. 232.

HOME IMPROVEMENT AT THE WHITE HOUSE

1. Seale, *The President's House*, pp. 90–91.
2. Jensen, *The White House and Its Thirty-four Families*, p. 72.
3. Seale, *The President's House*, p. 579; Frank and Melick, *The Presidents: Tidbits and Trivia*, p. 39.
4. Seale, *The President's House*, p. 269.
5. Ibid., p. 494.
6. Ona Jeffries, *In and Out of the White House* (New York: Wilfred Frank, 1960), p. 254.
7. Seale, *The President's House*, p. 316.
8. Jensen, *The White House and Its Thirty-four Families*, pp. 252–253.
9. Moses, *Presidential Courage*, p. 116.
10: Jeffries, *In and Out of the White House*, p. 289.
11. Ibid., p. 227; Bess Furman, *White House Profile* (Indianapolis: Bobbs-Merrill, 1951), p. 231; Seale, *The President's House*, pp. 540–541.

FIRST CHILDREN

1. Jensen, *The White House and Its Thirty-four Families*, p. 168.
2. Boller, *Presidential Anecdotes*, p. 206.
4. Thomas, *Dateline: White House*, pp. 17–18; Editors of *The New York Times*, *The Kennedy Years* (New York: Viking Press, 1964), p. 226.
5. Jimmy Carter, *Keeping Faith* (New York: Bantam Books, 1982), pp. 29–30, 564.
6. Alfred Steinberg, *The Man from Missouri: The Life and Times of Harry S. Truman* (New York: Putnam, 1962), pp. 394–395.
7. Thomas, *Dateline: White House*, pp. 98, 100–101.

PART II: *Fortunes and Fates*

RUNAWAYS

1. Frank Luther Mott, editor, *A Gallery of Americans* (New York: New American Library, 1951), pp. 116–122; Richard Amacher, *Benjamin Franklin* (New York: Twayne Publishers, 1962), pp. 20–21.
2. Lately Thomas, *The First President Johnson* (New York: William Morrow, 1968), pp. 12–14.
3. Editors of *American Heritage, American Heritage Book of the Pioneer Spirit* (New York: American Heritage Publishing, 1959), pp. 172–173; Allen Johnson and Dumas Malone, editors, *Dictionary of American Biography* (New York: Scribner, 1958), Vol. II, pp. 530–532; Irving Stone, *Men to Match My Mountains: The Opening of the Far West, 1840–1900* (Garden City, N.Y.: Doubleday, 1956), p. 37.
4. Gene Caesar, *King of the Mountain Men* (New York: Dutton, 1961), pp. 22–24; Johnson and Malone, *Dictionary of American Biography*, Vol. II, p. 33.

5. Nathan Irvin Higgins, *Slave and Citizen: The Life of Frederick Douglass* (Boston: Little, Brown, 1980), pp. 13–15, 33–34.
6. M. K. Wisehart, *Sam Houston* (Washington, D.C.: Robert B. Luce, 1962), pp. 3–6; Marquis James, *The Raven* (Indianapolis, Bobbs-Merrill, 1929), pp. 15–18.
7. Editors of *American Heritage, American Heritage Book of the Pioneer Spirit*, pp. 55–56.

THEY DIED BROKE

1. William Howard Adams, *Jefferson's Monticello* (New York: Abbeville Press, 1983), p. 237; Fawn Brodie, *Thomas Jefferson* (New York: Norton, 1974), p. 43.
2. Oscar Lewis, *Sutter's Fort: Gateway to the Gold Fields* (Englewood Cliffs, New Jersey: Prentice-Hall, 1966), pp. 197–200; Richard Dillon, *Fool's Gold: A Biography of John Sutter* (New York: Coward-McCann, 1967), pp. 343–350.
3. Donald Dale Jackson, *Gold Dust* (New York: Alfred A. Knopf, 1980), p. 333; Editors of *American Heritage, American Heritage Book of the Pioneer Spirit*, p. 189.
4. Joseph and Frances Gies, *The Ingenious Yankees* (New York: Thomas Crowell, 1976), pp. 209–210; Mitchell Wilson, *American Science and Invention* (New York: Simon & Schuster, 1954), p. 124; National Geographic Society, *Those Inventive Americans* (Washington, D.C. : The National Geographic Society, 1971), p. 80.
5. Goldhurst, *Many Are the Hearts*, p. 21; Woodward, *Meet General Grant*, pp. 487–489; William S. McFeely, *Grant* (New York: Norton, 1981), p. 489.
6. William Walton, *The Evidence of Washington* (New York: Harper & Row, 1966), pp. 9–13, 45; Dumas Malone, ed., *Dictionary of American Biography* (New York: Scribner, 1961), Vol. VI, p. 169.

WILLS

1. Hudson Strode, *Jefferson Davis, Tragic Hero* (New York: Harcourt, Brace and World, 1964), pp. 421–443; Burke Davis, *The Long Surrender* (New York: Random House, 1985), p. 249–52; Clement Eaton, *Jefferson Davis* (New York: Free Press, 1977), p. 264.
2. Carl Van Doren, *Benjamin Franklin* (New York: Viking Press, 1938), p. 762; Bruce Bliven, *A Mirror for Greatness: Six Americans* (New York: McGraw-Hill, 1975), p. 47; Frank Donovan, *The Benjamin Franklin Papers* (New York: Dodd, Mead, 1962), pp. 290–291.
3. Burke Davis, *George Washington and the American Revolution* (New York: Random House, 1975), p. 428.
4. Ted Morgan, *FDR: A Biography*, p. 257.
5. Elisabeth Griffith, *In Her Own Right: The Life of Elizabeth Cady Stanton* (New York: Oxford University Press, 1984), pp. 89, 98.
7. Leonard Carmichael and J. C. Long, *James Smithson and the Smithson Story* (New York: Putnam, 1965), p. 14; Mark Sullivan, *Our Times*, Vol. 2, p. 614.

UNREWARDED HEROES

1. Page Smith, *The Nation Comes of Age: A People's History of the Ante-bellum Years* (New York: McGraw-Hill, 1981), pp. 220; Richard M. Ketchum, "The

Thankless Task of Nicholas Trist," *American Heritage,* Vol. XXI, No. 5 (Aug. 1970), pp. 13–14, 46–90.

2. Page Smith, *The Shaping of America: A People's History of the Young Republic* (New York: McGraw-Hill, 1980), p. 546; John Bakeless, *Background to Glory,* (Philadelphia: Lippincott, 1957), pp. 326–328; Johnson and Malone, *Dictionary of American Biography,* Vol. II, pp. 127–130; Richard Ketchum, "Men of the Revolution—XI," *American Heritage,* Vol. XXV, No. 1 (Dec. 1973), pp. 32–33, 78.

3. Hope Miller, *Scandals in the Highest Office,* p. 43; Eric Foner, *Tom Paine and Revolutionary America* (New York: Oxford University Press, 1976), p. 258; Editors of *American Heritage, The American Heritage Pictorial History of the Presidents,* p. 13.

4. Clay Blair, *Silent Victory* (Philadelphia: Lippincott, 1975), pp. 260–263; Gordon W. Prange, *Miracle at Midway* (New York: McGraw-Hill, 1982), pp. 45–46.

5. Bernard A. Weisburger, *The District of Columbia: The Seat of Government* (New York: Time/Life Books, 1968), pp. 65–66; Maymie R. Krythe, *What So Proudly We Hail: All About Our American Flag, Monuments and Symbols* (New York: Harper & Row, 1968), pp. 157–159.

PRIDE BEFORE A FALL

1. Editors of *American Heritage, The American Heritage Book of Indians* (New York, American Heritage Press, 1961), p. 344; Dee Brown, *Bury My Heart at Wounded Knee: An Indian History of the American West* (New York: Holt, Rinehart and Winston, 1970), pp. 136–137; Jacob Dunn, *Massacres of the Mountains: A History of the Indian Wars of the Far West, 1815–1875* (New York: Archer House, 1958), pp. 423–424.

2. Donald Barr Chidsey, *The French and Indian War* (New York: Crown, 1969), p. 43.

3. W. E. Woodward, *Meet General Grant,* p. 313.

4. Harry Coles, *The War of 1812* (Chicago: University of Chicago Press), p. 184; Walter Lord, *The Dawn's Early Light* (New York: Norton, 1972), pp. 261–263.

5. Edwin Hoyt, *The Vanderbilts and Their Fortunes* (Garden City, N.Y.; Doubleday, 1962), p. 360.

6. Dale Carnegie, *Lincoln the Unknown* (Forest Hills, N.Y.: Forest Hills Publishing, 1932), p. 121.

VISIONS, DREAMS, AND OMENS

1. Fawn Brodie, *No Man Knows My History: The Life of Joseph Smith the Mormon Prophet* (New York: Alfred A. Knopf, 1971), p. 39.

2. Johanna Johnston, *Runaway to Heaven: The Story of Harriet Beecher Stowe* (Garden City, N.Y.: Doubleday, 1963) p. 201.

3. Brown, *Bury My Heart at Wounded Knee,* pp. 432–438.

4. Carnegie, *Lincoln the Unknown,* p. 166; Jensen, *The White House,* p. 90.

5. Page Smith, *The Rise of Industrial America: A People's History of the Post-Reconstruction Era* (New York: McGraw-Hill, 1984), p. 68.

6. John Moses, *Presidential Courage,* p. 80.; Stephen B. Oates, *With Malice Toward*

None: The Life of Abraham Lincoln (New York: Harper & Row, 1977), pp. 425–426.

7. Joseph L. Gardner, *Departing Glory: Theodore Roosevelt as Ex-President* (New York: Scribner, 1973), pp. 88–89; Means, *The Woman in the White House*, p. 117.
8. James W. Clarke, *American Assassins: The Darker Side of Politics* (Princeton, N.J.: Princeton University Press, 1982), pp. 214–219; James McKinley, *Assassination in America* (New York: Harper & Row, 1977), p. 57.

LINCOLN'S SON: INVITED TO THREE ASSASSINATIONS

1. Ruth Randall, *Lincoln's Sons* (Boston: Little, Brown, 1955), pp. 210–218.
2. Ibid., p. 300.
3. Ibid., p. 300; Kane, *Facts About the Presidents*, p. 161.

ILLEGITIMACY IN AMERICA'S PAST

1. Webb Garrison, *Lost Pages from American History* (Harrisburg, Pa.: Stackpole Books, 1976), pp. 50–51.
2. Ibid., p. 19.
3. Robert A. Hendrickson, *The Rise and Fall of Alexander Hamilton* (New York: Dodd, Mead, 1985), p. 3; Johnson and Malone, *Dictionary of American Biography*, Vol. IV, p. 171.
4. Irving Stone, *Men to Match My Mountains*, p. 37.
5. Russell, *The Shadow of Blooming Grove*, pp. 317–319.

THANKS, BUT—

1. *The New York Times*, May 18, 1986, Vol. CXXXV, No. 46,788, Section 6, Part II, p. 38.
2. Walter Ross, *The Last Hero: Charles A. Lindbergh* (New York: Harper & Row, 1968), pp. 143–144.
3. W. A. Swanberg, *First Blood* (New York: Scribner, 1957), pp. 173–174.
4. Nellie Snyder Yost, *Buffalo Bill* (Chicago: Swallow Press, 1979), pp. 66–67.
5. Davis, *George Washington and the American Revolution*, p. 450.
6. Gardner, *Departing Glory*, pp. 370–373.

BETS

1. Russell, *The Shadow of Blooming Grove*, p. 448.
2. Editors of *American Heritage*, *American Heritage Book of the Revolution* (New York: American Heritage Publishing, 1971), p. 234.
3. Smith, *The Shaping of America*, p. 53.
4. Editors of *American Heritage*, *The American Heritage History of the Great West* (New York: American Heritage Publishing, 1969), p. 261.
5. Mott, *A Gallery of Americans*, pp. 124–125.
6. Boller, *Presidential Anecdotes*, pp. 240–241.

FIRED

1. Richard Kenin and Justin Wintle, eds., *The Dictionary of American Biographical Quotation* (New York: Alfred A. Knopf, 1978), p. 506.

2. Bates Lowry, *Building a National Image: Architectural Drawings for the American Democracy, 1798–1912* (Washington, D.C.: National Building Museum, 1985), pp. 17–18.
3. Benjamin Thomas, *Stanton: The Life and Times of Lincoln's Secretary of War* (New York: Alfred A. Knopf, 1962), pp. 586–591.
4. Hugh Gregory Gallagher, *FDR's Splendid Deception* (New York: Dodd, Mead, 1985), p. 115.
5. Otto Eisenschiml, *Why Was Lincoln Murdered?* (New York: Grosset & Dunlap, 1937), pp. 16–21.

PART III: *War Games*

THE ARMY-NAVY GAME IS PLAYED AT SANTIAGO DE CUBA

1. Walter Millis, *The Martial Spirit* (Cambridge, Mass.: The Riverside Press, 1931), p. 262.
2. Ibid., p. 327.
3. Ibid., pp. 328–329.

HOW THEY FOUGHT IN THE DAYS OF SAIL

4. C. Keith Wilbur, *Picture Book of the Revolution's Privateers* (Harrisburg, Pa.: Stackpole Books, 1972), p. 71.
6. Nathan Miller, *Sea of Glory* (New York: David McKay, 1974), pp. 380–385; John Walsh, *Night On Fire* (New York: McGraw-Hill, 1978), pp. 66–89.
7. Wilbur, *Picture Book of the Revolution's Privateers*, p. 56.

WHEN WARS WERE MORE GENTLEMANLY

1. Lord, *The Dawn's Early Light*, pp. 175–176.
2. Burke Davis, *Our Incredible Civil War* (New York: Holt, 1960), p. 106.
3. Editors of *American Heritage*, *The American Heritage History of the Thirteen Colonies* (New York: American Heritage Publishing, 1967), p. 257.
5. Bowers, *Young Thomas Jefferson*, pp. 229–235.
6. Lord, *The Dawn's Early Light*, pp. 138–139.
7. Robert Henry, *"First with the Most," Forrest* (Indianapolis: Bobbs-Merrill, 1944), pp. 338–340.
8. Truman, *Women of Courage*, pp. 31–35.
9. Davis, *George Washington and the American Revolution*, p. 443.
10. Swanberg, *First Blood*, p. 327; Bruce Catton, *The Coming Fury* (Garden City, N.Y.: Doubleday, 1961), p. 311.

RUSES THAT WORKED

1. H. P. Willmott, *June 1944* (Poole, Dorset, United Kingdom: Blanford Press, 1984), pp. 64–66; Editors of *Army Times*, *D-Day: The Greatest Invasion* (New York; Putnam, 1969), pp. 33–44.
2. Page Smith, *A New Age Now Begins* (New York: McGraw-Hill, 1976), pp. 832–834.
3. Stanley Falk, *Decision at Leyte* (New York: Norton, 1966), p. 77; John Costello, *The Pacific War* (New York: Quill, 1982), pp. 502–519.

4. Davis, *George Washington and the American Revolution*, p. 392: Smith, *A New Age Now Begins*, p. 1,659.
5. Editors of *American Heritage*, *The American Heritage Picture History of the Civil War* (New York: American Heritage Publishing, 1960), p. 117.
6. Editors of *American Heritage*, *American Heritage Book of the Revolution*, p. 250.
7. Bakeless, *Background to Glory*, pp. 177–210; Dale Van Every, *A Company of Heroes: The American Frontier, 1775–1783* (New York: William Morrow, 1982), p. 188.

RIVALRY IN THE MILITARY

2. Editors of *American Heritage*, *The American Heritage Pictorial History of the Presidents of the United States*, p. 905; William Manchester, *American Caesar* (Boston: Little, Brown, 1978), p. 478.
3. Lengyl, *I, Benedict Arnold* (Garden City, N.Y.: Doubleday, 1960), p. 17; Smith, *A New Age Now Begins*, p. 589.
4. Evan Connell, *Son of the Morning Star* (San Francisco: North Point Press, 1984), p. 12.
5. Lengyl, *I, Benedict Arnold*, p. 22.

RAISING AN ARMY

1. Richard Ketchum, *The Winter Soldiers* (Garden City, N.Y.: Doubleday, 1973), pp. 83–89.
2. Davis, *George Washington and the American Revolution*, p. 179.
3. Tugwell, *Grover Cleveland*, p. 34; Roy Basher, *A Short History of the American Civil War* (New York: Basic Books, 1967), pp. 69–70.
4. Millis, *The Martial Spirit*, pp. 148–159.

LINCOLN'S GENERALS: FOUR LOSERS AND A WINNER

3. Malone, *Dictionary of American Biography*, Vol. V, pp. 196–198.
4. Editors of *American Heritage*, *The American Heritage Pictorial History of the Presidents of the United States*, p. 394.
5. Woodward, *Meet General Grant*, p. 309; Bruce Catton, *Grant Takes Command* (Boston: Little, Brown, 1969), pp. 124–143.

BATTLE CRIES

1. Leonard Guttridge, *The Commodores* (New York: Harper & Row, 1969), p. 212.
3. Millis, *The Martial Spirit*, p. 274.
4. Walsh, *Night On Fire*, pp. 78–81.
5. Bern Andersen, *By Sea and River* (New York: Alfred A. Knopf, 1962), pp. 240–243.
6. Dumas Malone, *Dictionary of American Biography* (New York: Scribner, 1934), Vol. XIV, pp. 232–233.

FAMOUS SURPRISE ATTACKS

1. Editors of *American Heritage*, *American Heritage History of the American Revolution*, pp. 189–190.

3. Edward Stackpole, *Chancellorsville: Lee's Greatest Battle* (Harrisburg, Pa.: Stackpole Books, 1958), pp. 266–267.
4. Walter Lord, *Day of Infamy* (New York: Holt, 1957), pp. 174–175.

PART IV: *Signposts of America's Past*

PAPER CHASE: THE TRAVELS OF THE DECLARATION OF INDEPENDENCE

1. David Hawke, *Honorable Treason* (New York: Viking Press, 1976), p. 172.
3. Dumas Malone, *Story of the Declaration of Independence* (New York: Oxford University Press, 1954), p. 89.
4. Ibid., pp. 89–92.
5. Ibid., p. 251.
6. Ibid., p. 248.
7. Ibid., p. 257.
8. Ibid.
9. Ibid.
10. Ibid.
11. Ibid., p. 262.
12. Ibid., p. 263.
13. Ibid.
14. Alfred Meyer, "Daily Rise and Fall of the Nation's Revered Documents," *Smithsonian*, Vol. 17, No. 7 (Oct. 1986), p. 135.

ENSHRINING OF AMERICANA

2. Adams, *Jefferson's Monticello*, pp. 248–259.
3. Stanley W. McClure, *The Lincoln Museum and the House Where Lincoln Died* (Washington, D.C.: National Park Service, 1949), p. 16.
4. Ketchum, *The Winter Soldiers*, p. 21.
5. Krythe, *What So Proudly We Hail*, pp. 60–88.
6. The United States Capitol Historical Society, *We the People* (Washington, D.C.: The United States Capitol Historical Society, 1963), pp. 90–96.
7. "Continuing Battles for the Alamo," *American History Illustrated*, Vol. XX, No. 11 (March 1986), pp. 52–57.
8. Norman Richards, *The Story of Old Ironsides* (Chicago: Children's Press, 1967), pp. 25–26.
9. Edward Hamilton, *Fort Ticonderoga, Key to a Continent* (Boston: Little, Brown, 1964), pp. 225–230.

WHAT WE ALMOST GOT

1. Krythe, *What So Proudly We Hail*, pp. 188–192.
2. Ibid., p. 213; Daniel Boorstin, *The Americans: The National Experience* (New York: Random House, 1973), p. 355; The United States Capitol Historical Society, *We the People*, p. 96.
3. Krythe, *What So Proudly We Hail*, p. 151.
4. Alistair Cooke, *Alistair Cooke's America* (New York: Alfred A. Knopf, 1973), p. 134.

5. James Bishop, *The Birth of the United States* (New York: William Morrow, 1976), pp. 217–224, p. 335.
6. Boorstin, *The Americans: The National Experience*, pp. 349–351; The United States Capitol Historical Society, *We the People*, p. 98.
7. Page Smith, *John Adams* (Garden City, N.Y.: Doubleday, 1962), pp. 296–297; Krythe, *What So Proudly We Hail*, pp. 27–30.
8. J. Earl Massey, *America's Money* (New York: Crowell, 1968), pp. 76–83, 90; Don Taxay, *The U.S. Mint and Coinage* (New York: Arco Publishing, 1966), pp. 15–20.
9. Krythe, *What So Proudly We Hail*, pp. 30, 40–43.

MEMORABLE MARKERS

1. Cooke, *Alistair Cooke's America*, p. 109.
4. Stackpole, *Chancellorsville, Lee's Greatest Battle*, p. 273.
5. Jay Robert Nash, *Bloodletters and Badmen: A Narrative Encyclopedia of American Criminals from the Pilgrims to the Present* (New York: M. Evans, 1973), p. 283.
6. Russell, *The Shadow of Blooming Grove*, p. 633.
7. Bernard Mayo, *Myths and Men: Patrick Henry, George Washington, Thomas Jefferson* (Athens, Ga.: University of Georgia Press, 1959), p. 77.

FLAGS

1. Lord, *The Dawn's Early Light*, p. 191.
2. Seale, *The President's House*, pp. 372–373;
3. Davis, *The Long Surrender*, p. 8; Strode, *Jefferson Davis, Tragic Hero*, p. 525.
4. Krythe, *What So Proudly We Hail*, pp. 16–17; Swanberg, *First Blood*, p. 339.
5. Milo Quaife, *The History of the United States Flag from the Revolution to the Present, Including a Guide to Its Use and Display* (New York: Harper & Row, 1961), p. 41.
6. Randall, *Lincoln's Sons*, p. 100.
7. Ibid., pp. 44, 87, 108.
8. Ibid., pp. 44–87; Boorstin, *The Americans: The National Experience*, p. 375.
9. Krythe, *What So Proudly We Hail*, p. 24; John Costello, *The Pacific War* (New York: Rawson, Wade, 1981), pp. 545–546.
10. Krythe, *What So Proudly We Hail*, p. 6.
11. Ibid., p. 7.
12. Davis, *George Washington and the American Revolution*, pp. 454–455.

PART V: *Mixed Media: Communication at Its Best*

ANYTHING FOR A STORY

1. Davis, *The Long Surrender*, p. 145.
2. Ross, *The Last Hero*, p. 223.
3. Charles Brown, *The Correspondents' War: Journalists in the Spanish-American War* (New York: Scribner, 1967), p. 81; Millis, *The Martial Spirit*, p. 67.
4. Marcus Cunliffe and the editors of *American Heritage*, *The American Heritage History of the Presidency*, p. 566.

5. Boller, *Presidential Anecdotes*, pp. 63–64; Jack Shepherd, *The Adams Chronicles* (Boston: Little, Brown, 1975), p. 302.
6. Lois W. Banner, *Elizabeth Cady Stanton: A Radical for Women's Rights* (Boston: Little, Brown, 1980), p. 83.

THE U.S. VERSUS SPAIN: THE WAR THE NEWSPAPERS WON

1. Brown, *The Correspondents' War*, p. 78.
2. Ibid.; B. J. A. O'Toole, *The Spanish War: A Compact History* (New York: Norton, 1984), p. 190.
3. Brown, *The Correspondents' War*, pp. 212–220; Allan Keller, *The Spanish-American War: A Compact History* (New York: Hawthorn Books, 1969), pp. 88–93.
4. O'Toole, *The Spanish War*, p. 276.
5. Brown, *The Correspondents' War*, pp. 389–390; John Tebbel, *The Life and Good Times of William Randolph Hearst* (New York: Dutton, 1952), pp. 190–195.
6. O'Toole, *The Spanish War: A Compact History*, pp. 251–252.
7. Millis, *The Martial Spirit*, pp. 326–327.

SIGNING THEIR NAMES

1. David Freeman Hawke, *Benjamin Rush: Revolutionary Gadfly* (Indianapolis: Bobbs-Merrill, 1971), p. 164.
2. Jay Monaghan, *The Book of the American West* (New York: Messner, 1963), p. 31.
4. Weisburger, *The District of Columbia: The Seat of Government*, pp. 65–75.
5. Banner, *Elizabeth Cady Stanton: A Radical for Women's Rights*, p. 10; Elisabeth Griffith, *In Her Own Right*, p. 58.
7. Woodward, *Meet General Grant*, pp. 484–485.
8. Editors of *American Heritage*, *The American Heritage Book of Great Adventures of the Old West*, p. 183.
9. Morgan, *FDR: A Biography*, p. 146.

SIGNALS, CODES, AND CUES

1. Dorothy Kunhardt, *Twenty Days* (New York: Harper & Row, 1965), p. 75.
2. Editors of *American Heritage*, *American Heritage Book of the Revolution*, p. 246.
3. Walter Lord, *A Time to Stand* (New York: Harper & Row, 1961), p. 101.
4. George Condon, *Stars in the Water* (Garden City, N.Y.: Doubleday, 1974), pp. 8–9.
5. George Stimpson, *The Book About American History* (Greenwich, Conn.: Fawcett Publications, 1956), pp. 394–395.
6. Rodman Gilder, *Battery* (Boston: Houghton Mifflin, 1936), p. 220; Marvin Trachtenberg, *The Statue of Liberty* (New York: Viking Press, 1976), p. 186.
8. Smith, *The Shaping of America*, p. 519.
9. Editors of *American Heritage*, *American Heritage Book of Great Adventures of the Old West*, pp. 241–242.
10. Whalen, *The Longest Debate*, pp. 202–203.
12. Bruce Lancaster, *From Lexington to Liberty* (Garden City, N.Y.: Doubleday, 1955), p. 94; Richard Wheeler, *Voices of 1776*, p. 3.

THE ART OF SHAKING HANDS

1. Seale, *The President's House*, p. 8.
2. Jeffries, *In and Out of the White House*, p. 42.
3. Smith, *The Shaping of America*, pp. 803–805.
4. Jensen, *The White House and Its Thirty-four Families*, p. 60.
5. Aikman, *The Living White House*, p. 300.
6. Reader's Digest, *Great Lives, Great Deeds* (Pleasantville, N.Y.: Reader's Digest Association, 1964), p. 340.
7. Boller, *Presidential Anecdotes*, p. 143.
8. Goldhurst, *Many Are the Hearts*, p. 85.
9. Aikman, *The Living White House*, p. 51.
10. Boller, *Presidential Anecdotes*, pp. 188–189.
12. Page Smith, *America Enters the World: A People's History of the Progressive Era and World War I* (New York: McGraw-Hill, 1985), p. 312.
13. Means, *The Woman in the White House*, p. 169; Russell, *The Shadow of Blooming Grove*, pp. 437–438.
14. McCoy, *Calvin Coolidge*, pp. 287–288.

TOKENS OF APPRECIATION

1. Davis, *Old Hickory*, pp. 74–75, 304.
2. Cunliffe, *George Washington: Man and Monument*, pp. 16, 148.
3. Morgan, *FDR: A Biography*, p. 109; Editors of *American Heritage*, *The American Heritage Pictorial History of the Presidents of the United States*, pp. 789–790.
4. Woodward, *Meet General Grant*, pp. 368–369.
5. Thomas A. Bailey, *Presidential Saints and Sinners* (New York: The Free Press, 1981), pp. 239–240.
6. John Terrell, *Zebulon Pike: The Life and Times of a Great Adventurer* (New York: Weybright and Talley, 1968), pp. 175–176, 224–225.
7. Morison, *Christopher Columbus, Mariner* (Boston: Little, Brown, 1955), pp. 53–54.
8. Krythe, *What So Proudly We Hail*, pp. 201–202.
9. Linda McMurray, *George Washington Carver: Scientist and Symbol* (New York: Oxford University Press, 1981), p. 291.
10. Robert Howard, *The Horse in America* (Englewood Cliffs, N.J.: Follet, 1965), p. 96.
11. Gerald Ford, *A Time to Heal* (New York: Harper & Row, 1979), pp. 171–172.

TWENTY-ONE-GUN AND OTHER SALUTES

3. O'Toole, *The Spanish War*, p. 252.
4. Swanberg, *First Blood*, pp. 327–328; Catton, *The Coming Fury*, p. 324.
5. McFeely, *Grant*, p. 220.

PART VI: *Morality and Immorality, Ethics and Beliefs*

NEVER A DULL SUNDAY

1. Douglas Southall Freeman, *Lee's Lieutenants* (New York: Scribner, 1942), pp. 488–489; Burke Davis, *They Called Him Stonewall* (New York: Holt, Rinehart & Winston, 1954), p. 172.
2. Seale, *The President's House*, pp. 488–489; Louise Durbin, *Inaugural Cavalcade* (New York: Dodd, Mead, 1971), pp. 101–102.
3. Francis Dillon, *The Pilgrims* (Garden City, N.Y.: Doubleday, 1975), pp. 154–155.
4. David Loth, *The People's General* (New York: Scribner, 1951), p. 296.
5. Strode, *Jefferson Davis, Tragic Hero*, pp. 165–166.
6. Clifford Clark, *Henry Ward Beecher: Spokesman for a Middle-Class America* (Urbana, Ill.: University of Illinois Press, 1978), p. 124.

INFIDELITY

1. Miller, *Scandals in the Highest Office*, p. 230.
2. Forrest McDonald, *Alexander Hamilton* (New York: Norton, 1979), pp. 258–259; Philip Burr, *The Great American Rascal* (New York: Hawthorn, 1973), p. 220; Richard B. Morris, *Alexander Hamilton and the Founding of the Nation* (New York: Dial, 1957), p. 580.
3. Miller, *Scandals in the Highest Office*, pp. 242–245.
4. Boller, *Presidential Anecdotes*, pp. 80–81; Amy Jensen, *The White House and Its Thirty-three Families* (New York: McGraw-Hill, 1962), pp. 52–54; Alfred Kazin, *An American Procession* (New York: Alfred A. Knopf, 1984), p. 86.
5. Clark, *Henry Ward Beecher*, pp. 197–224; Allen Johnson, ed., *Dictionary of American Biography* (New York: Scribner, 1957), Vol. I, p. 134.
6. Milton Lomask, *Aaron Burr: The Conspiracy and the Years of Exile, 1805–1836* (New York: Farrar, Straus, Giroux, 1982), pp. 396–405.

INVOKING THE ALMIGHTY

1. Mott, *A Gallery of Americans*, p. 151.
2. Boller, *Presidential Anecdotes*, p. 217.
3. Walter Lord, *The Good Years: From 1900 to the First World War* (New York: Harper & Row, 1960), p. 84.
4. Strode, *Jefferson Davis, Tragic Hero*, p. 279.
5. Carnegie, *Lincoln the Unknown*, p. 172.
7. Bailey, *Presidential Saints and Sinners*, p. 194.
8. Bailey, *Presidential Saints and Sinners*, p. 271.
9. John Murray Allison, *Adams and Jefferson: The Story of a Friendship* (Norman: University of Oklahoma Press, 1966), p. 210.
10. Stephen J. Wagner, *The Road to the White House, the Politics of Presidential Elections* (New York: St. Martin's Press, 1984), p. 17; Paul F. Boller, *Presidential Campaigns* (New York: Oxford University Press, 1984), p. 38; Smith, *The Shaping of America*, p. 728.

PRAYER

1. Alistair Cooke, *Alistair Cooke's America* (New York: Knopf, 1973), p. 33.
2. Boller, *Presidential Anecdotes,* p. 278.
3. Van Doren, *Benjamin Franklin,* p. 17.
4. Swanberg, *First Blood,* p. 115.
5. Smith, *America Enters the World,* p. 730.
6. Smith, *The Shaping of America,* p. 80.
7. Thomas, *Dateline: White House,* pp. 119–120.
8. Lord, *A Time to Stand,* p. 207; Editors of *American Heritage, The American Heritage Book of Great Adventures of the Old West,* p. 123.

DO'S AND DON'TS

1. Alice Earle, *Stage-Coach and Tavern Days* (New York: Blom, 1969), p. 4.
2. Ibid., p. 2.
3. Bliven, *A Mirror for Greatness: Six Americans,* p. 55.
4. Smith, *The Nation Comes of Age,* p. 10.
5. Frank Moore, *The Diary of the American Revolution, 1775–1781* (New York: Washington Square Press, 1967), p. 221.
6. Howard, *The Horse in America,* p. 194.
7. John Morgan, *Robert Fulton* (New York: Mason/Charter, 1977), p. 153.
8. Editors of American Heritage, *The American Heritage Book of Great Adventures of the Old West,* pp. 177–178.

LIES AND OTHER MISTRUTHS

1. Russell, *The Shadow of Blooming Grove,* p. 383; Cooke, *Alistair Cooke's America,* p. 314.
2. Walter Lord, *The Past That Would Not Die* (New York: Harper & Row, 1965), p. 106.
3. Bailey, *Presidential Saints and Sinners,* pp. 256–257.
4. Samuel Eliot Morison, *Christopher Columbus, Mariner* (Boston: Little, Brown, 1955), p. 44.
5. Edwin Palmer, *The Vanderbilts and Their Fortunes* (Garden City, N.Y.: Doubleday, 1962), p. 206.
6. Stewart Holbrook, *Age of Moguls* (Garden City, N.Y.: Doubleday, 1956), p. 67; Mathew Josephson, *The Robber Barons; the Great American Capitalists, 1861–1901* (New York: Harcourt, Brace, 1934), pp. 187, 275.
7. Gallagher, *FDR's Splendid Deception,* pp. 91–92.
8. Means, *The Woman in the White House,* pp. 177–178; Mark Sullivan, *Our Times* (New York: Scribner, 1935), Vol. VI, pp. 293–312.
9. Allison, *Adams and Jefferson,* pp. 318–320.

THROUGH INDIAN EYES

1. Denis McLoughlin, *Wild & Wooly: An Encyclopedia of the Old West* (Garden City, N.Y.: Doubleday, 1975), pp. 445–446.
2. Editors of *American Heritage, American Heritage Book of Great Adventures of the Old West,* p. 254.

3. Monaghan, *The Book of the American West*, p. 391.
4. Smith, *A New Age Now Begins*, pp. 498–499.
5. Donald Chidsey, *Lewis and Clark* (New York: Crown, 1970), p. 78.

TO ERR IS HUMAN

1. Editors of *American Heritage*, *The American Heritage Book of Great Adventures of the Old West*, p. 30.
2. Ibid., p. 214; Stone, *Men to Match My Mountains*, p. 39.
3. Yost, *Buffalo Bill*, pp. 131–133.
4. Ferol Egan, *Fremont: Explorer for a Restless Nation* (Garden City, N.Y.; Doubleday, 1977), pp. 515–517.
5. Robert Lacey, *Ford: The Men and the Machine* (Boston: Little, Brown, 1986), p. 43.
6. Editors of *American Heritage*, *The American Heritage Book of Great Adventures of the Old West*, p. 184.
7. Nash, *Bloodletters and Badmen*, p. 299.
8. Means, *The Woman in the White House*, p. 114.

PART VII: *Life-styles*

LIVING WAGES

1. Bishop, *The Birth of the United States*, p. 215.
2. Condon, *Stars in the Water*, pp. 66–68.
3. Sandburg, *Abraham Lincoln: The Prairie Years and the War Years*, p. 69.
4. Wayne Gard, *The Chisholm Trail* (Norman, Okla.: University of Oklahoma Press, 1954), p. 89.
5. Ibid., p. 175.
6. Connell, *Son of the Morning Star*, p. 18.
7. Smith, *The Rise of Industrial America*, p. 219.
9. Lord, *The Good Years*, p. 161.
10. Cooke, *Alistair Cooke's America*, p. 317.

SCHOOLING

1. Carnegie, *Lincoln the Unknown*, p. 18.
2. Booker T. Washington, *Up from Slavery* (Williamstown, Mass.: Corner House Publishers, 1978), pp. 26–35; Louis R. Harlan, *Booker T. Washington: The Making of a Black Leader, 1856–1901* (New York: Oxford University Press, 1972), p. 36.
3. Mathew Josephson, *Edison* (New York: McGraw-Hill, 1959), p. 20.
4. Jim Burke, *Buffalo Bill: The Noblest Whiteskin* (New York: Putnam, 1973), p. 34.
5. Rockham Holt, *George Washington Carver: An American Biography* (Garden City, N.Y.: Doubleday, 1943), pp. 31–52, 72; McMurray, *George Washington Carver*, p. 19; Lawrence Elliot, *George Washington Carver: The Man Who Overcame* (Englewood Cliffs, N.J.: Prentice-Hall, 1966), pp. 23–26, 55.
6. Smith, *The Rise of Industrial America*, p. 347.
7. Van Doren, *Benjamin Franklin*, pp. 10–11.

TRAVELING IN STYLE

1. Editors of *American Heritage, American Heritage Book of the Revolution*, p. 239.
2. Lord, *A Time to Stand*, pp. 112–113.
3. Davis, *George Washington and the American Revolution*, p. 269.
4. Ibid., p. 282.
5. Editors of *American Heritage, The American Heritage Book of Great Adventures of the Old West*, p. 347.
6. Smith, *John Adams*, pp. 352–356.

THE TOBACCO HABIT

1. Kane, *Facts About the Presidents*, pp. 177–178.
2. Smith, *The Shaping of America*, p. 541.
3. Robert Taylor, *Vessel of Wrath: the Life and Times of Carry Nation* (New York: New American Library, 1966), p. 137.
4. Hadley, *Power's Human Face*, p. 128.
5. Moses, *Presidential Courage*, p. 64.
6. Ibid., p. 198.
7. Nash, *Bloodletters and Badmen*, pp. 43–44.

OH, HOW THEY DANCED

1. Davis, *George Washington and the American Revolution*, p. 311.
2. Seale, *The President's House*, p. 261.
3. Dee Brown, *Trail Driving Days* (New York: Bonanza Books, 1952), p. 64; Gard, *The Chisholm Trail*, p. 165.
4. Frank and Melick, *The Presidents: Tidbits and Trivia*, p. 33.
5. Hatch, *Woodrow Wilson*, p. 170; Richard Shenkman and Kurt Reiger, *One Night Stands with American History* (New York: William Morrow, 1980), p. 175.
6. Lacey, *Ford: The Men and the Machine*, pp. 242–243.
7. Thomas, *Dateline: White House*, p. 182.
8. Ibid., p. 83.

BED TIMES

1. Vernon Heaton, *The Mayflower* (New York: Mayflower Books, 1980), p. 138.
2. Flexner, *George Washington*, p. 35; Editors of *American Heritage, The American Heritage Pictorial History of the Presidents of the United States*, p. 13.
3. Sandburg, *Abraham Lincoln: the Prairie Years and the War Years*, p. 104; Carnegie, *Lincoln the Unknown*, p. 47.
4. Moses, *Presidential Courage*, p. 115.
5. Jeffries, *In and Out of the White House*, p. 149.
6. F. C. Hanighen, *Santa Anna, the Napoleon of the West* (New York: Coward-McCann, 1934), pp. 112–121.
7. Mott, *A Gallery of Americans*, p. 193.
8. Smith, *The Shaping of America*, pp. 775–776.
9. Mary Oakley, *Elizabeth Cady Stanton* (Old Westbury, N.Y.: The Feminist Press, 1972), p. 82.
10. James Bishop, *The Day Lincoln Was Shot* (New York: Harper & Row, 1955),

p. 213; Louis J. Weichmann, *A True History of the Assassination of Abraham Lincoln and of the Conspiracy of 1865* (New York: Alfred A. Knopf, 1952), p. 156.

MAN AND HIS DOG

1. Traphes Bryant, *Dog Days at the White House* (New York: Macmillan, 1975), p. 97.
2. Ibid., p. 27.
3. Gallagher, *FDR's Splendid Deception*, p. 174.
4. Editors of *American Heritage*, *To the Pacific with Lewis and Clark* (New York: American Heritage Publishing, 1967), p. 113.
5. Seale, *The President's House*, p. 330.

WHAT'S IN A NAME?

1. Woodward, *Meet General Grant*, p. 14; Carnegie, *Lincoln the Unknown*, p. 206.
2. Washington, *Up from Slavery*, pp. 34–35.
3. Hatch, *Woodrow Wilson*, p. 37.
4. Smith, *A New Age Now Begins*, pp. 1,097–1,098.
5. Editors of *American Heritage*, *The American Heritage Pictorial History of the Presidency*, pp. 313–318.
6. Robert Riegel, *American Feminists* (Lawrence, Kan.: University of Kansas Press, 1963), pp. 87–88.
8. Editors of *American Heritage*, *The American Heritage Pictorial History of the Presidents of the United States*, p. 200; Coles, *The War of 1812*, p. 191.
9. Shenkman and Reiger, *One Night Stands With American History*, p. 245; Editors of *American Heritage*, *The American Heritage History of the Presidents of the United States*, p. 972.
11. Peter Lyon, *Eisenhower—Portrait of the Hero* (Boston: Little, Brown, 1984), p. 268; Stephen Ambrose, *Eisenhower* (New York: Simon & Schuster, 1984), p. 18.
12. Nash, *Bloodletters and Badmen*, p. 98.
13. Ford, *A Time to Heal*, pp. 47–48.

DRESSED FOR THE OCCASION

1. Walter Lord, *The Good Years* (New York: Harper & Row, 1965), p. 94.
2. Louise Durbin, *Inaugural Cavalcade* (New York: Dodd, Mead, 1971), p. 9.
3. Bliven, *A Mirror for Greatness*, p. 35; Editors of *American Heritage*, *American Heritage Book of the Revolution*, p. 260.
4. Walter Lord, *A Night to Remember* (New York: Holt, 1955), p. 83.
5. Walton, *The Evidence of Washington*, p. 15.
6. Gene Smith, *Lee and Grant: A Dual Biography* (New York: McGraw Hill, 1984), pp. 267–269.
7. Mott, *A Gallery of Americans*, p. 195.
8. Gard, *The Chisholm Trail*, p. 174.
9. Goldhurst, *Many Are the Hearts*, pp. 49–50.
10. Thomas J. Fleming, *Now We Are Enemies* (New York: St. Martin's Press, 1960), p. 228.
12. Griffith, *In Her Own Right*, pp. 70–71.

13. Davis, *George Washington and the American Revolution*, p. 413; Flexner, *George Washington*, p. 7.
14. Charles A. Lindbergh, *Autobiography of Values* (New York: Harcourt Brace Jovanovich, 1977), p. 313.

INSIGHTS ON EYESIGHT

1. Van Doren, *Benjamin Franklin*, p. 637.
2. Morris, *The Rise of Theodore Roosevelt*, p. 62.
3. Margaret Truman, *Harry S. Truman* (New York: William Morrow, 1972), p. 47.
4. Moses, *Presidential Courage*, p. 70.
5. Ibid., pp. 78–79.
6. Ibid., p. 103.
7. Davis, *George Washington and the American Revolution*, p. 451.

NAPPING ON THE JOB

1. Matthew Josephson, *Edison: A Biography* (New York: McGraw-Hill, 1959), pp. 43–44.
2. Carnegie, *Lincoln the Unknown*, p. 151; T. Harry Williams, *Lincoln and His Generals* (New York: Alfred A. Knopf, 1952), p. 22.
3. Means, *The Woman in the White House*, p. 120; Donald F. Anderson, *William Howard Taft: A Conservative's Conception of the Presidency* (Ithaca, N.Y.: Cornell University Press, 1973), p. 126.
4. Thomas, *Dateline: White House*, p. 67.
5. Gallagher, *FDR's Splendid Deception*, p. 99.
6. Ned Bradford, *Battles and Leaders of the Civil War* (New York: Appleton-Century-Crofts, 1956), p. 39.
7. Diana Healy, *America's Vice-presidents: Our First Forty-three Vice-presidents and How They Got to Be Number Two* (New York: Atheneum, 1984), pp. 159–161.

PRICE TAGS

3. Butterfield, *American Past*, p. 76.
4. Editors of *American Heritage*, *The American Heritage Book of Great Adventures of the Old West*, pp. 206–209.
6. Ibid., pp. 214–215.
7. Louise Hail Tharp, *Three Saints and a Sinner* (Boston: Little, Brown, 1956), p. 245.
8. Haines, *Horses in America*, p. 115.
9. George Stimpson, *A Book About American History* (Greenwich, Conn.: Fawcett, 1956), pp. 278–279.
10. Mark Sullivan, *Our Times*, Vol. VI (New York: Scribner, 1935), p. 620.
11. Smith, *The Rise of Industrial America*, p. 219; Lord, *The Good Years*, pp. 4, 321.
12. National Geographic Society, *Those Inventive Americans*, p. 172.
13. Lindbergh, *The Spirit of St. Louis*, p. 93.

PART VIII: *Words and Wisdom*

TOASTS

1. Bulkey S. Griffin, comp., *Offbeat History: A Compendium of Lively Americana* (Cleveland: World Publishing, 1967), p. 122.
2. Thomas, *Dateline: White House*, p. 15.
3. Hadley, *Power's Human Face*, p. 134.
4. Smith, *John Adams*, pp. 111–112.
5. Smith, *A New Age Now Begins*, p. 1,790.
6. Butterfield, *American Past*, p. 86.
7. Marquis James, *The Life of Andrew Jackson* (Indianapolis: Babbs-Merrill, 1938), p. 719.
8. Allen Johnson and Dumas Malone, *Dictionary of American Biography* (New York: Scribner, 1931), p. 189.
9. Swanberg, *First Blood*, p. 339.
10. Smith, *The Shaping of America*, p. 811.
11. Allison, *Adams and Jefferson*, p. 320.

OH, HELL

1. Kenin and Wintle, *The Dictionary of Biographical Quotation*, p. 743.
2. Caesar, *King of the Mountain Men*, p. 73.
3. Butterfield, *American Past*, p. 122.
4. Cooke, *Alistair Cooke's America*, p. 218.
5. Kenneth S. Davis, "In the Name of the Great Jehovah and the Continental Congress!" *American Heritage*, Vol. XIV, No. 6 (Oct. 1963), p. 77.
6. Shenkman and Reiger, *One Night Stands With American History*, pp. 220–221.
7. Carnegie, *Lincoln the Unknown*, pp. 102–103.
8. Nash, *Bloodletters and Badmen*, pp. 168–169.

LAST WORDS

1. Butterfield, *American Past*, p. 106.
2. Page Smith, *Trial By Fire: A People's History of the Civil War and Reconstruction* (New York: McGraw-Hill, 1982), p. 579.
3. Editors of *American Heritage*, *The American Heritage Book of the Pioneer Spirit*, p. 589.
4. Butterfield, *American Past*, p. 140; Russell, *The Shadow of Blooming Grove*, p. 591.
5. Ibid., p. 385.
6. Desmond Morris, *The Book of Ages* (New York: Viking, 1983), p. 75.
7. Josephson, *Edison*, p. 484.
8. Smith, *The Nation Comes of Age*, p. 226; Marie Hecht, *John Quincy Adams: A Personal History of an Independent Man* (New York: Macmillan, 1972), pp. 626–627.
9. Lenoir Chambers, *Stonewall Jackson*, Vol. II (New York: William Morrow, 1959), p. 447.

10. Elliot, *George Washington Carver: The Man Who Overcame*, p. 249.
11. Moses, *Presidential Courage*, p. 71.
12. Tugwell, *Grover Cleveland*, p. 290.
13. Burr, *The Great American Rascal*, p. 226.

MATTERS OF SEMANTICS

1. Lord, *The Good Years*, p. 86; Josephson, *The Robber Barons*, p. 374.
2. Taylor, *Vessel of Wrath*, p. 137.
3. Smith, *A New Age Now Begins*, p. 726; Ketchum, *The Winter Soldiers*, p. 104; Davis, *George Washington and the American Revolution*, p. 93.
4. Nash, *Bloodletters and Badmen*, pp. 299–300.
5. Charles B. MacDonald, *A Time for Trumpets: The Untold Story of the Battle of the Bulge* (New York: William Morrow, 1985), pp. 512–513.

THE INDIAN SPEAKS

1. Kenin and Wintle, *The Dictionary of Biographical Quotation*, p. 204.
2. Ibid., p. 437.
3. Ibid., p. 727.
4. Ibid., p. 690.
5. Brown, *Bury My Heart at Wounded Knee*, p. 21.
6. Ibid., p. 38.
7. Ibid., p. 103.
8. Ibid., p. 144.
9. Ibid., p. 241.
10. Ibid., pp. 79–80.
11. Ibid., p. 446.

ADVICE

1. Editors of *American Heritage*, *The American Heritage Pictorial History of the Presidents of the United States*, p. 768.
2. Bowers, *The Young Thomas Jefferson*, p. 321.
3. Hedley Donovan, *Roosevelt to Reagan: A Reporter's Encounters with Nine Presidents* (New York: Harper & Row, 1985), p. 66.
4. Editors of *American Heritage*, *The American Heritage Book of Great Adventures of the Old West*, pp. 10–11.
5. Editors of *American Heritage*, *The American Heritage Pictorial History of the Presidents of the United States*, p. 728.
6. Means, *The Woman in the White House*, p. 21.
7. Morgan, *FDR: A Biography*, p. 176.
8. Boller, *Presidential Campaigns*, p. 113; Frank and Melick, *The Presidents: Tidbits and Trivia*, p. 50.
9. Morris, *The Rise of Theodore Roosevelt*, pp. 129, 148; Edward Wagenknecht, *The Seven Worlds of Theodore Roosevelt* (New York: Longmans, Green, 1958), p. 24.

GOOD REPLIES

1. Cooke, *Alistair Cooke's America*, p. 253.
2. Lord, *The Dawn's Early Light*, p. 331.

3. Wisehart, *Sam Houston*, p. 255.
4. Richard O'Connor, *Gould's Millions* (Garden City, N.Y.: Doubleday, 1962), p. 107.
5. Ross, *The Last Hero*, p. 92.
6. Oakley, *Elizabeth Cady Stanton*, p. 62.
7. Bliven, *A Mirror for Greatness*, p. 39.
8. Boller, *Presidential Campaigns*, p. 50.
9. Editors of *American Heritage*, *The American Heritage Book of the Great Adventures of the Old West*, pp. 357–358; Angie Debo, *Geronimo: The Man, His Time, His Place* (Norman, Okla.: University of Oklahoma Press, 1976), p. 29.
10. Boller, *Presidential Anecdotes*, p. 310.
11. Cannon, *Reagan*, p. 20.

"TRUBEL" WITH THE THREE R'S

1. Editors of *American Heritage*, *The American Heritage History of the Great West*, p. 59.
2. Lacey, *Ford: The Men and the Machine*, p. 165.
3. Smith, *America Enters the World*, p. 805; Shenkman, *One-Night Stands*, p. 216.
4. Frank, *The Presidents: Tidbits and Trivia*, p. 26.
6. Robert G. Ferriss, *Lewis and Clark* (Washington, D.C.: National Park Service, 1975), p. 107.
7. DiSalle, *Second Choice*, p. 38; Editors of *American Heritage*, *The American Heritage Pictorial History of the Presidents of the United States*, p. 241.
8. Randall, *Lincoln's Sons*, pp. 122–123; Carnegie, *Lincoln the Unknown*, p. 290; Kunhardt, *Twenty Days*, p. 75.

PART IX: *The Political Process*

SPEECHES

1. Kane, *Facts About the Presidents*, pp. 95–96; Boller, *Presidential Anecdote*, pp. 92–93.
2. Davis, *Our Incredible Civil War*, pp. 151–153; Griffin, *Offbeat History*, p. 24.
3. McFeely, *Grant*, p. 234.
4. Boller, *Presidential Campaigns*, p. 246.
5. William Manchester, *American Caesar* (Boston: Little, Brown, 1978), pp. 661–662.
6. Editors of *American Heritage*, *The American Heritage Pictorial History of the Presidents of the United States*, p. 900; Butterfield, *The American Past*, p. 480.
7. Fawn Brodie, *Thaddeus Stevens, Scourge of the South* (New York: Norton, 1959), p. 348.
8. Smith, *John Adams*, pp. 268–269; Whalen, *The Longest Debate*, pp. 24–26.
9. Smith, *The Rise of Industrial America*, p. 547.
10. Whalen, *The Longest Debate*, pp. 24–26.
11. Boller, *Presidential Campaigns*, p. 213.
12. Kittler, *Hail to the Chief*, pp. 71–73.

PARDONABLE OFFENSES

1. Truman, *Women of Courage*, p. 161.
2. Oates, *With Malice Toward None: The Life of Abraham Lincoln*, p. 288.
3. Davis, *The Long Surrender*, pp. 258–259.
4. Ford, *A Time to Heal*, pp. 175–178.
5. Larry Starkey, *Wilkes Booth Came to Washington* (New York: Random House, 1976), p. 165; Eisenschiml, *Why Was Lincoln Murdered?*, pp. 180–184; Bishop, *The Day Lincoln Was Shot*, p. 294.
6. Lyle Saxon, *Lafitte the Pirate* (New Orleans: Robert L. Crager, 1950), pp. 156–185; Malone, *Dictionary of American Biography*, Vol. V, pp. 540–541.

POLITICAL MUDSLINGING

1. Boller, *Presidential Campaigns*, p. 7.
2. Bryant, *Dog Days at the White House*, p. 65.
3. Hadley, *Power's Human Face*, p. 129.
4. Smith, *The Shaping of America*, p. 282.
5. Smith, *The Nation Comes of Age*, p. 10.
6. Moses, *Presidential Courage*, pp. 169–170.
7. Ibid., p. 42.

ON THE VICE-PRESIDENCY

2. Healy, *America's Vice-presidents*, pp. 7–8.
3. DiSalle, *Second Choice*, p. 14.
4. Healy, *America's Vice-presidents*, p. 136.
5. Henry F. Graff, "A Heartbeat Away," *American Heritage*, August 1961, Vol. XV, Number 5, p. 86.
6. Joseph E. Persico, *The Imperial Rockefeller* (New York: Simon & Schuster, 1981), p. 245.
7. Doris Kearns, *Lyndon Johnson and the American Dream* (New York: Harper & Row, 1976), p. 164.
8. Will Yolen and Kenneth Giniger, eds., *Heroes for Our Times* (Harrisburg, Pa.: Stackpole Books, 1968), p. 176.
9. Editors of *American Heritage*, *The American Heritage Pictorial History of the Presidents of the United States*, p. 799.
10. Healy, *America's Vice-presidents*, pp. 71–74.
11. Ibid., p. 156.

DEMOCRACY IN ACTION

1. Smith, *The Rise of Industrial America*, p. 465.
2. Josephson, *The Robber Barons*, pp. 129–131; Richard O'Connor, *Gould's Millions*, p. 76.
3. Shenkman and Reiger, *One Night Stands With American History*, p. 129.
4. Smith, *The Nation Comes of Age*, p. 84.
5. Smith, *John Adams*, pp. 183–184.
6. Wagner, *The Road to the White House*, pp. 15–16.

7. Reinhard Luthin, *The Real Abraham Lincoln* (Englewood Cliffs, N.J.: Prentice-Hall, 1960), pp. 56–57.
8. Durbin, *Inaugural Cavalcade*, p. 4.
9. Truman, *Women of Courage*, p. 20.
10. Wagner, *The Road to the White House*, p. 17.

PART X: *Joys and Sorrows, Love and Death*

WAR-TORN LOYALTIES

1. Benjamin Botkin, *A Civil War Treasury of Tales, Legends, and Folklore* (New York: Random House, 1960), pp. 511–512.
2. Ibid., p. 201.
3. Smith, *A New Age Now Begins*, p. 498.
4. McFeely, *Grant*, p. 101.
5. Swanberg, *First Blood*, p. 327.
6. Fleming, *Now We Are Enemies*, p. 269; Bishop, *The Birth of the United States*, p. 151.
7. Seale, *The President's House*, pp. 409–410.

GUNS AGAINST THE HELPLESS

1. Smith, *A New Age Now Begins*, p. 336.
2. Brown, *Bury My Heart at Wounded Knee*, pp. 87–92; Smith, *The Rise of Industrial America*, p. 12; Editors of *American Heritage*, *The American Heritage Book of Indians*, p. 345.
3. Brown, *Bury My Heart at Wounded Knee*, pp. 444–446.
4. Seymour M. Hersh, *My Lai 4: A Report on the Massacre and Its Aftermath* (New York: Random House, 1970), pp. 22–50; Seymour M. Hersh, *Cover-up* (New York: Random House, 1972), pp. 3–49.
5. Joe Eszterhas and Michael Roberts. *Thirteen Seconds* (New York: Dodd, Mead, 1970), pp. 145–176; Peter Davies, *The Truth About Kent State* (New York: Farrar, Straus, Giroux, 1973), pp. 9–30.

TEARFUL TIMES

1. Smith, *A New Age Now Begins*, p. 1,584.
2. McFeely, *Grant*, p. 402; Butterfield, *American Past*, p. 196.
3. Connell, *Son of the Morning Star*, p. 1.
4. Miller, *Scandals in the Highest Office*, p. 138; Davis, *The Long Surrender*, p. 262.
5. Smith, *The Shaping of America*, p. 280.
6. Jensen, *The White House and Its Thirty-Three Families*, p. 170.
7. Smith, *The Nation Comes of Age*, pp. 94–100.
8. Miller, *Scandals in the Highest Office*, p. 135.
9. Gene Smith, *When the Cheering Stopped* (New York: William Morrow, 1964), pp. 81–82.
10. Smith, *The Nation Comes of Age*, pp. 808–809.
11. David Abrahamsen, *Nixon vs. Nixon: An Emotional Tragedy* (New York: Farrar, Straus and Giroux, 1977), p. 164.

12. Robert H. Ferrell, ed., *Dear Bess: The Letters from Harry to Bess Truman, 1910–1959* (New York: Norton, 1983), p. 298.
13. Stephen B. Oates, *Let the Trumpet Sound* (New York: Harper & Row, 1982), pp. 162–164; Boller, *Presidential Campaigns*, p. 300; Lerone Bennett, *What Manner of Man; A Biography of Martin Luther King, Jr.* (Chicago: Johnson Publishing, 1964), pp. 117–119; David J. Garrow, *Bearing the Cross: Martin Luther King, Jr., and the Southern Christian Leadership Conference, 1955–1968* (New York: William Morrow, 1986), pp. 143–149.

CELEBRATIONS

1. Jeffries, *In and Out of the White House*, p. 99; Seale, *The President's House*, p. 192.
2. Ross, *The Last Hero*, pp. 134–135.
3. Swanberg, *First Blood*, p. 80; Catton, *The Coming Fury*, p. 134.
4. Jensen, *The White House and Its Thirty-four Families*, p. 47; Smith, *The Nation Comes of Age*, p. 19; Seale, *The President's House*, p. 192.
5. Don Russell, *The Lives and Legends of Buffalo Bill* (Norman, Okla.: University of Oklahoma Press, 1960), pp. 178–179.
6. Krythe, *What So Proudly We Hail*, pp. 144–145; The United States Capitol Historical Society, *We the People*, p. 22; Walton, *Evidence of Washington*, p. 11.
7. Margaret Pumphreys, *Pilgrim Stories* (Chicago: Rand, McNally, 1961), pp. 153–161; Thomas Fleming, *One Small Candle* (New York: Norton, 1964), pp. 211, 216.

POPPING THE QUESTION

1. Hatch, *Woodrow Wilson*, pp. 164–167.
2. Allison, *Adams and Jefferson*, p. 33.
3. James Flexner, *The Traitor and the Spy* (New York: Harcourt, Brace, 1953), pp. 232–235.
4. Oakley, *Elizabeth Cady Stanton*, p. 25.
5. Thomas, *Dateline: White House*, p. 179.

UNLIKELY MARRIAGES

1. Malone, *Dictionary of American Biography*, Vol. VIII, pp. 18–19.
2. Sandburg, *Abraham Lincoln: The Prairie Years and the War Years*, pp. 127–139.
3. Miller, *Scandals in the Highest Office*, p. 163; Aikman, *The Living White House*, p. 51; Butterfield, *The American Past*, p. 242; Seale, *The President's House*, pp. 559–560.
4. Jeffries, *In and Out of the White House*, p. 118; Jensen, *The White House and Its Thirty-four Families*, pp. 64–71.
5. Morris, *The Book of Ages*, pp. 69, 76.
6. Irving Wallace, *The Fabulous Showman: The Life and Times of P. T. Barnum* (New York: Knopf), 1959, pp. 108–110.

MAN AND HIS HORSE

1. Russell, *The Lives and Legends of Buffalo Bill*, pp. 362–363.
2. Margaret Truman, *White House Pets* (New York: McKay, 1969), pp. 149–53.

3. Shenkman and Reiger, *One Night Stands With American History*, p. 78.
4. Jensen, *The White House and Its Thirty-three Families*, p. 181; *Dog Days at the White House*, p. 29.
5. Sullivan, *Our Times*, Vol. III, p. 14.
6. Davis, *The Long Surrender*, pp. 284–285.
7. Stanley, Vestal, *Jim Bridger, Mountain Man* (Lincoln, Neb.: University of Nebraska Press, 1946), pp. 297–298.
8. Yost, *Buffalo Bill*, pp. 208–209.
9. Carnegie, *Lincoln the Unknown*, p. 166; Seale, *The President's House*, p. 411.

PART XI: *Adventure and Intrigue*

JAILBREAKS, ESCAPES, AND QUICK GETAWAYS

1. Jon Tuska, *Billy the Kid, A Bio-Bibliography* (Westport, Conn.: Greenwood Press, 1983), pp. 97–99; Pat F. Garrett, *The Authentic Life of Billy the Kid* (Norman, Okla.: University of Oklahoma Press, 1954), pp. 136–139.
2. Alexander B. Callow, *The Tweed Ring* (New York: Oxford University Press, 1966), p. 290; Denis Lynch, *Boss Tweed* (New York: Boni and Liverright, 1927), pp. 377–396.
3. John Bakeless, *Daniel Boone* (Harrisburg, Pa.: Stackpole Books, 1965), pp. 158–185.
4. Fawn Brodie, *Thomas Jefferson* (New York: Norton, 1974), p. 146; Dumas Malone, *Jefferson the Virginian* (Boston: Little, Brown, 1948), pp. 356–358; Randolph, *The Domestic Life of Thomas Jefferson* (Cambridge, Mass.: University Press, 1939), p. 34.
5. Nash, *Bloodletters and Badmen*, p. 41.
6. Hadley, *Power's Human Face*, pp. 42–43; Jensen, *The White House and Its Thirty-three Families*, p. 47; Smith, *The Nation Comes of Age*, p. 19.
7. Holbrook, *Age of Moguls*, pp. 30–31; Josephson, *The Robber Barons*, pp. 122–127; O'Connor, *Gould's Millions*, pp. 68–71.
8. Truman, *Women of Courage*, pp. 53–55.
9. Nash, *Bloodletters and Badmen*, p. 170–172.

RUNNING UP THE WHITE FLAG

1. Davis, *George Washington and the American Revolution*, p. 429; Editors of *American Heritage*, *American Heritage Book of the Revolution*, pp. 358–359; Smith, *A New Age Now Begins*, p. 1,704.
2. Lord, *The Dawn's Early Light*, pp. 239–244, 295–296.
3. Gene Smith, *Lee and Grant, A Dual Biography* (New York: McGraw-Hill, 1984), pp. 264–268; Editors of *American Heritage*, *American Heritage Book of the Pioneer Spirit*, p. 566.
4. Garrett, *The Authentic Life of Billy the Kid*, pp. 125–127; Tuska, *Billy the Kid, A Bio-Bibliography*, p. 91.
5. Keller, *The Spanish-American War*, pp. 231–233; David Trask, *The War With Spain in 1898* (New York: Macmillan, 1981), pp. 415–419.
6. Catton, *The Coming Fury*, pp. 322–323; Swanberg, *First Blood*, pp. 318–320.

DUELING: AN AMERICAN PASTIME

1. Smith, *The Shaping of America*, p. 499.
2. Johnson and Malone, *Dictionary of American Biography*, Vol. III, pp. 187–189.
3. James, *The Raven*, pp. 64–67; Donald Braider, *Solitary Star* (New York: Putnam, 1974), pp. 60–62.
4. Oates, *With Malice Toward None*, pp. 61–62.
5. Glyndon G. Van Deusen, *The Life of Henry Clay* (Boston: Little, Brown, 1937), pp. 220–222; Boller, *Presidential Campaigns*, p. 40.
6. Davis, *Old Hickory*, pp. 46–49.

CLOSE CALLS

1. Wagenknecht, *The Seven Worlds of Theodore Roosevelt*, p. 15.
2. Blair, *The Search for JFK*, pp. 570–571.
3. Hadley, *Power's Human Face*, pp. 168–169; Russell, *The Shadow of Blooming Grove*, pp. 465–467.
4. Dumas Malone, *Jefferson and His Time* (Boston: Little, Brown, 1981), p. 469.
5. Bennett, *What Manner of Man*, p. 98.
6. Donovan, *The Benjamin Franklin Papers*, p. 265; Van Doren, *Benjamin Franklin*, pp. 161–162.
7. Editors of *American Heritage*, *The American Heritage Pictorial History of the Presidents of the United States*, p. 898; Alden Hatch, *General Ike: A Biography of Dwight D. Eisenhower* (New York: Holt, 1944), pp. 15–16.

RANSOMS AND OTHER PAYOFFS

1. Elliott, *George Washington Carver, The Man Who Overcame*, pp. 11–14.
2. Ross, *The Last Hero*, pp. 195–223.
3. Lord, *The Dawn's Early Light*, pp. 198–200.
4. Glenn Tucker, *Dawn Like Thunder: The Barbary Wars and the Birth of the U.S. Navy* (Indianapolis: Bobbs-Merrill, 1963), pp. 98–99.
5. Peter Wyden, *Bay of Pigs* (New York: Simon & Schuster, 1979), p. 303; Edwin Tetlow, *Eye on Cuba* (New York: Harcourt, Brace and World, 1966), p. 180.
6. *The New York Times*, October 3, 1986, Vol. CXXXVI, No. 46,916, p. 7.

SUNKEN SHIPS

1. Morrison, *Christopher Columbus, Mariner*, pp. 61–64; Samuel Eliot Morison, *Admiral of the Ocean Sea: A Life of Christopher Columbus* (Boston: Little, Brown, 1942), pp. 300–317.
2. O'Toole, *The Spanish War*, p. 124; Millis, *The Martial Spirit*, p. 127; Trask, *War with Spain*, pp. xii, 35.
3. Yost, *Buffalo Bill*, p. 146.
4. William White, *Tin Can on a Shingle* (New York: Dutton, 1957), pp. 142–151.

SOUVENIR HUNTERS

2. Margaret Truman, *White House Pets*, p. 152; Jensen, *The White House and Its Thirty-four Families*, p. 71.

3. Davis, *Our Incredible Civil War*, pp. 19–23.
4. Jensen, *The White House and Its Thirty-four Families*, p. 93.
6. Goldhurst, *Many Are the Hearts*, p. 233.
7. Adams, *Jefferson's Monticello*, pp. 248, 259.
8. Carnegie, *Lincoln the Unknown*, p. 260.
9. Lindbergh, *Autobiography of Values*, pp. 312–313.

HOAXES, DECEPTIONS, AND PUT-ONS

1. Weinstein, *Woodrow Wilson*, pp. 291–292; Jensen, *The White House and Its Thirty-four Families*, p. 205.
2. Van Doren, *Benjamin Franklin*, pp. 574–575.
3. Stimpson, *The Book About American History*, pp. 139–143; Davis, *George Washington and the American Revolution*, p. 270.
4. Shenkman and Reiger, *One Night Stands with American History*, p. 211.
5. Ronald Reagan, *Where's the Rest of Me?* (New York: Karz Publishers, 1981), p. 68.

LOST, MISPLACED, OR LED ASTRAY

1. Kane, *Facts About the Presidents*, p. 31.
2. Garrison, *Lost Pages from American History*, pp. 39–41.
3. Editors of *American Heritage, The American Heritage History of the Thirteen Colonies* (New York: American Heritage Publishing Co., 1967), pp. 41–48.
4. Malone, *Dictionary of American Biography*, Vol. VII, pp. 163–164.
5. Eisenschiml, *Why Was Lincoln Murdered?*, pp. 138–144.
6. Charles A. Lindbergh, *The Spirit of St. Louis* (New York: Scribner, 1953), p. 459.
7. Editors of *American Heritage, The American Heritage Picture History of the Civil War*, p. 561.
8. Editors of *American Heritage, The American Heritage History of the Great West* (New York: American Heritage, Publishing Co., 1965), pp. 67–72; Terrell, *Zebulon Pike*, p. 173.
9. Davis, *The Long Surrender*, p. 285.
10. Heaton, *The Mayflower*, pp. 139–140.
11. Editors of *American Heritage, American Heritage Book of the Pioneer Spirit*, p. 93.

FAKE BURIALS AND OTHER GRAVE SITUATIONS

1. Malone, *Dictionary of American Biography*, Vol. V, p. 188.
2. Sullivan, *Our Times*, Vol. VI, p. 614.
3. Fawn Brodie, *No Man Knows My History: The Life of Joseph Smith the Mormon Prophet* (New York: Knopf, 1971), p. 397.
4. Davis, *The Long Surrender*, pp. 240–241.
5. Carnegie, *Lincoln the Unknown*, pp. 301–302; Kane, *Facts About the Presidents*, pp. 160–161.
6. Davis, *George Washington and the American Revolution*, p. 76; Fleming, *Now We Are Enemies*, p. 322; Smith, *A New Age Now Begins*, p. 536.
7. Samuel Carter, *The Riddle of Dr. Mudd* (New York: Putnam, 1974), p. 336; Johnson, *Dictionary of American Biography*, Vol. I, p. 452.

ROYAL ENCOUNTERS

1. Aikman, *The Living White House*, p. 57.
2. Russell, *The Lives and Legends of Buffalo Bill*, pp. 74–79.
3. Lacey, *Ford: The Men and the Machine*, p. 405.
4. Jeffries, *In and Out of the White House*, p. 35.
7. Russell, *The Lives and Legends of Buffalo Bill*, pp. 330–331.
8. Wallace, *The Fabulous Showman*, pp. 82–83.
9. Jensen, *The White House and Its Thirty-four Families*, pp. 39–40; Peter Buckman, *Lafayette* (New York: Paddington Press, 1977), pp. 261–263.

PART XII: *How It Happened*

PLAYING CARDS

1. Cass Canfield, *Incredible Pierpont Morgan* (New York: Harper & Row, 1974); p. 81; Editors of *American Heritage*, *The American Heritage Pictorial History of the Presidents of the United States*, p. 561.
2. Holbrook, *Age of Moguls*, p. 27; Josephson, *The Robber Baron*, p. 71.
3. Bliven, *A Mirror for Greatness*, p. 41.
4. Richard O'Connor, *Wild Bill Hickok* (Garden City, N.Y.: Doubleday, 1959), pp. 257–260; Denis McLaughlin, *Wild and Woolly: An Encyclopedia of Western Gunfighters* (Garden City, New York: Doubleday, 1975), pp. 221–225.
5. Ambrose, *Eisenhower*, p. 31.

NAKED

1. Lord, *The Good Years*, p. 224; Smith, *America Enters the World*, p. 44.
2. Donald Chidsey, *The Siege of Boston: An On-the-Scene Account of the Beginning of the Revolution* (New York: Crown, 1966), p. 113.
3. Jacob Wasserman, *Columbus: Don Quixote of the Seas* (Boston: Little, Brown, 1930), pp. 90–91.
4. Van Doren, *Benjamin Franklin*, pp. 404–405.
5. Burton Harris, *John Colter: His Years in the Rockies* (New York: Scribner, 1952), pp. 128–131.
6. Griffin, *Offbeat History*, p. 8; Shepherd, *The Adams Chronicles*, p. 302.
7. Means, *The Woman in the White House*, p. 110; Randall, *Lincoln's Sons*, pp. 282–283.

UPLIFTING MOMENTS: PEOPLE WHO WERE CARRIED

1. Lindbergh, *The Spirit of St. Louis*, pp. 495–497.
2. Brodie, *Thomas Jefferson*, pp. 247–248.
3. Brodie, *Thaddeus Stevens*, p. 354; Editors of *American Heritage*, *The American Heritage History of the Confident Years* (New York: American Heritage Publishing Co., 1969), p. 34.
4. Editors of *American Heritage*, *The American Heritage History of the Making of the Nation*, p. 35
5. Lon Tinkle, *13 Days to Glory: The Seige of the Alamo* (New York: McGraw-Hill, 1958), pp. 182–183.

6. Carnegie, *Lincoln the Unknown*, p. 238.
7. James MacGregor Burns, *Roosevelt—The Soldier of Freedom* (New York: Harcourt Brace Jovanovich, 1970), p. 324.

ON FOOT

1. Wallace Stegner, *The Story of the Mormon Trail* (New York: McGraw-Hill, 1964), pp. 221–237.
2. Durbin, *Inaugural Cavalcade*, pp. 16–19.
3. Gallagher, *FDR's Splendid Deception*, pp. 62–67.
4. Yost, *Buffalo Bill*, p. 386.
6. Alfred Steinberg, *The Man from Missouri* (New York: Putnam, 1962), p. 345.

OUT IN THE COLD

1. Tebbel, *George Washington's America*, p. 36.
2. Durbin, *Inaugural Cavalcade*, p. 99.
3. Bower, *The Young Thomas Jefferson*, p. 48.
4. Gallagher, *FDR's Splendid Deception*, p. 195.
5. Wagenknecht, *The Seven Worlds of Theodore Roosevelt*, p. 235.

UP IN SMOKE

1. Tinkle, *13 Days to Glory*, pp. 236–237.
2. Fleming, *Now We Are Enemies*, p. 241; Bishop, *The Birth of the United States*, pp. 141–144.
3. Seale, *The President's House*, pp. 135–136.
4. McCoy, *Calvin Coolidge*, p. 147; Boller, *Presidential Anecdotes*, pp. 239–240.

IT HAPPENED WHILE THE BAND PLAYED

1. Editors of *American Heritage*, *American Heritage Book of the Revolution*, p. 373.
2. Ibid., p. 102.
3. Lord, *A Time to Stand*, p. 159; Tinkle, *13 Days to Glory*, p. 198.
4. Charles Strong, *Story of American Sailing Ships* (New York: Grosset & Dunlap, 1957), pp. 58–59.
5. Lord, *A Night to Remember*, pp. 52, 96–101, 174.
6. Seale, *The President's House*, p. 267.
7. Editors of *American Heritage*, *American Heritage Book of the Revolution*, p. 238; Ketchum, *The Winter Soldiers*, p. 311.
8. Connell, *Son of the Morning Star*, p. 294.
9. Seale, *The President's House*, p. 416.
10. Ibid., p. 564.
11. Walter Lord, *Day of Infamy* (New York: Holt, 1957), pp. 70–76.

OCCASIONS FOR A SONG

1. Milton Viorst, *Fire in the Streets* (New York: Simon & Schuster, 1979), pp. 218–219; Whalen, *The Longest Debate*, pp. xix–xx.
2. Arnold Madison, *Carry Nation* (Nashville, Tenn.: Thomas Nelson, 1977), pp. 132–136.

3. Judith Nies, *Seven Women: Portraits from the American Radical Tradition* (New York: Viking Press, 1977), pp. 54–55.
4. Russell, *The Lives and Legends of Buffalo Bill*, p. 327.
5. Stefan Lorant, *The Life and Times of Theodore Roosevelt* (Garden City, N.Y.: Doubleday, 1959), p. 317.

PART XIII: *Crime, Punishment and the Law*

ASSASSINATIONS THAT FAILED

1. Davis, *Old Hickory*, pp. 345–346; James Clarke, *American Assassins* (Princeton, N.J.: Princeton University Press, 1982), pp. 194–198; Marcus Cunliffe and the editors of *American Heritage*, *The American Heritage History of the Presidency*, p. 87.
2. Clarke, *American Assassins*, pp. 214–220.
3. Ibid., pp. 167–174.
4. Ibid., pp. 69–73; Truman, *Harry S. Truman*, pp. 487–488.
5. Clarke, *American Assassins*, pp. 156–165; Ford, *A Time to Heal*, pp. 309–312.
6. Lou Cannon, *Reagan* (New York: Putnam, 1982), pp. 402–405.

ASSASSINATIONS THAT SUCCEEDED

1. Jim Bishop, *The Day Lincoln Was Shot* (New York: Bantam, 1962), pp. 196–206.
2. Moses, *Presidential Courage*, pp. 110–119.
3. Clarke, *American Assassins*, pp. 55–57.
4. Ibid., pp. 107–126; McKinley, *Assassination in America*, pp. 104–128.

ARRESTING PREDICAMENTS

1. Butterfield, *American Past*, p. 117.
2. Callow, *The Tweed Ring*, p. 241; Lynch, *Boss Tweed*, p. 402; Albert Paine, *Th. Nast* (Princeton, N.J.: The Pyne Press), p. 335.
3. Carnegie, *Lincoln the Unknown*, pp. 297–302.
4. Alma Lutz, *Susan B. Anthony: Rebel, Crusader, Humanitarian* (Boston: Beacon Press, 1959), pp. 200–201; Godfrey D. Lehman, "Susan B. Anthony Cast Her Ballot for Ulysses S. Grant," *American Heritage*, December 1985, Vol. 37/No. 1, pp. 25–31.
5. Griffith, *In Her Own Right*, p. 156.
6. Russell, *The Lives and Legends of Buffalo Bill*, p. 369.
7. Taylor, *Vessel of Wrath*, p. 135.
8. Wisehart, *Sam Houston*, pp. 11–12; James, *The Raven*, p. 20.

HANGED MEN (AND A WOMAN)

1. Katherine and John Bakeless, *Spies of the Revolution* (New York: Scholastic Books, 1962), pp. 95–106.
2. Davis, *George Washington and the American Revolution*, p. 343; Flexner, *The Traitor and the Spy*, p. 390.
3. Dorothy Meserve Kunhardt and Philip B. Kunhardt, *Twelve Days* (New York: Castle Books, 1965), pp. 208–211.

4. Bishop, *The Birth of the United States*, p. 140.
5. Miller, *Scandals in the Highest Office*, p. 261; Flexner, *George Washington*, p. 92; Davis, *George Washington's America*, pp. 25–26.
6. Bruce Catton, "Prison Camps of the Civil War," *American Heritage*, Vol. X, No. 5 (Aug. 1959), pp. 5–8, 96–97.
7. Stephen B. Oates, *To Purge This Land with Blood* (Amherst, Mass.: University of Massachusetts Press, 1984), p. 335.
8. Clarke, *American Assassins*, pp. 208–209; McKinley, *Assassination in America*, pp. 45–48.
9. Burton Schindler, "The Haymarket Bomb," *American History Illustrated*, Vol. XXI, Number 4 (June 1986), pp. 20–27.
10. Stephen Oates, *The Fries of Jubliee* (New York: Harper & Row, 1975), pp. 124–125.

PRISON STORIES

1. Strode, *Jefferson Davis, Tragic Hero*, pp. 229–235.
2. Eisenschiml, *Why Was Lincoln Murdered?*, pp. 175–179; Samuel Carter, *The Riddle of Dr. Mudd* (New York: Putnam, 1974), p. 162.
3. Callow, *The Tweed Ring*, pp. 291, 197; Lynch, *Boss Tweed*, p. 1.
4. Eleanor Young, *Forgotten Patriot—Robert Morris* (New York: Macmillan, 1950), pp. 243–252.

PART XIV: *History in Perspective*

SHORTSIGHTED REACTIONS TO GREAT LEAPS FORWARD

1. Peter Baido, "The Business of America," *American Heritage*, Vol. 36, No. 4 (June/July 1985), p. 18.
2. Christopher Cerf and Victor Navasky, *The Experts Speak the Definitive Compendium of Authorative Misinformation* (New York: Pantheon Books, 1984), p. 207.
3. Sullivan, *Our Times*, Vol. II, p. 604.
4. Gies, *Ingenious Yankees*, pp. 103–104; Wilson, *American Science and Invention*, p. 68.
5. Thomas Fleming, *The Man Who Dared Lightning: A New Look at Benjamin Franklin* (New York: William Morrow, 1971), p. 10; Clark, *Benjamin Franklin*, p. 88.
6. Editors of *American Heritage*, *The American Heritage Picture History of the Civil War*, p. 179; Ruth White, *Yankee From Sweden* (New York: Holt, 1960), p. 199.

THE CLOUDED CRYSTAL BALL

1. Ivan Jones and the editors of Time/Life Books, *The Plains States* (New York: Time/Life Books, 1968), p. 37.
3. Hadley, *Power's Human Face*, p. 197.
4. Editors of *American Heritage*, *The American Heritage Pictorial History of the Presidents of the United States*, p. 729.
5. Editors of *American Heritage*, *The American Heritage History of the Making of a Nation* (New York: American Heritage Publishing Co., 1968), p. 258; Butterfield, *American Past*, p. 108.

6. Boller, *Presidential Campaigns*, pp. 248–249.
7. Nixon, *The Memoirs of Richard Nixon*, pp. 244–245.

HAD THEY ONLY KNOWN

1. Davis, *George Washington and the American Revolution*, pp. 160–174.
4. O'Toole, *The Spanish War*, pp. 190, 371; Millis, *The Martial Spirit*, p. 360.
5. Lord, *Day of Infamy*, pp. 44–48.

WHAT THEY WERE DOING WHEN

1. Hermann Hagedoren, *The Roosevelt Family of Sagamore Hill* (New York: Macmillan, 1954), p. 117.
2. Cunliffe, *George Washington: Man and Monument*, p. 123.
3. Hatch, *Woodrow Wilson*, p. 12.
4. Whalen, *The Longest Debate*, pp. 164–165.
5. Thomas, *Dateline: White House*, p. 97.
6. David McCullough, *Mornings on Horseback* (New York: Simon & Schuster, 1981), p. 64.
7. Nixon, *The Memoirs of Richard Nixon*, p. 1,053.

HISTORIC MOMENTS ON THE NIGHT SHIFT

1. Butterfield, *American Past*, p. 192.
2. James Morgan, *Our Presidents* (New York: Macmillan, 1969), pp. 304–307; McCoy, *Calvin Coolidge*, pp. 146–149; Ishbel Ross, *Grace Coolidge and Her Era* (New York: Dodd, Mead, 1962), pp. 77–81.
3. O'Toole, *The Spanish War*, pp. 385–386.
4. Butterfield, *American Past*, p. 383; Sullivan, *Our Times*, Vol. VI, p. 37; DiSalle, *Second Choice*, pp. 130–131.
5. Catton, *The Coming Fury*, pp. 314–315; Swanberg, *First Blood*, p. 294.

WHAT ELSE HAPPENED ON THE FOURTH OF JULY?

1. Allison, *Adams and Jefferson*, p. 36.
2. Editors of *American Heritage*, *The American Heritage Book of Great Adventures of the Old West*, p. 13; Smith, *The Shaping of America*, p. 526.
3. Editors of *American Heritage*, *The American Heritage History of the Making of a Nation*, p. 187.
4. Harry Ammon, *James Monroe* (New York: McGraw-Hill, 1971), pp. 572–573.
5. Dumas Malone, *Dictionary of American Biography*, Vol. IX (New York: Scribner, 1936), p. 353.
6. Editors of *American Heritage*, *The American Heritage Picture History of the Civil War*, p. 324; James McPherson, *Ordeal by Fire: The Civil War and Reconstruction* (New York: Alfred A. Knopf, 1982), p. 333.
7. Claude M. Fuess, *Calvin Coolidge, The Man from Vermont* (Boston: Little, Brown), pp. 20–22.
9. Brown, *The Correspondents' War*, p. 386.

BUFFALO FACTS

1. Larry Barness, *Heads, Hides and Herds: The Compleat Buffalo Book* (Fort Worth, Texas: Texas Christian University Press, 1985), p. 26.

2. Horan, *The Great American West*, p. 208.
6. Barness, *Heads, Hides and Herds*, p. 8; Horan, *The Great American West*, p. 208.
8. Ibid.
10. Barness, *Heads, Hides and Herds*, p. 135; Horan, *The Great American West*, p. 209.
11. Ibid., p. 353.
12. Ibid., p. 208.

THE RISE AND FALL OF THE HORSE IN AMERICA

1. Howard, *The Horse in America*, pp. 20–21; Francis Haines, *Horses in America* (New York: Crowell, 1971), p. 25.
2. Otto Bettman, *The Good Old Days—They Were Terrible!* (New York: Random House, 1974), p. 3.
3. Haines, *Horses in America*, p. 123.
5. Howard, *The Horse in America*, p. 70.
6. Ibid., p. 215.
8. Ibid., p. 228.
9. Russell, *Buffalo Bill*, p. 94.

Index